Pocket in back —

Stage 3

Stage 4

Stage 5

Stage 6

Stage 7

Stage 8

Pocket in back

Communications
in the
Modern Corporate
Environment

124015

Daniel Abelow
Edwin J. Hilpert

PRENTICE-HALL, Englewood Cliffs, N.J. 07632

Library of Congress Cataloging-in-Publication Data

Abelow, Daniel. 1948–
  Communications in the modern corporate environment.

  Includes index.
  1. Business—Data processing.   2. Management—
Communication systems.   I. Hilpert, Edwin J.   II. Title.
HF5548.2.A24   1985   658'.0546   85-16942
ISBN   0-13-153842-X

Editorial/production supervision and interior design: TKM Productions
Cover design: Photo Plus Art
Manufacturing buyer: Gordon Osbourne

    This book was written on a multiuser Cromemco™ microcomputer running Cromix™, Cromemco's operating system based on UNIX™ from AT&T. WordStar™ was the word processing software. Ten chapters of the book's initial draft were dictated, transcribed by a word processing service, and downloaded to the micro by means of its Racal modem.
    Because it is a multiuser system, this micro can be used locally for word and data processing while a remote user is accessing and using the computer for electronic mail, to transfer files, or to run applications stored on its twenty-megabyte hard disk. This computer is used frequently via tele-communications from remote locations, to work on the book as well as for other jobs.

Printed in the United States of America

10   9   8   7   6   5   4   3   2   1

ISBN   0-13-153842-X   01

PRENTICE-HALL INTERNATIONAL (UK) LIMITED, *London*
PRENTICE-HALL OF AUSTRALIA PTY. LIMITED, *Sydney*
PRENTICE-HALL CANADA INC., *Toronto*
PRENTICE-HALL HISPANOAMERICANA, S.A., *Mexico*
PRENTICE-HALL OF INDIA PRIVATE LIMITED, *New Delhi*
PRENTICE-HALL OF JAPAN, INC., *Tokyo*
PRENTICE-HALL OF SOUTHEAST ASIA PTE. LTD., *Singapore*
EDITORA PRENTICE-HALL DO BRASIL, LTDA., *Rio de Janeiro*
WHITEHALL BOOKS LIMITED, *Wellington, New Zealand*

*This book is dedicated
by Dan Abelow to his parents for encouraging him to be all he can be
and by Ed Hilpert to his wife, Carol Ann, for her many years of loving support.*

CONTENTS

PREFACE

For most people who work for a living, the quality of information rapidly available to them from their office and company determines their success and effectiveness. Timely and relevant information directly supports most people's work, whether their job is in management, sales, manufacturing, purchasing, or another area.

There is a critical relationship between an organization's information resources, its communications capabilities, and its business success. This is a dynamic equation that is now undergoing profound changes. These changes are due to the introduction of computing throughout organizations, including the full range of systems from microcomputers, workstations, and word processors through terminals linked to minicomputers and mainframes.

Because of the powerful communications capabilities of these systems, the speed at which business information can be transmitted inexpensively over dozens or thousands of miles has been reduced from days to minutes. In addition, the range and scope of useful business information stored in and processed by all types of computers and word processors is growing at the speed of a tidal wave.

In most organizations, each microcomputer, word processor, computer terminal, or workstation is usually purchased to provide one or two business functions, instead of impacting the overall environment. Adding communications between these systems, however, can affect most users of the systems. It may also have a variety of impacts on the overall environment. These may range from reducing the time needed for certain business functions to improving the way a company manages its operations.

Both business planners and users face a variety of problems during the selection and implementation of communications for an organization's complete range of computer and word processing systems. First, no "turnkey" solutions are available that will satisfy all functional requirements. Second, the best communications system for each company cannot be selected or implemented without careful planning.

Successful communications systems depend on a thorough understanding of business needs, communications hardware and software, and proper procedures for linking a company's systems to reach its objectives.

Literally hundreds of choices are possible in today's computer communications marketplace, including software and hardware links between systems of all sizes. How does an organization determine its communications needs and opportunities? What are the ways to manage communications planning and implementation, and who should be involved? How should a company plan solutions that take advantage of appropriate microcomputers and word processors? Effective decisions will yield communications that are accepted, instead of systems that are avoided.

This book is designed to provide guidance in this complex and rapidly expanding area of decision making. It divides these decisions into four clear stages: analysis, design, implementation, and application. It uses a detailed approach so each reader can extract the elements that apply to his or her situation.

In Part I, "Analysis," Chapter 1 provides an overview of business communications systems that include mainframe computers, minicomputers, microcomputers, word processors, and executive workstations. Chapter 2 covers management models for creating a communications planning team, and procedures for conducting a feasibility study. Chapter 3 offers criteria for selecting communications software. Chapter 4 reviews the characteristics and functions of communications hardware.

In Part II, "Design," Chapter 5 merges user requirements with communications options to yield a model that reflects both benefits and opportunities. Chapter 6 reviews methods for developing communications compatibility between different systems, including corporate standards for communications. Chapter 7 includes the valuable area of micro-mainframe communications. Chapter 8 extends this to the process of integrating word processing with computing and communications. Chapter 9 explains the potentially valuable role of local area networks.

In Part III, "Implementation," Chapter 10 begins with securing an authorization to proceed based on positive relationships with management. Chapter 11 continues with product selection and purchasing. Chapter 12 contains the areas of installation and testing. Chapter 13 focuses on the available choices for training end users. Chapter 14 provides the functional components of communications management.

In Part IV, "Application," Chapter 15 offers a spectrum of communications examples to provide insight into actual uses in modern organizations. Chapter 16 is about electronic mail and message systems. Chapter 17 emphasizes effective communications security procedures. Chapter 18 reveals the information resources in on-line data bases. Chapter 19 opens up the mainframe computer software available through time sharing. Chapter 20 focuses on starting communications with external customers, suppliers, and clients.

This book is intended to be a practical tool for data processing and data communications professionals who are managing the introduction of a modern information environment in their organizations. These individuals may work in an information center, a project group in the MIS department, an office automation task force, an in-house computer store, or even a "microcomputer department." While most of these individuals' expertise is considerable, this book offers the spectrum of issues and decisions surrounding communications on micros, word processors, workstations, mainframes, and minicomputers. This is an area that is only now being widely developed from an integrated corporate perspective.

The book also addresses the needs of office and administrative managers who are relied upon for input during planning, implementation, and use of communications using the micros, workstations, word processors, and computer terminals in their departments. Users who have not had formal computer training will understand and benefit from this book if they have had some experience in using a business microcomputer, word processor, or a larger computer.

For students, the coverage meets a growing need of computer science, business, management, and related courses. This book helps prepare today's students to work in the types of advanced information environments now being built by many corporations. It treats the subject broadly by including both concepts and applications. It also offers the specifics of analyzing, designing, implementing, and applying effective business communications using microcomputers and word processors, the types of systems with which so many students are familiar.

Now that more than 25 million microcomputers and word processors will be in corporations by the end of the decade, many companies and users are interested in linking micros and word processors to other systems to produce a variety of business goals. Left to themselves, users tend to make these connections in ad hoc ways. This will obstruct uniform communications in most companies within a few years.

There are two important reasons to develop a modern information environment systematically in each company. First, a significant body of knowledge is available for designing well-planned communications, to avoid future problems and realize business benefits. Second, substantial advantages result from systematic solutions including cost and time savings, accelerated learning curves, and centralized control.

ACKNOWLEDGMENTS

This book is the result of years of experience in data communications and computing, and in addition to the people who provided those experiences, many highly skilled people have shared their expertise with us. The authors would above all like to thank the engineering and marketing staffs of Racal-Milgo, whose contributions have been both essential and superb. Since it is not possible to thank all those who assisted individually, we would like this book to be our way of saying "thank you."

Those involved with the development of this book also deserve thanks. They include Richard Nathanson, Vice-President of Racal-Milgo, who had the original idea to write the book and repeatedly gave his time and energy to help it grow; John Steele, who was the godfather of the book during its birth and made essential early contributions; Alex Durr, who offered strong assistance and support during the middle stages of the writing; Oscar Collier, whose advice about the literary handling of this project helped more than he may ever realize; and the book's editor, Karl Karlstrom, whose interest, professional support, and guidance steered this book from its inception until it had become the best book the authors could create.

The credit for the successes of this book belongs to all those who helped, while responsibility for flaws belongs to the authors.

Last but not least are those who, in their own way, made the writing of this book possible: Marcy Abelow, who was extraordinarily patient because she knew what she was in for, and was unusually helpful since she is responsible for integrating microcomputers, minicomputers, and mainframes in her professional work; Don Lewis, for maintaining at peak performance the computer on which the book was written; Alan Weiselberg, for his unwavering support in seeing this book's cause advanced; Stanley Kuperstein, for his inimitable method of proving how sophisticated an enthusiastic user's achievements may be; and Sunset, for keeping the terminal free of cat hair while spending countless hours on the desk during the writing.

Daniel Abelow
Edwin J. Hilpert

Part I
ANALYSIS

1

INTRODUCTION AND OVERVIEW

By the mid- to late 1980s, what will be the biggest "computer" in a typical billion-dollar corporation? The corporation may acquire 1000 microcomputers, word processors, and workstations. End users will then have more computing power than even a data processing (DP) department that is running three mainframes and more than a dozen minis. There will also be more "computer people" who are end users than there is staff in the MIS department. See Figure 1.1.

End-Users:		Data Processing:	
Computers and Word Processors	RAM Memory (processing power)	Computers and Word Processors	Megabytes of RAM
300 micros with	64K RAM each	3 mainframes	Each computer:
150 micros with	128K RAM each		36 Megabytes RAM
200 micros with	256K RAM each		
50 micros with	512K RAM each	15 minicomputers	Each minicomputer:
250 multi-user	2 Megabytes of RAM		2 Megabytes RAM
micros with	in each micro		
50 word processors	64K RAM each	16 word processors	128K RAM each
200 word processors	128K RAM each		
Total End-Users: 1,200 systems	Total RAM: 644 Megabytes	Total DP: 34 systems	Total RAM: 140 Megabytes

Figure 1.1 Even large DP departments may soon be passed in size by the numbers of end users doing various kinds of computing and word processing, and the combined magnitude of their local office systems.

The managers and staff of DP departments are literally being thrown into a situation where the "personal computing department" may soon outgrow their own. When a large corporation has acquired 1000 IBM PCs, it has generally added between 256 megabytes and 640 megabytes of processing power (RAM memory), a staggering amount to put rapidly in the hands of end users. It does not matter whether an organization is small or large. The introduction and everyday use of microcomputers and word processors is not a passing fad. It is a fundamental change in the computing environment of many organizations.

1.1 REASONS FOR COMMUNICATIONS

Because of the growing size and complexity of many organizations, employees require rapid access to up-to-date information from other operating areas in order to complete transactions, manage everyday operations, meet government regulations, make significant decisions, review performance, and develop strategic plans and budgets for the future.

In an increasing number of organizations, there is an accelerating use of micros, word processors, and workstations to enhance the business capabilities of the organization to capture and process larger amounts of information. This is now being followed by responsible attempts to link these distributed desktop systems with the organization's main data center and with each other, so that business performance can be increased rapidly.

Executives, for example, no longer require a central data processing department to continually provide new custom reports. Summarized data is increasingly downloaded to a desktop system from a mainframe computer. Executives then use a micro or a workstation as a tool to help make improved decisions; to develop plans, budgets and forecasts; to formulate policies and objectives; and to manage the enterprise's activities.

The introduction of computing throughout organizations has been compared to the development of factories and the industrial revolution, on which our economy and society have depended for over a century. This is an accurate comparison. There is probably no greater business advantage available today than the effective combination of personal computing and rapid communications. Both individuals and organizations are exploring these opportunities, to gain the increased competitive performance abilities that are now available.

1.2 BENEFITS FROM COMMUNICATIONS

Perhaps the largest impact of micros, word processors, and workstations is that they combine easily learned computer systems with the business needs and work structure of local offices throughout an organization. As a result, computing is now being dispersed rapidly to appropriate employees, enabling them to be more effective.

Modern organizations are highly specialized. Typical functions include marketing, accounting, manufacturing, personnel, and the like. All of these functions may be present in one division of an enterprise, and one enterprise may contain multiple divisions in areas as diverse as lumbering, construction, and consumer products.

There is an organizational structure within each functional activity, such as in one division's marketing, and this contains its own management system and information requirements. Daily business operations require the most detailed information for functions such as transaction processing, inventory, and order entry. In many small and larger organizations today, these are being computerized in local offices using small local systems.

The operating data in each department generally resembles the business information needed by other departments in the same division. Customer data is needed by marketing, accounting, and shipping. Detailed summaries of current sales are needed by inventory control, manufacturing, and purchasing. While the overall operating data is the same, each area has its own way of looking at and using the enterprises's information. Since data that is sent from one system to another is only copied, it can be sent to all locations where it is needed. Personal computing combined with communications can provide numerous ways to view the same data.

For competitive and logistical reasons, increasing computerization is required to process the high volume of data that is present in each functional area. Once installed, the local computer systems in a sales office, for example, can rapidly produce and transmit one extract of each day's transactions for accounting, another for product shipping, one for management summaries, and so on. When communications is added to appropriate local systems, these daily reports can be generated and sent at high speed to appropriate workers and offices in other departments in the organization.

Compared to the mail or even to overnight delivery, there is much faster turnaround time for computer communications. At a moderate speed of communications, it takes six seconds to send one page over a standard telephone dial-up link between two systems. That means up to ten pages of business information can be sent in less than a minute, and many companies already use faster communications speeds than this.

By marrying local computing with rapid communications, each office's operating and management information can be more responsive to the business needs of other functional areas, and to central management. Transaction information and summary data can be sent swiftly from dispersed local systems to the main data center and to other offices and departments. A great deal more current operating information can now be made rapidly available, in specific beneficial information flows, to improve operations and decisions throughout an enterprise.

In each company there is a hierarchy of information needs in which detailed customer and transaction requirements are on the bottom. At this level, local computer systems process the detailed information that comprises the work flow of an individual or an office. The information is aggregated as it moves upward from offices to regional and division management until it is transformed into operating summaries for those at the top of the pyramid. These individuals need general information that affects the total organization.

What is emerging today is the ability to process, store, retrieve, and rapidly transmit current operating data by using small local computers and communications throughout an organization. As the information is transmitted upward through the organization's information hierarchy, the size of the computer systems that process it also increase. The information is generally aggregated in larger, centralized computer systems. There it is available for senior executives to access, using micros and workstations, to prepare operating summaries and presentations that include word processing, computer graphics, and numerical analyses.

1.3   MANAGEMENT ASPECTS OF COMMUNICATIONS

The overall impact of introducing computing to local offices is to shift power and responsibility to the department, executives, and employees who properly manage and benefit from their own systems. After micros have been introduced, one clear management responsibility is to plan and justify adding communications to appropriate micros and word processors. In most cases, this will be done by end users and staff from the central data processing department together.

Effective coordination is required because communications shrink the working distance between the different offices in one department, or between departments. The primary objective is to plan high-speed communications to support business operations, management control, planning, and other functions of an organization.

Computer-to-computer communications therefore becomes part of the central business system of an enterprise, and it matches the requirements of operating areas like accounting, manufacturing, marketing, and management. As a result, there are multiple operating objectives in designing communications and evolving requirements over time.

These communications objectives generally fall into four areas: Information sharing, responsiveness, reliability, and decision making. As in all periods of organizational development, coordinated planning is the essential prerequisite to achieving significant goals and objectives.

1.3.1   Information Sharing

Information sharing is the effective management of the organization's information resources to realize specific operating and business benefits. This can be initiated from a top-down perspective by a DP department or by senior management. It may also be requested from the bottom up, by users who can make a case for benefits they would receive from greater access to extracts of computerized information in the main data center, or in the local systems in other offices.

One example is off-loading processing and information storage from a main center to local micros. This provides economies of scale from easier-to-use microcomputer software, and distributes the processing load to the offices in which information is used. Because more relevant computerized data is stored locally in the office in which it is used, there is often faster access than if it were available only in the corporate data center.

As a result of local storage, however, there are greater needs to share portions of this information with others who need it. This may reduce communications costs. When data is processed locally, summaries of the data can often be sent between systems instead of large volumes of raw data.

1.3.2 Responsiveness

Responsiveness is a key reason why personal computing has spread so rapidly. It is the capability of local systems to directly satisfy local computing needs. This same benefit results from adding planned computer communications to small local systems: The computerized data inputs to an office meet its current requirements, and its data outputs correspond to the information needs of specific other offices, departments, and managers in the organization.

In addition, the growth of communications responds to the needs of local applications that are done with micros, word processors, and workstations. Once a communications link has been proven for each type of system and application—such as the consolidation of one division's budgets on a mainframe, after local budgets have been prepared on micros—it can be spread rapidly to other offices that have similar systems. It is no longer necessary to design a new application or a new communications link. Consider four examples:

- A nationwide computerized order entry system may have been wanted for years. By using microcomputer software available for some industries that includes or can have communications added to it, it may be implemented on micros in a few months.

- An electronic mail network may be needed, but it might be too expensive to add to a mainframe computer. If a few micros or word processors are already used in most offices around the country, lower-cost electronic mail is within reach.

- Only the most sophisticated mainframes allow managers to call up data in the data base, and then to graph it to show current trends and business performance. There are many packages that do this on micros, however, using data from other computers throughout a corporation. Since these graphs can be sent between compatible micros, senior and middle management can be given a "results at a glance" graphic management information system without a major investment by the DP department.

- Departmental applications such as personnel records, parts lists, and marketing performance reports can be off-loaded from mainframe computers. Departmental processing and communications lighten the main data center's work load, while giving users local systems tailored to their unique needs.

1.3.3 Reliability

Reliability involves three capabilities. The first is the ability to add effective communications without having to scrap existing computer systems and purchase new, compatible ones. While a single compatibility solution is not available, an increasing number of organizations have proven that it is possible, within reasonable cost and performance limits, to achieve reliable communications with incompatible systems.

The second reliability objective is the ease with which users can manage communications. With recent and current generations of communications software and hardware, it has become possible to bury the complexities of communications so that they are, in the main, invisible to users. Instead of focusing on "how to do it," users may now direct their attention to the more useful question, "How much can I accomplish today?"

Third, the reliability of communications between multiple systems is generally high. In a corporation with a single large mainframe, the words "The system is down" affects the entire enterprise. With local computing, duplication of hardware and software is built in throughout the organization. Since communications hardware and software are also highly reliable once tested and proven, a high degree of data independence and operating protection are built into organizations that use micros, word processors, and workstations.

1.3.4 Decision Making

As in other areas of computer technology, rapid advances are being made in communications during this decade. The price of communications hardware is falling, for instance. This decline is about 10 to 15 percent per year, about the same rate of decline as micros.

This complicates purchase decisions, because it sometimes seems wiser to wait for tomorrow's system than it is to purchase today's. Technological advances are not slowing in the communications field, so there isn't any "best time" to buy; next year's hot new system will be as vulnerable to change as the one available right now. One profitable rule of thumb is to determine if the payback period from a specific communications investment is less than two years, and to add the communications if it is.

1.4 SYSTEM COMPONENTS

In the 1960s it took an entire corporation to afford a mainframe computer. In the 1970s, that same amount of computing power was put into a minicomputer, and it could be afforded by a department. Today, an equal amount of computing power can be put in a micro that fits on one person's desk, and thousands of these can be used in a large corporation.

At this moment, the technology of these smaller systems continues to mature rapidly. In 1975, when the microcomputer was introduced, it was an 8-bit computer that had 4K to 16K of RAM memory and ran at one or two megahertz. (A megahertz is one million cycles per second of clock frequency.) During the 1980s, the performance standard is becoming the 16-bit or 32-bit micro with up to four megabytes of RAM, running at up to 10 megahertz, which allows millions of computer operations per second. See Figure 1.2.

Micros and workstations are increasingly replacing intelligent terminals in corporate networks for three reasons. First, when local systems are not on-line with a mainframe computer, they can serve user departments with a wide variety of local computer applications. Second, they relieve the host mainframe of processing tasks that local systems can perform equally well, such as applications that frequently repeat screens or entering and validating data at the local level. Third, most reasonably powerful micros and workstations can access

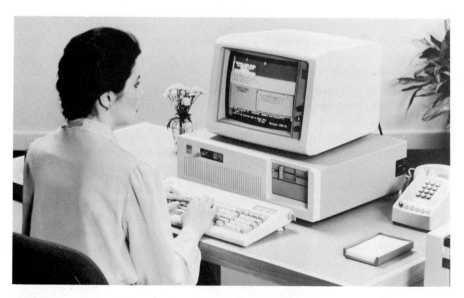

Figure 1.2   The IBM Personal Computer AT combines word processing, data processing, and storage for 20 million characters of software and information on its hard disk, and a multiuser system in one desktop computer. Photograph courtesy IBM Corporation.

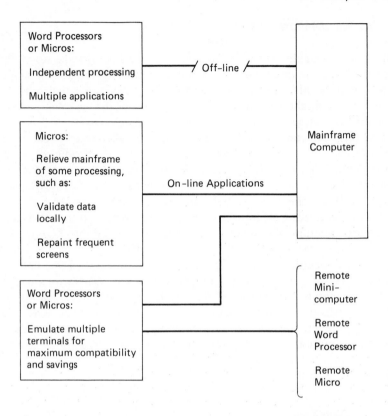

Figure 1.3   Reasons why desktop systems are replacing intelligent terminals in corporate networks.

more than one network or computer by emulating different kinds of intelligent or dumb terminals. See Figure 1.3.

By adding communications between appropriate micros, workstations, and word processors, a company builds a modern information system that spreads across time zones and thousands of miles. It becomes as easy to send a memo across a continent as it is to send it down the hall. As a result, the foundation is built for a new concept the authors call a *nationwide office.*

A nationwide office is an extended environment in which people have the instant computer and telephone communications they need to work together as if they were located in the same building, though they may not be connected by either geography or time zone. The main reason for rapid communications is not to gain computer processing, as it is with remote terminals linked to a central mainframe computer. The main benefit from communications is sending and receiving operating business information and summaries at higher speeds than has been possible before.

Among the most powerful beliefs are those that govern attitudes toward time and space. In 1902, a year before the Wright brothers' first airplane flight and six years before Henry Ford's Model T, a child sitting in a horse-drawn carriage would have imagined expressways, airports, and five-hour transcontinental flights ridiculous. The idea that people would walk on the moon during his or her lifetime might have been laughable.

Today's emerging information environment points toward the same scale of advances. As communications between computers of all sizes and word processors becomes normal, the meanings of time and distance may change again. Potentially, few offices in a company will be independent from each other, and this may be a change of age as well as an age of change.

From a planning perspective, the system components in a nationwide office start from the base of an organization's existing and planned computer systems and word processors, applications software, data files, and operating procedures. To this is added communications hardware, communications software, communications management, user procedures, and links between some workstations and a company's data network(s).

A growing need to develop capable end users should not be ignored. New skills expectations are affecting executives and employees in many organizations. New computer literacy requirements, computer usage expectations, and computer communications responsibilities have started to arrive as essential personal skills. In most companies, increasing efforts are being devoted to helping employees become sophisticated end users. Over the coming years, the most sophisticated users of communications using micros, workstations, and word processors will slide into the driver's seat of local information management.

1.5 REALISTIC EXPECTATIONS

Because micros, workstations and word processors are new members of data networks, their arrival presents problems as well as benefits. Data processing managers would prefer a single solution that links all their company's local office systems into their networks. Their impossible dream is finding one product that links all the different systems with one step.

On a technical level computer communications works better if different types of communications have different standards, while maintaining compatibility. Users often need to share data bases and files within each office. This requires multiuser micros or local area networks (whose speed is one megabit, one million bits per second, or greater). The need to send an office's work to other departments within a company calls for remote communications over the telephone network, or over a private data network. Remote communications are substantially slower than local communications. In addition, a private network can be built in a number of ways, and these also differ from public networks that link computers in many companies.

There are too many unique communication needs for one standard product to satisfy them all. A more realistic goal is for a company to develop communication standards that match its systems and its needs. Developing some of these solutions has become quick and easy, while others remain difficult, but most parts of them are technically possible today.

In many organizations, effective communications are being built by taking the available elements and piecing them together into workable solutions. This satisifies the technical questions, though the answers are not ideal. Still, more choices are available each year in a faster, bigger, and cheaper "black box," or in rapidly improving communications software.

While the lack of sophisticated software for micros was a typical DP complaint in the 1970s, it has become a reason for optimism in the 1980s. With millions of dollars in profits possible from one microcomputer software package, the battle to write and sell better software has attracted major computer companies and venture capitalists. Some of the newer packages rival software that costs tens of thousands of dollars on mainframes, yet they cost only a few hundred dollars. One area of furious growth is new software that supports compatible corporate communications between micros and mainframes.

By selecting and testing appropriate hardware and software, uniform standards can be created for communications by an organization. This results in a "building block" approach to the use and growth of communications. Each office can add local office systems as needed in small low-cost steps while enjoying compatible high-speed communications with the rest of the company.

With the promise of compatible communications, a more difficult objective can be considered: building a shared information infrastructure based on planned and coordinated business operations. This is the real bridge between stand-alone personal systems and an emerging era of accessible computerized information. Communications hardware and software are smaller obstacles than creating and developing planning projects that answer a company's data organization questions.

Successfully managing each stage in the transition to a new era is the real challenge raised when powerful desktop workstations pose the questions of "What can't we do better? Where have we computerized the information we need today? How do we extract it and make it available to those who need it? What new computerized information resources are we going to have next year, based on the new systems we're installing now? Where will we be in five years, and how will we operate then?"

This is not an easy situation, but new opportunities are rarely simple. This new era will continue to grow rapidly, with or without systematic planning and participation by users and DP professionals in any particular company.

The spread of a modern information environment is a major business de-velopment that cannot be ignored. In an increasing number of companies, the combination of computing and communications is starting to become the busi-ness, and business systems are being built around strategic uses of these technologies. This will go much more smoothly and produce better results if those affected, including both users and DP professionals, start using the best techniques to develop this new era.

2

THE FEASIBILITY STUDY

The first step in telecommunications planning is to reduce the project to a series of clear steps that are carried out in sequence and yield the desired results. Many of these steps are mainly routine and can be handled by capable end users. The procedures are similar to those followed in other types of business planning. Each step should be pursued with the level of precision appropriate for an organization before moving on to the next step.

When computer communications is added between micros, word processors, workstations, and computer terminals—whether to two word processors or to an entire corporation—data is needed from inside the organization. What is the company's situation? What needs will be satisfied by computer communications? What business objectives will be achieved? What is the specific program required to achieve them?

Determining this requires, first, selecting those responsible for planning and implementation, and second, a feasibility study.

2.1 MANAGEMENT MODELS FOR COMMUNICATIONS PLANNING

The everyday use of micros, word processors, and workstations changes the relationship between the DP department and end users. As executives, clerks, bookkeepers, lawyers, and secretaries use all types of personal systems, the mystery of computing disappears. As user experience grows, their authority over the use of their systems expands.

The ownership of computerized business data is also following the use of personal computing. Control is spreading from DP to the end-user community that creates and stores the data on its own systems. As the number of local systems increases throughout a department in a company, the need expands to share the data with other local systems in the department and company, including the DP department.

When users and DP start sharing computerized business data, the pattern of control is shaped by the politics and culture of each company. Depending on each company's needs, five kinds of management models may be followed. An information center, steering committee, in-house consultants, joint task force, or microcomputer department can guide the information compatibility and hardware/software selection so that information transfers and data structures are compatible throughout the corporation.

No matter which pattern the DP-user effort follows, the overall modern information environment rapidly develops increasing complexity. Successful management combines the technical understanding possessed by DP with the business understanding of users. Contributions from both are essential if the evolution of a computerized corporation is to succeed. Any management approach must be a team effort between end users and DP staff, if the quality of the company's business information is to be protected.

For example, users in departments like accounting, marketing, finance, law, and manufacturing should help define their own needs for computer communications. DP specialists can guide and assist users with the technical details of installing and operating the communications on the users' business micros, workstations, and word processors.

2.1.1 The Information Center

In most companies, the information center is part of the DP department and is staffed by DP personnel. The information center assists users in most of the phases of planning, purchasing, and expanding the scope of their computing, whether the mainframe computer, micros, word processors, or workstations are used.

The information center was developed by IBM in Canada to bridge the gap between the DP department and the end user. A DP department with a multimillion-dollar budget often takes over a year to meet new or changing user needs, while one user with a powerful business micro can start seeing results in a few hours or days. The purpose of the information center is to give the users the computing tools they need on both the mainframe computer and, with an increasing number of companies, on whatever system they may be using.

The staff of the information center usually starts with one or more in-house consultants, but then grows on the basis of the amount of user needs stimulated. Eventually, there can be managers, coordinators, and consultants supporting the computing of hundreds or thousands of end users.

Classroom training and seminars are usually offered, covering the how-tos of basic end-user computing. Hands-on training can include retrieving data from the mainframe computer, creating screens on terminals or micros, producing reports desired, electronic mail, and how to use computer communications. The point of access to the company's larger computer systems can be a terminal, a micro, a word processor, or a workstation.

The information center offers services that it must "sell" to users. To do this it may send out a newsletter, hold an open house when it introduces a major new tool or microcomputer system, or offer seminars in end-user departments when their data on the mainframe is made more accessible to them. With each group of users, the information center often starts working with the users who are both interested and motivated, and these users in turn spread the word in their offices.

2.1.2 Steering Committee

In this approach, DP staff and users work together to develop written objectives for the use of communications between appropriate systems throughout the company. A plan is developed and signed by all groups, and the systems are implemented and used according to the guidelines. The guidelines are reviewed periodically to ensure that they match current needs. The steering committee should meet regularly to maintain the compatibility and usefulness or the data on the different systems, as they change over time, so that the data can be communicated between appropriate users throughout the company.

The steering committee can give end users considerably more responsibility than an information center. A general model for this approach is:

1. Consider having the committee chaired by an end user. If the DP department causes a problem or a slowdown, it should accept the blame at once. If the DP department is not at fault, the responsibility is then clearly on the users. The impact of this approach is that the use, maintainance, and training needed for new systems becomes steadily more of a user responsibility. Expenses related to workstations and communications between them are assumed by end users in their department budgets. Department managers will watch their computing expenses closely, and make sure that these tools are both useful and cost-effective.

2. The steering committee sets overall priorities and approves the corporate standards for hardware, software, and communications. These standards reflect the business needs of users.

3. Individual projects that use or communicate between micros, word processors, or workstations should be approved by the steering committee only if users want it. Where possible, a user should be named project

manager, and should be responsible for seeing that planned deadlines are met.

4. If users want an application on the mainframe computer but face a wait of more than a year, they should be encouraged to consider their local systems for their application.

5. As a base of sophisticated end users develops, they can be encouraged to form advanced user groups and start independent planning. The DP department can set up a training program for advanced users, to introduce them to the life cycle of developing an application, and the responsibility involved at all stages, including maintaining it after it has been installed.

   Their plans, proposed systems, and user-written manuals should be submitted to the steering committee, but advanced users should be supported in moving faster and contributing more to the company. Their major limits should be adhering to corporate-wide information, hardware, software, and communications standards to insure compatibility.

Some of today's DP departments may consider this too high a level of user involvement, but a high level of user self-sufficiency offers benefits that cannot be ignored.

2.1.3 In-House Consultants

These specialists are company employees who may have a variety of titles, such as "business sytems consultant" or "end-user service coordinator." They are organized either as a formal group, or as individuals assigned to specific departments, offices, or projects. Their responsibilities include two-way communications between DP and end users. When end users have a problem or expand their use of workstations, they work with these consultants to plan purchases, receive training, develop new applications on their systems, or solve problems. These consultants may come from the DP departments, or they may be knowledgeable end users.

2.1.4 Task Force Management

A task force includes both end users and DP staff who tackle a specific project together, such as the companywide communication of one type of business transaction: How accurate is the data in it, who owns the data, and how it is communicated from one department to the next so that it can be used in the local computer systems in each office?

2.1.5 Microcomputer Department

This may be a separate department (or a new "microcomputer manager" position), or it might operate under the control of the DP department. It develops standards for buying and using micros, workstations, and sometimes word processors. When users want to add one or more systems, this group helps them evaluate their needs and planned uses. It often helps users get their new systems up and running properly.

A microcomputer department may not formally recognize the communications needs of personal computer systems, including communications with larger company computers, but this can be included as a specific responsibility. These responsibilities generally involve:

- Evaluating communications software and hardware.
- Helping develop appropriate communications procedures and standards, and encouring their use.
- Forming user groups for regular information exchange.
- Offering training, support, and service for end-user systems and business applications.

2.2 FEASIBIILITY STUDY PROCEDURES

In general, the larger the company, the more departments that may become involved in communications planning. Most organizations are also developing control over end-user computing, including both selection of systems and applications, which leads to greater centralization of decisions. The DP department is usually the leader of these efforts, and most end-user managers follow the approach suggested by the DP department.

At the same time, there is a greater effort by DP to involve end users. Increasingly, solutions are viewed from user points of view, and are not preconceived technical decisions. This offers greater concern for improving the business effectiveness of the users and the organization, by fitting the users' business information needs instead of the DP department's technical systems.

This can only occur if users contribute significantly to all phases of planning during the (in general) seven-step feasibility study. Depending on each company's needs, some of the steps can be skipped, if appropriate.

2.2.1 Preliminary Steps

In most organizations, it is important to request written authority to conduct a feasibility study before it is begun. This authorization can be as informal as a memo, or it can be a formal project brief. In general, however, it should include the following elements:

- The feasibility study's name.
- Who initiated it and authorized it.

- Its purpose and duration.
- The group responsible for the study, including its manager and staff.
- A list of the departments included in the study.
- A budget figure if expenditures will be made (such as travel to various cities).

A second preliminary task is to create a standard meeting note-taking form that will document what is learned in each of the study's interviews, help assemble the recommendations, and prove critical if specific facts must be confirmed later. One format for this form is in Figure 2.1, though it should be adapted to the political needs of each company.

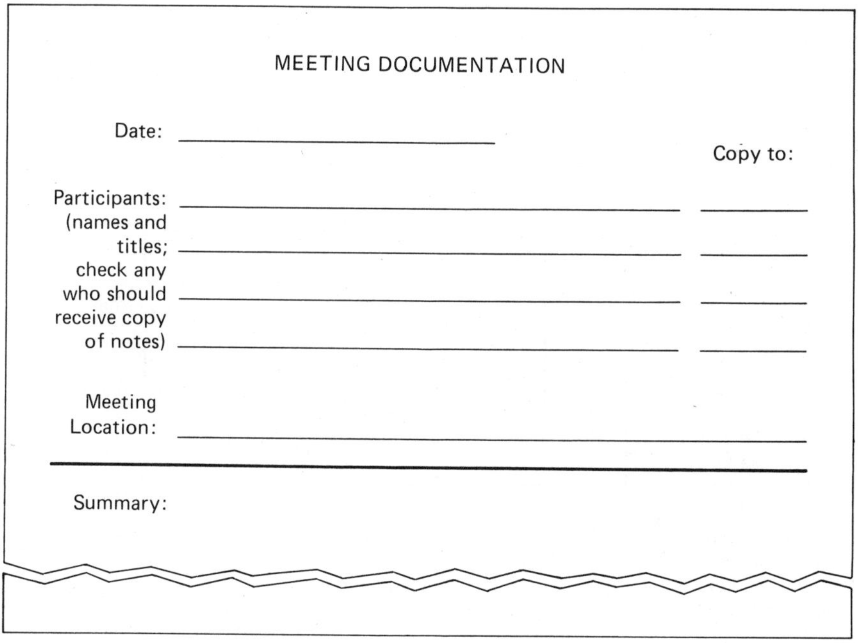
MEETING DOCUMENTATION

Date: ____________

Copy to:

Participants: (names and titles; check any who should receive copy of notes) ____________

Meeting Location: ____________

Summary:

Figure 2.1 Standard meeting notes documentation form.

2.2.2 Data Collection

Next, determine the appropriate part(s) of the department(s) where computer communications should be added. The information needed to decide this will be gathered in three steps of the feasibility study, which will together create four documents:

- An organization chart that also lists computer and word processing systems and terminals.
- Diagrams of the physical layouts of the offices in which computer communications are being added.
- Job descriptions of the areas already computerized and those that will be computerized in the near future.
- A flowchart of paperwork that illustrates the use of computers and word processors.

Organization charts and office layouts can often be acquired by interviewing appropriate department or office managers. In the interviews, have the managers explain the size of the staff in each area and the computer or word processing equipment used. See Figure 2.2.

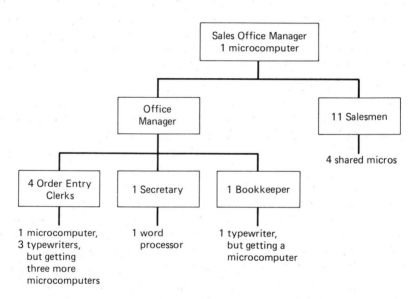

Figure 2.2   Sample organization chart, with numbers of staff and all computers, terminals, and workstations added.

If possible, conclude each interview with a tour of the offices in which the staff works, and draw pictures of the physical arrangements of the word processor and computer equipment they use. Note already installed communications links to off-site computers on the diagrams. See Figure 2.3.

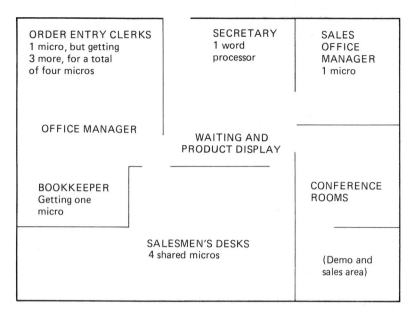

Figure 2.3 Sample office layout, showing locations of current and potential micros, word processors, workstations, and terminals.

2.2.3 Office Environment

Once the physical arrangements of the offices are known, it is time to concentrate on the areas that are computerized (or soon will be computerized) with microcomputers, word processors, workstations, and terminals. The definition of "soon will be computerized" should match the organization's business planning horizon.

These will generally be the areas in which computer communications can be started, since the purpose of this feasibility study is to add computer communications where needed, *not* to add more micros, workstations, and word processors to the organization.

Now interview appropriate users and their supervisors. Develop a list of their computer-related activities. This list should include short job descriptions and the ways that communications applies to each activity. See Figure 2.4.

If one of these job description lists can be attached to each word processor or microcomputer on the office layout, the next document can be created. This is a flowchart of work that might be linked electronically in the departments or offices in the study. This can be developed with the aid of an activity survey.

Jobs done on the micro now, or planned for the next three micros, after installation	Does telecommunications apply to this activity?
Enter new orders	Yes — send them in daily via phone, saving express courier costs
Maintain current price list	Yes — price changes can be received via telecommunications
Answer questions from salesmen and customers	Yes — access answers in the computers of other departments (such as shipping date info. in shipping, available inventory, and credit status)
Provide summary totals to Sales Office Manager and Corporate HQ	Yes — send formatted data to his micro through a possible local area network and to the main data center
Filing copies of orders	Yes — archiving sales orders in main data center, in weekly batches; stored on tape
Maintain customer history for sales tracking and planning	Yes — offload previous history from DP computer into local hard disk, for faster access (if a shared hard disk or a local area network can be obtained)

Figure 2.4   Sample job description list, for order entry clerks.

2.2.4 Activity Surveys

The last document, the paperwork flowchart, shows how paperwork flows throughout the department. Activity surveys use interviews with the people who supervise the use of micros, word processors, workstations, or terminals on larger computers, to determine the quantity of each type of paperwork. Quite often, managers or their staff will know roughly how many documents or entries are completed per month in each area.

If they do not know, numbered documents may yield that information. For example, record the invoice numbers from the first day of each month for the past few months to compute an average month's volume of invoices. (Numbers of sales or customers can be derived from documents such as invoices, also.)

During the activity survey, acquire a sample of each kind of paperwork or document processed (those on the paperwork flowchart).

Current Turnaround Time: 10 to 14 days from receipt of order to shipping and billing
On-line Turnaround Time: 1 to 3 days from receipt of order to shipping and billing

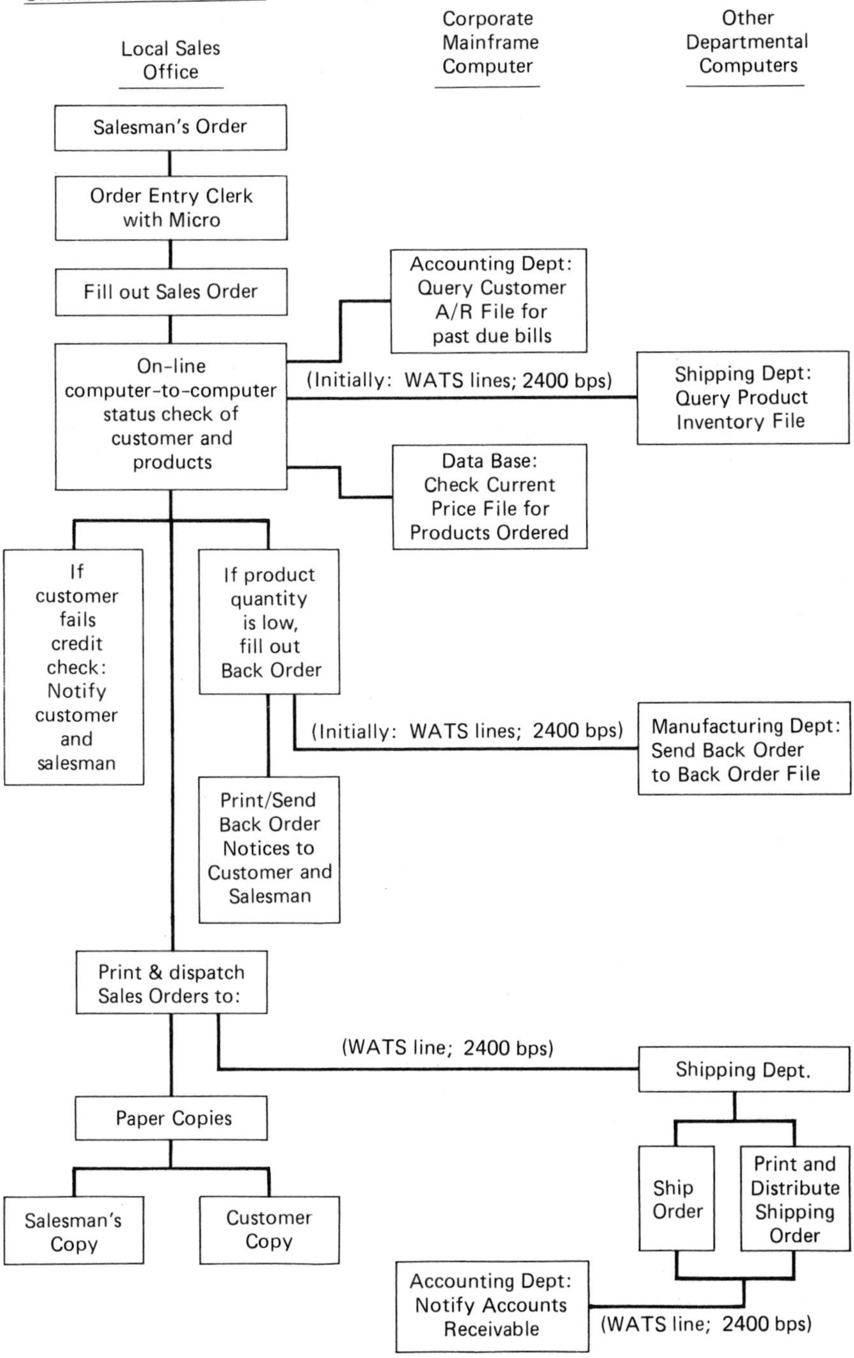

Figure 2.5 Work flow diagram including projected communications with other computers.

Also, ask the amount of time in days that it takes for the finished paperwork from each type of job to be transmitted to its next department and entered into the next computer system (if a computer is used there).

By adding this time information, the activity survey helps show the benefits from computer communications. The final work flow diagram should be something like the example in Figure 2.5.

2.2.5 Confirm Gathered Data

Enough information has now been collected to begin serious planning, but there is one more step before starting. The basic facts should be confirmed with the appropriate department managers, especially the facts on their area in the four initial planning documents.

Since the main recommendations are going to be based on these documents, this confirmation will help support the recommendations. Use the standard meeting notes form to record each confirmation, and send a copy of the meeting notes to the department manager after he or she confirms the gathered facts.

2.2.6 Data Analysis

Planning can begin once there is a basic overview of the departments, people, computer systems, and how the work is done. The next problem is the most important one: knowing what really needs to be accomplished.

If the imagined goal is to add communications to all the microcomputers and word processors in all the departments in the study, this is wrong. Networking a business is not the purpose of planning.

The goal of planning is to develop specific information access and transmission that these departments will use to achieve their business objectives. If it is available, analyze the company's business plan, especially where it describes the departments in the study. Tailor the proposed solutions to help achieve these business goals, and communications is more likely to be implemented.

For instance, look at the differences between the business purposes of departments. Every department's name tells you about its primary goal: accounting, marketing, shipping, manufacturing, management.

Each company is also unique. For example, a frozen foods shipping company is different from an automobile parts shipping company, even though both may have computing needs. Within one industry, the shipping department at a publisher of mass market paperbacks has different needs from a publisher of limited edition art books, yet they may both track their inventory with computers.

Communications planning should be as specific as each department is unique, and it should fit the business goals of each company and user as closely as possible.

2.2.7 Developing an Initial Model

Instead of only one answer, several recommendations should be developed and compared to each other. The best few solutions, together, are the goal, so that the appropriate executives can make the final choice. A method to arrive at these solutions is as follows:

1. Determine where direct electronic communication using micros, computer terminals, or word processors can accelerate the work flow.

2. List in adequate detail the different possible solutions that appear appropriate. Many companies have adopted a communications structure where micros, word processors, and workstations are linked to each other *through* a mainframe or minicomputer(s) that handles the communications. In other companies there are existing data networks that have excess capacity. It is usually desirable to fit the overall corporate pattern, unless there are specific reasons to offer another solution.

3. If the paperwork flowchart can be improved, determine the most logical flow of paperwork according to the specific objectives described in the interviews. If changes in existing work flows will be suggested, these need to be reviewed with appropriate managers before continuing with planning, since such changes may not be acceptable.

4. Link together with communications groups of jobs and activities that can be performed by the same piece of computer equipment, communications hardware, or transmission line(s), even if these are located in different offices. This is not always obvious. Communications hardware does not care whether it is transmitting manufacturing or accounting data, for example.

5. Calculate the total time savings that result from each possible solution.

6. Determine if each possible solution helps achieve the business objectives of the department, the people working in it, and the company as a whole.

7. How will each solution work in actual use? Is it easy for the current staff to learn? Will they find it reliable? Who will maintain the hardware? Is the necessary software available, or will it have to be developed? How will users handle problems?

8. How long will it take to introduce each solution? Can the implementation be scheduled to match the company's business plan for that department?

Are any elements new, unproven technologies? If some employees may be displaced, will the company's personnel department help find them jobs in other sections of the organization?

9. Determine the specific items of hardware, software, and transmission lines that are needed to implement each possible solution, and estimate their cost. These decisions may be made with the assistance of Chapter 3, "Criteria for Selecting Communications Software," and Chapter 4, "Characteristics and Functions of Communications Hardware."

10. Which of the solutions offers the most flexibility or capacity to meet changing conditions or future growth?

11. After reviewing the solutions, eliminate those with serious problems.

12. Write a short summary of each remaining solution, including both its features and its faults. Let this sit for several days, then read all the summaries together, as if they were presented for the first time, for a decision.

2.2.8 Refining the Model

Key people should be consulted at this stage in each department and office, to review the best available solutions and offer their suggestions. These key people are the manager of the work that is done in each office, and the manager of the department. If possible, also meet with line and staff members of divisions over the departments.

If the possible solutions are reviewed widely at this point, these managers will not feel that the new systems have been imposed on them. If top management must approve implementation (which is likely if the project is large enough), verifying that one or more recommendations are widely considered desirable and realistic will help them gain acceptance.

These meetings should follow a standard format, described in Figure 2.6. The meetings should confirm the planners' understanding and proposed solutions. The comments received help determine which are the best solutions for the final proposal.

If contradictions develop between the opinions received in these review meetings and previous statements from research, the initial meeting notes may prove valuable. They document the views of managers and staff on the facts in question.

This sequence leads to clear specifications for the proposed communications, and a list of business benefits expected. With this understanding, it is possible to tackle the software and hardware decisions on which the users' performance will depend.

Date:_____	Dept./Office:_____ Attending: _____ _____ _____
Presentation Areas and Sequence:	(use back for more names) **Notes:**

1. Briefly describe feasibility study
   a. Planning goals
   b. Scope of project
   c. People consulted
   d. Areas reviewed/studied	

2. Show understanding of situation
   a. Use organization chart, office
      layout, job descriptions, and
      work flowchart
   b. Use office's and company's
      business plans and goals	

3. Proposed solutions
   a. The recommended alternative
      — benefits
      — phases
      — cost
      — features or problems
   b. Other major alternatives	

4. Record meeting summary
   a. Points of agreement
   b. Points of disagreement
   c. Send key attendees a copy of
      the meeting notes	

Figure 2.6 Use a standard sequence for the presentations on the feasibility study, and a standard form for recording notes from the meetings.

3

CRITERIA FOR SELECTING
COMMUNICATIONS SOFTWARE

The criterion against which software should be evaluated is people, because people are the most important (and usually the most expensive) element in the work environment. It is people who decide what is done with communications, and their range of choices expands as they use micros, word processors, workstations, and terminals in new ways: data bases, spreadsheets, word processor documents, graphics, financial reports, forecasts, customer records, order entry, product inventories, and the like.

By itself, computer communications is a tool that parallels the telephone. Phones sit on millions of desks, but they gain meaning only when two people call each other and solve a problem, make an appointment, place an order, or employ them in countless other ways.

In the broadest sense, virtually anything that is done with computers or word processors can be a candidate for communications, because all kinds of data and text files can be sent from one system to another. A manager may spend hours using a micro to develop a spreadsheet, but only 30 seconds to send his conclusions to another manager's workstation. It is that 30 seconds that saves days before action is taken, since every decision must be communicated before it has an impact.

3.1 IDENTIFYING COMMUNICATIONS USERS

The first-line user is anyone who has a personal system or a terminal that he or she can use to communicate with other individuals who have a system, whether the remote systems are on another floor of the same building or on another continent. For example, most executives do not have access to their department's information in their corporation's main computer data base. If they had a user view of their area's performance that they could include in their decisions, one improved decision might pay for communications on all of their office's systems.

The second-line user is a person who has a local system or a terminal nearby. The system may be on a secretary's desk or at someone else's desk in the same office. In either case, computer communications can still provide access to the systems of remote individuals or access to information on remote computers. Second-line users might not need to know how to run the communications directly, but they should understand what can be accomplished with computer communications, so it can help them do their jobs better.

Second-line users often need immediate text communication with others with whom they work on joint projects. These combined efforts are constant in corporations: New product introductions forge intense team efforts that span several departments at once. Cost-cutting programs touch virtually every area of most companies at one time or another. Solving problems at remote locations requires frequent detailed communications with key individuals. Instant text delivery can speed business performance along with the information sent back and forth.

3.2 EVALUATION OF COMMUNICATIONS SOFTWARE

The software that sends recorded data from one system to another is called communications software. There is a wide range of quality between different communications software packages, just as with every other kind of software. The single most important feature that an end user needs is auto-dial/auto-answer capability, so that the user can avoid the complexities of putting systems on-line with each other.

Ideally, calling another computer should be as easy as dialing the phone. This is the value of auto-dialing, and there are two ways to achieve it. First, an "intelligent" auto-dial modem can be used, which is a modem that stores phone numbers and dials them with one keystroke. Second, it can be a feature of the communications software, which uses command files to control communications.

Command files are one key to simple end-user communications. They save users from having to learn how to run communications software. Second, the user doesn't have to know the phone number for any remote computer systems, or technical details for making different types of systems talk to each other. This is all determined in advance, entered into the command files, and performed automatically by the microcomputer or word processor under the control of the command file.

Most of today's users have grown up B.C., "Before Computers," and they don't want to know how a computer works. Many users may need computer communications, but they want their computer to dial another system automatically, or have their computer answer another system's call, without having to bother with complicated instructions.

Error checking is also a desirable feature, and it is included in some communications software. When error checking is used, the receiving system sends an acknowledgement after each block of data that is received correctly, so the sending system can transmit the next block of data. If a transmission error occurs, the receiving system asks for the last block of data to be retransmitted until it is received correctly. This is especially important when sending numerical data that must be error-free, such as a customer's order or a financial report.

Another useful feature is the ability of the communications software to change the protocol. For example, the Ethernet local area network uses only 7-bit data bytes, while most communications software for micros defaults to an 8-bit data byte. Since some software can be automatically configured when needed to 7-bit bytes by the command file that runs each call, this would be better software for workstations linked to an Ethernet network.

The communications speed that the software can handle without losing characters may also need evaluation. In most large organizations, existing communications networks are faster than 300 bps or 1200 bps.* In fact, many organizations that have a private data network may prefer a standard speed as high as 9600 bps. At these speeds, not all communications software can keep up with the data network.

3.3 USER INTERFACES

Another type of software that can be used in communications doesn't actually communicate—it is "menu" software that offers an easier interface between the user and the workstation, as illustrated in Figures 3.1 and 3.2.

There are various software packages on the market that provide menus, and some of these can be easily customized with titles, attractive screen layouts, and command lines that run software without users having to know the commands involved. Or a software program can be custom written to serve this purpose.

In Figure 3.2, when a user types "59" to call the Montreal office a series of steps takes place. The menu program runs the communications software. The communications software looks for a command file named MONTREAL. When it finds MONTREAL, it reads the telephone number and other commu-

---

*The abbreviation "bps" stands for bits per second, which is the number of bits of information that can be transmitted in one second. The *baud rate* (as in 300 baud) is also defined as the number of bits of data that can be transmitted in one second. In this book, bps is used to describe communications speeds. It is easier for many readers to understand 2400 bits per second than 2400 baud.

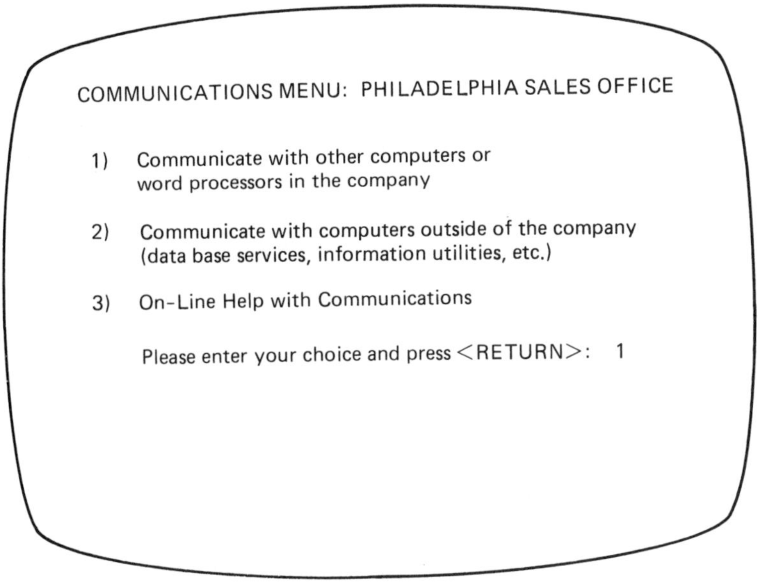

```
COMMUNICATIONS MENU:  PHILADELPHIA SALES OFFICE


     1)   Communicate with other computers or
          word processors in the company

     2)   Communicate with computers outside of the company
          (data base services, information utilities, etc.)

     3)   On-Line Help with Communications

          Please enter your choice and press <RETURN>:   1
```

Figure 3.1 A user selects in-company computer communications from the communications menu of the microcomputer, word processor, workstation, or terminal.

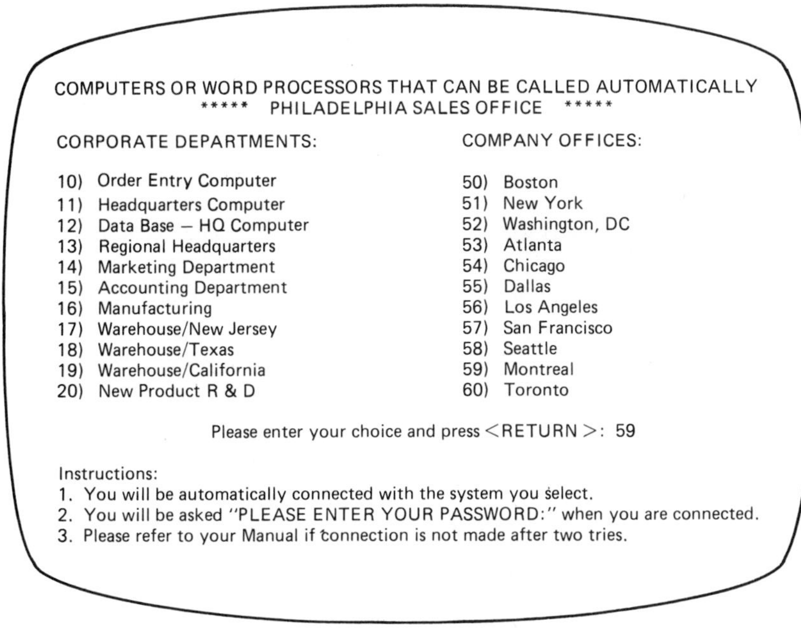

```
COMPUTERS OR WORD PROCESSORS THAT CAN BE CALLED AUTOMATICALLY
              *****   PHILADELPHIA SALES OFFICE   *****
    CORPORATE DEPARTMENTS:                COMPANY OFFICES:

    10)  Order Entry Computer             50)  Boston
    11)  Headquarters Computer            51)  New York
    12)  Data Base — HQ Computer          52)  Washington, DC
    13)  Regional Headquarters            53)  Atlanta
    14)  Marketing Department             54)  Chicago
    15)  Accounting Department            55)  Dallas
    16)  Manufacturing                    56)  Los Angeles
    17)  Warehouse/New Jersey             57)  San Francisco
    18)  Warehouse/Texas                  58)  Seattle
    19)  Warehouse/California             59)  Montreal
    20)  New Product R & D                60)  Toronto

          Please enter your choice and press <RETURN >:  59

Instructions:
1. You will be automatically connected with the system you select.
2. You will be asked "PLEASE ENTER YOUR PASSWORD:" when you are connected.
3. Please refer to your Manual if connection is not made after two tries.
```

Figure 3.2 A user selects an international call from the standard communications menu configured for his or her local office.

nications commands in the file as if they were entered from the keyboard. These commands are set up for the type of system in the Montreal office. An auto-dial modem establishes the connection automatically.

Since communications simplicity can be achieved for users, there is a rule of thumb that can help guide planning for end-user computer communications. If this criterion is met (through it may take some work on some personal systems and be impossible on others), the success of computer communications will be improved enormously:

> Computer users prefer simplicity over sophistication. The best kind of simplicity is to make the complexities of computer communications *invisible* to the user.

This is a high ideal, and it is difficult to achieve. As standard communications menus and communications procedures are developed and tested in a company, initial estimates of the time required before installation may have to be modified to match each situation as it develops.

Simple end-user operation is becoming easier with each passing year, however. An increasing number of user-friendly features are being built into many communications software packages. The best already have command file capabilities. Many can be menu-driven. Today, with mainstream, popular systems such as the IBM PC, a variety of communications software choices are available, and even better software is being introduced.

If communications simplicity can be achieved, users will say, "Hey, that's not hard. I just sent five pages of transactions 2000 miles in a minute!" Sparking *this* reaction will help computer communications take hold throughout an entire company.

3.4 SOFTWARE COMPATABILITY

Nothing is worse than having micros and word processors in a company that is trying to add communications, and then discovering that the systems are not compatible with each other. The only choices are (1) to replace some of the in-place hardware or software, (2) to leave these as stand-alone systems, or (3) to develop compatible communications.

Communications software controls the data sent by using a specific protocol, and communications will work only when two systems are using the same protocol. The protocol is the set of codes or rules that controls the transmission between the systems, so they both understand what has been sent and what has been received. As a result, one micro, word processor, or workstation may need several different communications software packages if each offers a protocol that is compatible with a different type of remote system.

Both hardware and software are available to convert many business micro protocols to standard mainframe and communications protocols such as BSC,

EBCDIC, X.25, and others. Since the choices of protocol translation hardware and software are expanding rapidly, micro-to-mainframe links are becoming easier all the time.

This proliferation of communications choices also spans the gap between most of the popular business micros, such as between Apple, IBM-compatible, and CP/M systems. Many word processors have optional communications or microcomputer operating systems, and most of these may be able to join this growing information environment with other micros, word processors, work-stations, and larger computers.

3.5 FINAL SELECTION OF A SOFTWARE PACKAGE

When selecting software that will run on a budding network of systems throughout a company, see the products selected transmit typical applications files successfully, on the types of hardware that will be used, before buying. If the vendor cannot demonstrate installations up and running, the appropriate modems and communications software may be brought in and demonstrated on the company's systems. If not, there is no alternative but to run the tests in-house. For a product with a low cost, such as a full-featured communications software package for a micro, it might be purchased and tried.

This is the only way to confirm that the communications being bought will meet the users' requirements. If the time and funds are available, several soft-ware/hardware options may be tested before buying, so that the best one can be chosen.

Because links between different systems can be complex, each type of link must be tested before it is bought in quantity and turned over to inexperienced users for routine use. The developers, not the users, should do the testing.

Communications testing and development should not stop with an in-stalled system. Someone should be responsible for keeping up with the latest hardware and software. New products are frequently introduced that offer improved compatibility, additional communications functions, and enhanced productivity. These can reduce the costs of communications while increasing performance, the reason personal computers are having such an impact today.

If the computer communications and user interfaces are designed well, the criteria of employee adaptation and acceptance may be met within a shorter time horizon. Effective communications software selection and use allows com-puter communications to be introduced as an extension of the present environ-ment: There is already instant nationwide voice communications through the phone, and computer communications adds business information to this. With easy-to-use computer communications, employees may soon start thinking that this is as normal as our jet plane/television age seems today. When employees have adopted this revolution, their company will be able to enter the growing age of accelerated business performance.

4

CHARACTERISTICS AND FUNCTIONS

OF COMMUNICATIONS HARDWARE

The rapid spread of microcomputers, word processors, workstations, and terminals linked to larger computers is drawing most corporations toward a business environment permeated with computing. While stand-alone systems improve an individual's performance, communications alters both the company's and the individual's ability to keep up with, and perhaps outperform, their competition.

The need to operate in a modern business information environment is driving the growing need to link appropriate systems with communications. When effective communications is added, a company's systems speak the same high-speed business language, instead of remaining stand-alone devices.

As the feasibility study develops a clear concept of the planned communications, this must be applied to selecting uniform standards for communications hardware. Clear standards will prove invaluable as communications becomes the foundation for a company's high-speed information environment, and more local systems, employees, and departments must become part of it.

Because communications hardware uses the same technology as microcomputers, prices are declining while the range of choices is rising. As these costs continue to fall and business advantages grow, planners must transform communications hardware from a customized option into a standardized set of choices for users throughout a company.

Communications hardware is sophisticated, however, so it answers more questions than the modem, which is the device that links two remote devices over telephone lines. Specialized hardware supports many additional facets of communications:

- Multiplexers share lines and lower costs by transmitting the signals from up to 32 systems on one line.

- Protocol converters contribute to both savings and network building, by allowing incompatible systems to communicate with each other.

- Data encryptors provide the best security available for computer communications.

- Network control systems allow a small staff at a central site to monitor, manage, and maintain multiple communications networks for a corporation.

- The communications lines themselves offer options from simple direct dial to satellite links.

Since increased performance is becoming available at lower cost in each of these areas, it is important to understand the expanding range of choices. The communications hardware selected will shape each company's growth by determining the communications features it will enjoy—or miss—as its users build a modern business information environment.

4.1 MODEMS

Look at a nearby telephone. When you make a phone call, you use that phone—a device that converts your voice into a signal that travels over a phone line. At the other end, another phone converts this signal back into a voice.

When a computer makes a phone call, its telephone is a *modem*—a device that converts the computer's data into a signal that travels over the phone line. At the remote end, another modem converts the signal back into data that the distant computer can understand.

If you install a phone in your home or office, it is like adding a modem to a computer. You use the phone to make the telephone network handle voice calls. Your computer uses the modem and communications software to make the phone network handle calls to other computers. In fact, the modem industry evolved because companies wanted to send computer data over telephone lines. See Figures 4.1 and 4.2.

Though every phone will talk to every other phone, modems can communicate only with certain other modems. One of the main differences between modems is the speed at which they operate. There is a spectrum of communications speeds available, ranging from 110 bps (bits per second) to, in most uses, 56,000 bps. Each modem can communicate only with another modem of the same speed, or else "speed conversion" must be used.

Until recently, the communications speed chosen was based on the volume of data that needed to be sent between two computer systems. Often, end users were told to select the slowest speeds: 300 bps and 1200 bps. Since users

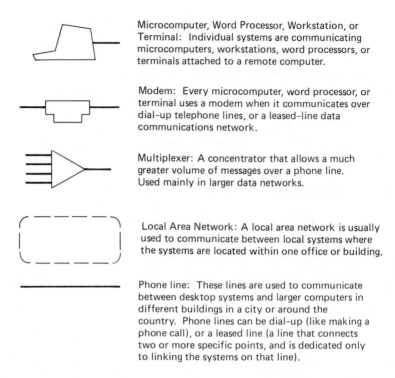

Microcomputer, Word Processor, Workstation, or Terminal: Individual systems are communicating microcomputers, workstations, word processors, or terminals attached to a remote computer.

Modem: Every microcomputer, word processor, or terminal uses a modem when it communicates over dial-up telephone lines, or a leased-line data communications network.

Multiplexer: A concentrator that allows a much greater volume of messages over a phone line. Used mainly in larger data networks.

Local Area Network: A local area network is usually used to communicate between local systems where the systems are located within one office or building.

Phone line: These lines are used to communicate between desktop systems and larger computers in different buildings in a city or around the country. Phone lines can be dial-up (like making a phone call), or a leased line (a line that connects two or more specific points, and is dedicated only to linking the systems on that line).

Figure 4.1   The basic kinds of telecommunications hardware. These symbols are used to illustrate the charts and diagrams in this book.

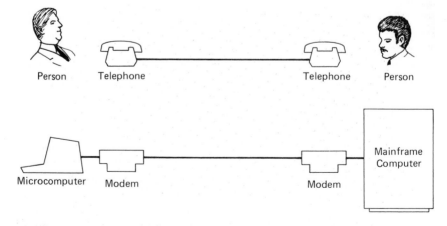

Figure 4.2   A modem is a computer's coupling device to a telephone.

often find these low speeds slow and frustrating when they try to accomplish a large volume of computer communications, end users are steadily pressing for faster communications speeds. Users of the slowest speeds, those at 300 bps, are moving to 1200 bps in large numbers. Those who are used to 1200 bps find that this is fine for line-by-line interactive work with other computers. It is slow, however, when whole screens have to be sent repeatedly from one system to another. These users are starting to step up to 2400 bps and even faster speeds, to accelerate their work. Figure 4.3 shows modems currently in use.

Figure 4.3   The state of Illinois operates one of the largest individual state data communications networks in the nation. Installed throughout the network are Racal-Milgo Omnimode Series intelligent modems operating at 4800 bps and 9600 bps. Courtesy of Racal-Milgo.

A second difference between modems is the diagnostic tests built into better-quality modems. The ability to do these tests is what stands between end users and a total communications failure.

Think of developing an action plan when computer communications goes down. Is the problem a bad transmission line? A faulty modem? The workstations in a remote office? When there is a problem and service is called, will those called point a finger at another component? How can the problem be isolated to prevent this finger-pointing?

You know your company's business cannot stop. Diagnostic tests are the only way to move rapidly and accurately toward a solution. Three kinds of problems generally cause communications failures. First are line problems. The quality of the transmission line is cited by data communications users as their biggest problem by far. Second are equipment problems—the communications hardware might not send or receive the data accurately. Users report major differences in the number of hardware problems they have, depending on the communications hardware vendor they choose. Third is the computers or terminals at either end of the line.

If computer communications are going to be run successfully by nontechnical users, modems should have built-in diagnostics so that the area causing trouble can be identified.

The diagnostics in reasonably priced modems can be surprisingly sophisticated. The most important diagnostic test is the loopback test. This allows the user to send a test message so that it "loops back" from significant points along the communications path, as illustrated in Figure 4.4. The problem's source can be determined from the specific area where loopback errors occur.

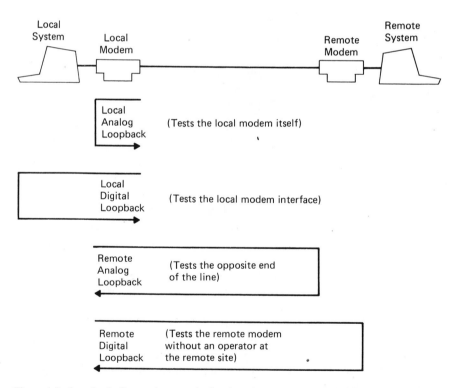

Figure 4.4 Loopback diagnostics tests the local modem, the transmission line, and the remote modem from one local site.

Beyond the modem's speed and diagnostics, modems offer a wide variety of features that can be matched to the user's needs. Two examples will show some of the more sophisticated possibilities in modem selection.

The first example is the Omnimode 48 from Racal-Milgo, which is a high-speed modem designed to allow the management of a network of local and remote modems from one site by trained end users or by specialists. By using the controls on its front panel and its built-in menus, modems throughout a network can be monitored, tested, and the network reconfigured. Omnimode itself operates at 1200, 2400, 3600, or 4800 bps, allowing it to work with a network of remote modems. Since its network management abilities are upward-compatible with larger network management systems, a growth path is available when needed.

The second example is the "triple modem" (VA3480) from Racal-Vadic. This triple modem is designed for computers in regional and central headquarters, where dial-in communications arrive at low transmission speeds (300 and 1200 bps). Rack mounting is available for up to 48 modems per rack, in nests of one to eight modems each, so central computers can be accessed immediately by multiple workstations throughout a company. This modem automatically answers and determines the speed of the modem calling in, the type of modem, and other characteristics. It adjusts its protocol to match the calling-in modem without needing instructions from software or an operator, within its range of speeds and protocols (four models are available, for wide compatibility). One telephone rotary can be used to dial into all the modem ports, simplifying dial-in for multiple end users.

It quickly becomes obvious: When a telephone is selected, a few questions are asked: How many lines are needed? Would you like a speaker phone? Do you need a simple phone or the model with a variety of features?

Today's sophisticated modems, on the other hand, offer a wider range of features every year. These new features simplify communications both for end users and for those responsible for planning and supporting computer communications. Those doing the planning should learn the state of the art in modem technology from an in-house specialist, a consultant, or a quality vendor when choosing the right modems for their needs.

4.2 MULTIPLEXERS

Suppose you are in a large office in Atlanta and its 35 workstations and terminals use frequent communications with your company's data processing center in Chicago, so the traffic on that line is heavy. With one line, only eight terminal hours are available per day (if we assume that the office is open from nine to five).

A multiplexer takes the data that would be sent over many lines and concentrates it to fit on one line, providing immediate cost savings along with improved communications performance. With a multiplexer that concentrates 16 channels on one line, 128 terminal hours per day would be available to the Atlanta office, with the expense of only one dedicated communications line.

In general, multiplexers are used on high-traffic lines. The remote sites in a region may have medium-speed lines into one hub city, with a multiplexed high-speed line to the main computer center. Cities in the Southeast may feed into Atlanta, for example. A high-speed leased line with the right type of multiplexers could carry a wide variety of computer communications between Atlanta and Chicago, as illustrated in Figure 4.5. As a result, multiplexers are usually selected by staff at the main computer center.

There are different types of multiplexers, but the statistical multiplexer is best for uses from 1200 bps to 9600 bps. Wide acceptance has greeted this type of multiplexer, because it provides a variety of advanced features such as automatic accuracy checking with error correction.

Error checking is so reliable that statistical multiplexers are sometimes used for low-speed applications, simply because of their accuracy. A buffer

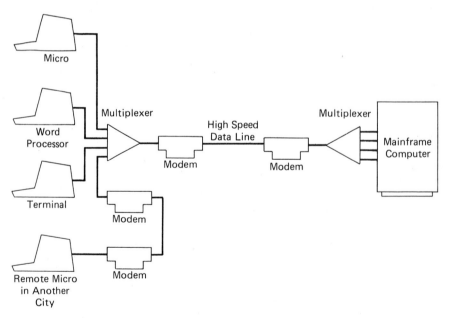

Figure 4.5 Statistical multiplexers support different systems over the same line, even if their protocols and communication speeds are different.

Figure 4.6   The Omnimux 320 illustrates the current generation of statistical multiplexers. It offers 32 channels with detailed statistical reporting, error correction, speeds up to 9600 bps, and support for all protocols. Courtesy of Racal-Milgo.

stores each frame of data sent, and waits for an acknowledgement that it has been received accurately before sending the next frame. If a request for retransmission is received, it sends the same frame until an "accurate transmission acknowledgement" is received. This allows multiplexers to get data through, even on noisy lines.

The statistical multiplexer also serves more devices than traditional multiplexers. Many different types of systems can use the same line, even if their communications speeds and protocols are not the same as each others. The statistical features offer an accurate picture of the total use of each available channel and the entire transmission line. This information shows the usage of the communications network, which aids network management.

Extensive diagnostics are usually available to support both local and remote monitoring and testing. Since trained technicians are usually available only at one site that may not even be at one end of a line, remote diagnostics are needed to rapidly isolate problems when they occur.

The higher the transmission speed, the more important error checking becomes. Some users select statistical multiplexers starting at 1200 bps, and many switch to them at 2400 bps.

4.3 PROTOCOL CONVERTERS

Protocols are used in communications so that sending and receiving systems understand each other. The communications protocol indicates the start and the end of the data transmission, acknowledges that the data has been received, and other control signals. The data protocol is the language each system uses, such as ASCII for most micros, workstations, word processors, and many minicomputers, and EBCDIC for IBM mainframes.

Unfortunately, many communication protocols are incompatible and different kinds of systems cannot communicate with each other, though broad families of systems are compatible.

Today, the increasing availability of nearly every type of protocol conversion offers users reasonably priced, flexible ways to link the different kinds of systems in a company. The simplest kind of protocol conversion is software that is run in a computer or word processor. The next level of speed and sophistication is a protocol converter, a hardware device that is usually controlled by a microprocessor and offers many features in one small device. Either of these solutions provides translation from one protocol to another, such as between ASCII and EBCDIC.

Considerable cost savings are possible from protocol conversion. It is certainly cheaper to add protocol conversion than it is to replace micros or word processors when different systems are linked into a mainframe computer. By using protocol conversion, many different types of micros, word processors, and workstations can be made to look like IBM 3270s, DEC VT100s, or a dumb terminal to a mainframe computer. This allows smaller systems to communicate with larger computers. The small systems are then turned back into stand-alone micros or word processors when the connection is ended.

Many conversion options are available. For example, part of the line from just one company, PCI, includes six protocol converters that support a wide range of ways to communicate into or out of IBM mainframe and minicomputer environments.

Additional savings may come from designing the communications links in an organization carefully. A smaller number of protocol converters will create a network if the communications goes through a computer center. See Figure 4.7.

Finding a wide range of micros, word processors, and larger computers with the same protocol in an organization is unlikely, so protocol converters are a cost-effective way to turn them into a network. Different existing systems can be interconnected at lower cost and an earlier date than replacing them with new systems that use compatible protocols.

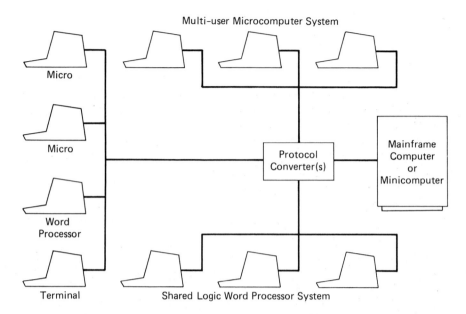

Figure 4.7 Centralized protocol conversion links many different systems at low cost. (Modems and multiplexers are not shown.)

4.4 DATA ENCRYPTORS

The need for everyday security is growing rapidly. Not only is computer crime increasing, but the amount of sensitive business data on computers grows constantly, so data security is more important every year. Responsibility for the security of transmitted data is placed squarely on the end user, not on the carrier that provides the transmission lines.

The best available answer is *data encryption*. This uses a computer-generated "key" to convert data to coded form when it is sent, and to decipher it when received. The method generally used is the National Bureau of Standards' Data Encryption Standard (DES), which is a 56-bit algorithm that can produce 72 *quadrillion* keys. This range of keys, plus key changes, protects data from unauthorized access.

The cheapest but most insecure way to protect data is with software that is resident in the computer systems at both ends. The problem lies in the possibility that this software can be tampered with by someone who has access to the computer system, whether a current employee or a recently discharged one. The National Bureau of Standards does not approve software encryption systems.

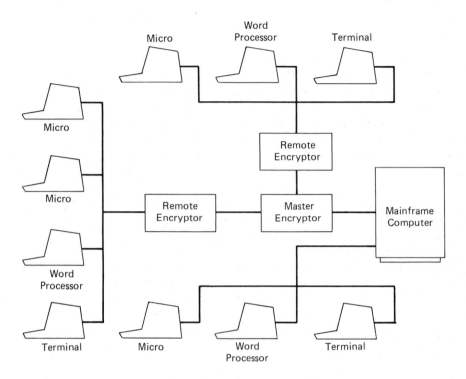

Figure 4.8   Parts of a network are protected with encryption devices, protecting only financial and other sensitive data. (Modems and multiplexers are not shown.)

Encryption hardware is virtually free from the threat of unauthorized, undetected tampering. As illustrated in Figure 4.8, a coding/decoding device is required at each location where data needs to be protected.

The National Bureau of Standards approves some hardware implementations of the DES, but also recommends frequent key changes. Keys can be changed by loading the new key into a hand-held transport module that is physically taken to each site. While this may be practical for a bank with local branches, large networks span thousands of miles and need a more flexible system.

For larger networks, the master encryption device should be able to download a unique key to each encryption device on the network. This allows the keys to be changed often, such as having daily working keys distributed online. To provide an additional layer of security, a master key should be used to encrypt the working keys during these transmissions.

Several vendors, including Racal-Milgo, provide these kinds of practical DES-based encryption systems. While suppliers of security systems will discuss their features and characteristics with customers, they will not provide detailed descriptions of specific uses of these systems or reveal their users, as is common for other kinds of communications products. This makes purchasing more complex, because users cannot be phoned for their opinions or their sites visited for inspection. After all, if you used a security system, would you describe in public how your communications are protected?

4.5 NETWORK CONTROL SYSTEMS

Though computer communications are advanced today, the normal state of networks is not trouble free. Most users encounter problems at one time or another, and users bear increased responsibility for maintaining their networks now that the Bell system has broken up. That is why hardware reliability, remote diagnostics, and nationwide maintenance contracts have large impacts on product selection. It also explains why network monitoring and control equipment has developed into a range of options, from portable test sets to network management systems. While there has been some movement toward simplification, the typical end user should not expect to be involved with selecting monitoring and control systems.

A network operations group is often responsible for maintaining larger networks. While the most common problem is the communications lines, there are also component problems (terminals, modems, multiplexers, etc.) and problems in locating the line or equipment causing the failure. As a result, network management systems have been developed that:

- Pinpoint failures at any site, whether local or remote.
- Automatically monitor the network in the background, over secondary channels on the lines, while the main communications activities continue.
- Measure the efficiency and performance of the total communications network or parts of the network.
- Allow total network control by operators at the central site, including both remote testing and backup by remote control, without technicians being needed in the field.
- Restore communications at the remote site, without local users ever knowing a problem occurred.

These systems work because every point in the network is assigned its own address and is equipped for remote control. The central management system scans each location, tests it, and reports its status. The operator can take any equipment with problems out of the network, and bring backup equipment online, including reconfiguring communications paths when a line is at fault. The most sophisticated systems notify the operator when a problem occurs, even before the communications goes down. See Figure 4.9.

Figure 4.9 At the Wachovia Bank in Winston-Salem, North Carolina, one Racal-Milgo network control system supports separate networks of office automation systems, internal information resources, and automated teller machines. Courtesy of Racal-Milgo.

For smaller networks, portable test equipment is available that can be used with the remote testing diagnostics built into better-quality modems. Again, test sets are generally used by communications specialists, but they are becoming easier to operate by knowledgeable end users. Their most valuable feature is their ability to determine whether a failure results from a terminal, a line, or a modem, so that the correct service organization can be called for prompt repair. They are also helpful in testing a communications link after a temporary failure, to make sure that it is working properly before computer systems are put back on-line.

4.6 COMMUNICATIONS LINES

Transmission lines are usually supplied by a carrier that is more concerned with voice communications than computer-to-computer messages.

While transmissions lines are not hardware, recommending the kinds of lines that should be used in a network may become part of end-user planning. Questions that should be answered include the network configuration, the transmission speeds, how many lines will be used, and what percentage of each line will be used during the time it is available.

The major kinds of lines are described here. They can be divided into five categories, so the appropriate ones should be researched by contacting their vendors when a network is being planned.

4.6.1 Direct Distance Dialing (DDD)

The telephone is often the first choice of users who need to test new communications links between locations. It is also the best choice for the lowest-volume users. Network planning is not required and placing the calls is as simple as dialing the phone—even easier when user-friendly autodial communications software is used.

The main problem with DDD is a one-minute minimum billing charge from the phone company. When 2400 bps is used as the communications speed, a one-page letter (240 words) can be sent in six seconds. This means that DDD may be fine for startup applications and low-volume uses, but cost savings quickly result from the next choice.

4.6.2 WATS Lines

WATS lines cover the entire United States, including Hawaii, Alaska, Puerto Rico, and the Virgin Islands. To save money, incoming WATS lines can be used at computer centers, or selected locations can be equipped with an outgoing WATS. A user's volume of calls and their length will determine the cost savings from WATS lines over Direct Distance Dialing.

While WATS billing is on a six-second basis, AT&T requires the average length of calls to be one minute or longer. If the calls on a WATS line average less than a minute, they are recalculated on a one-minute-per-call formula. This means that it may be a good idea to use the WATS line for some voice calls, since these will boost the average call to over a minute in length.

If a company already has WATS lines and does not expect a large volume of lengthy computer communications, the easiest solution to their transmission lines question may be to put microcomputer and word processor communications on their installed WATS lines. There are also many alternatives that are less expensive than WATS, from vendors such as MCI, ITT, US Telephone, and the like.

4.6.3 Leased Lines

A wide variety of leased line services are available. The available choices should be explored to determine the best option for each location.

AT&T's offerings include (1) Series 1000, a low-speed (30 to 150 bps) interstate service with charges based on the distances involved; (2) Series 2000 and 3000, which provide interstate service (up to 9600 bps with line conditioning at an extra charge) for both voice and data use, with three price schedules based on whether high- or low-traffic cities are interconnected; (3) Series 8000, a wide-band service supporting speeds up to 56,000 bps, with rates based on mileage charges, conditioning charges, and station termination charges; (4) Dataphone Digital Service (DDS), which offers AT&T's highest speeds on continuously leased lines (up to 1,544,000 bps), and is available from a limited number of cities (though extensions can be made to other cities).

A great deal of media attention has been given to competing leased-line vendors, who offer services at lower prices that AT&T. Their services are concentrated in urban areas, however, though most offer connections to every city (though at higher prices).

The most significant of these is MCI, because it won the landmark court battles that created substantial new segments of the communications industry. MCI offers leased line service for both voice and data, at speeds from the lowest used through 9600 bps from most high-traffic cities.

SPRINT is a well-known leased line service that also offers both voice and data communications with a pricing structure that resembles WATS line service. A limited number of cities form SPRINT's central network, with tie-ins to other major cities, and extension links to almost any city.

United States Transmission Systems (USTS), an ITT subsidiary, offers interstate leased lines for data and voice at speeds up to 9600 bps. A limited number of cities are available, but links to many additional cities are available through arrangements with local phone companies.

4.6.4 Value-Added Carriers

The most versatile alternative to leased lines is the value-added carriers such as GTE Telenet and Tymnet. Many time-sharing and private computer centers are connected to one or both of these networks. They offer transparent links between office systems of all sizes, on a nationwide basis, so long as the systems are connected to a phone line.

Using these networks is like receiving many of the advanced benefits forecast for private networks by the 1990s. They offer extensive protocol and speed conversions, allowing users to communicate immediately between different kinds of systems within their organization. They also provide error checking and network control management, including redundant systems and complete diagnostics for reliability. Users can focus on communications, instead of monitoring the network and fixing problems when they occur. This allows users to add new locations or upgrade computer systems rapidly, while having fewer problems.

These advantages have proved popular. In a typical month on Tymnet, for example, there are more than six million sessions, during which more than 50 billion characters are transmitted, accounting for 1.4 million hours of transmission time.

Nationwide electronic mail is also offered on these networks, with either instant message delivery, or store-and-forward "electronic mail boxes" that can be accessed from anywhere.

Other helpful features include connections to specialized services like Western Union's Telex, and frequent upgrades in the communication services available. Pricing is done in a number of ways, depending on each user's needs, so it is possible to accommodate both low- and high-volume users. (Low-volume users might consider networks like The Source or CompuServe, which provide many advanced services at reduced cost.)

Since value-added carriers offer end users access to state-of-the-art, fully supported networks, complete solutions are available that may prove helpful for planning sizable networks.

4.6.5   Satellite Services

Satellites offer two choices. There is the traditional high-speed network designed for medium- and high-volume users, and this is often a lower-cost alternative than terrestrial-based lines. Then there are satellite services designed specifically for microcomputers, including small earth stations that fit in a window and are a fraction of the cost of the large outdoor models.

For medium- and high-volume users, the traditional satellite services should be investigated first. RCA, the first company to offer commercial satellite service, now offers a Switched Satellite Service with speeds up to 9600 bps and charges based on actual use, over a monthly minimum. As a fictional example, a company may decide to link four regional headquarters offices: New York, Chicago, Los Angeles, and Atlanta. If these offices use 110 hours of high-speed data communications during a typical month (about 5 hours total per business day), the month's charge would be $1418.80. This can be viewed as an average cost of $354.70 per office, or a cost of $12.90 per hour.*

Two other vendors offering satellite services are Satellite Business Systems (SBS) and Western Union. SBS caters to high-volume users, and transmission speeds range up to 6.3 million bits per second. Western Union serves small users on a measured-use basis, and it also leases channels to major users. Each vendor has a unique price structure and does not charge for the same items as others, so cost comparisons are required.

---

*With deregulation, any tarriffs quoted are subject to rapid change. The current cost is calculated as follows: Each office must pay a $60 switch termination charge (which provides an access port), for a total of $240. Then, there is a $265 per month minimum for each access channel, which covers the first 22 hours (1320 minutes) of use. Finally, the metered use charge is 9 cents for each minute over the monthly minimum. One hundred ten hours is 6600 minutes, or 1650 minutes for an average channel. The usage charge is 9 cents times (1650 minutes minus 1320 minutes equals) 330 minutes, or $29.70 plus $265 per channel, for an average channel cost of $294.70. Four times $294.70, plus four terminations at $60 each, is $1,418.80—$354.70 per office or $12.90 per hour.

Satellite communications has other costs besides vendor charges, such as customer-owned Earth stations or transmission to carrier-owned Earth stations. Still, satellite communications sometimes produce real savings, and they should not be ignored. If communications satellites are used, virtually all the planning and maintenance should be turned over to specialists.

While satellite networks for micros and word processors are another alternative, the disadvantage of these networks is that they are one-way "broadcast" systems. One site sends data to a satellite, and then many receiving sites use small earth stations to receive the data. This is expensive for a point-to-point transmission, but if many receiving systems are involved, the costs fall dramatically. For example, the current cost of sending the amount of information in one day's *Wall Street Journal* is about $550 via satellites. If 1000 systems are receiving it, this averages only 55 cents per system.

Part II
DESIGNING YOUR SOLUTIONS

5

PHYSICAL DESIGN OF
COMMUNICATIONS

Designing effective communications means including a variety of elements. All are important and none can be ignored. The four main requirements are systematic planning, users, communications hardware and software, and the company's business procedures. When these are combined into a specific design, the overall communications network begins to emerge.

In many companies, DP staff will describe the emerging network in terms of its system objectives, and will produce diagrams of its inputs, outputs, and control systems.

It should never be forgotten, however, that the technical design must be developed with the aid of a user community where technical expertise is growing but still scarce. Above all, the main requirements for a successful team effort between DP specialists and end users are clear communications and a focus on meeting the users' business needs, not the communication network's technical needs.

5.1 DESIGN PROCEDURES

Most computer networks are based on separate calls that connect two computers at a time. If a network can be imagined as a list of separate calls made one at a time, this simple approach will produce an initial diagram of all the systems that need to be connected into one network.

A final network diagram comes from adding two more concepts, as illustrated in Figure 5.1: First, many systems can share one communications

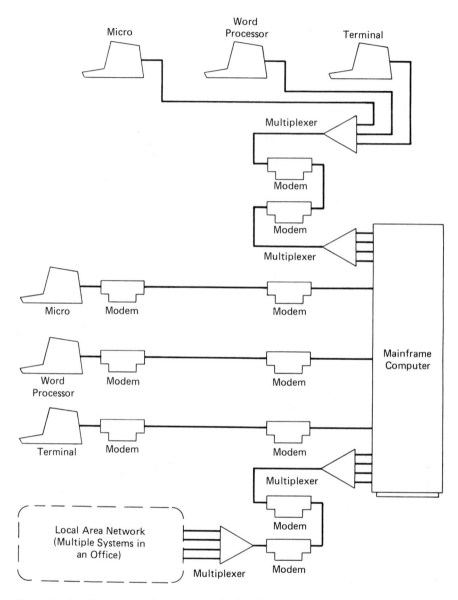

Figure 5.1   Small systems can share a communications line, and large computers can handle many communications lines at once.

line by using a multiplexer. Second, while single-user workstations can communicate with only one other system at a time, some multiuser micros and most larger computers can handle multiple communications lines and communicate with a number of other systems at one time.

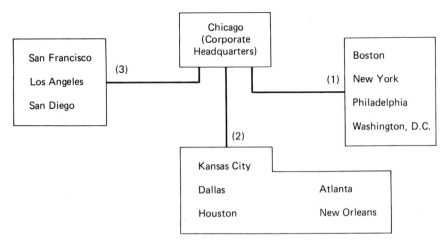

Projected microcomputer, terminal, workstation, and word processor communications by the end of the first year, by Region:

1. Eastern Region:
   550 calls per day, average three minutes long.
   Projected line use: 7.5 hours daily; 165 hours per month

2. Sunbelt Region:
   625 calls per day, average three minutes long.
   Projected line use: 8.5 hours daily; 190 hours per month

3. Western Region:
   500 calls per day, average three minutes long.
   Projected line use: 5.0 hours daily; 145 hours per month

Figure 5.2   Traffic volume estimates for network design.

The starting point for network planning is diagramming the network to be created. To begin a network diagram, mark all the locations on a map and label them. Put a small circle around each location where more than one communicating system (including terminals) is located in the same building. Then draw a box around groups of systems that are located in the same geographic area. In practice, this indicates where multiple locations might be linked to a local "hub" so that a multiplexer can support them together, on one high-speed line to the main computer center (or a regional center). This may be less expensive than running separate leased lines from each remote system to central points.

Next, add to the diagram the volume of traffic that is expected from each system, because this can range from a once-a-day direct-dial call over the phone system to a dedicated 9600 bps leased line. This information should be fairly easy to add, based on each location's numbers developed in the feasibility study. The initial sketch may resemble Figure 5.2.

5.2 TYPES OF NETWORKS

The network configuration will generally be only one of four choices, as shown in Figure 5.3.

5.2.1 Point-to-Point Network

The point-to-point network is usually for lower traffic networks that use only direct dial telephone links, or WATS lines. The lines shown are communications paths, not leased lines, and the telephone system provides the connections.

In a point-to-point network all the systems call the other systems directly. Since systems can communicate only with other systems that have the same speed and protocol, they should all have the same speed modems and use the same protocol. This is generally achieved by buying compatible modems and communications software.

5.2.2 Star Network

The star network is common where there is a mainframe computer and the remote systems are connected to it. The lines in a star network can be direct dial, incoming and outgoing WATS, or leased lines of various speeds (depending on the traffic volume).

In a star network, the communications goes through a computer center where varying speeds and protocols can be handled, so it is possible to mix communications speeds and protocols. For maintenance and control purposes it is still simpler to keep the number of speed and protocol choices to a minimum.

5.2.3 Hub Network

The hub network is used to save line costs in situations where multiple systems can be put on the same multiplexed high-speed lines.

The hub network offers the most flexibility, because statistical multiplexers allow mixing multiple speeds, protocols, and both synchronous and asynchronous systems on the same high-speed lines. Again, however, maintenance and management needs demand that the number of speed and protocol choices should be kept to the minimum that produces reliable communications.

5.2.4 Hierarchical Network

The fourth choice, the hierarchical network, is generally designed and managed by the DP department. The objective is to move the processing to the level in the hierarchy where it is most cost effective, such as departmental

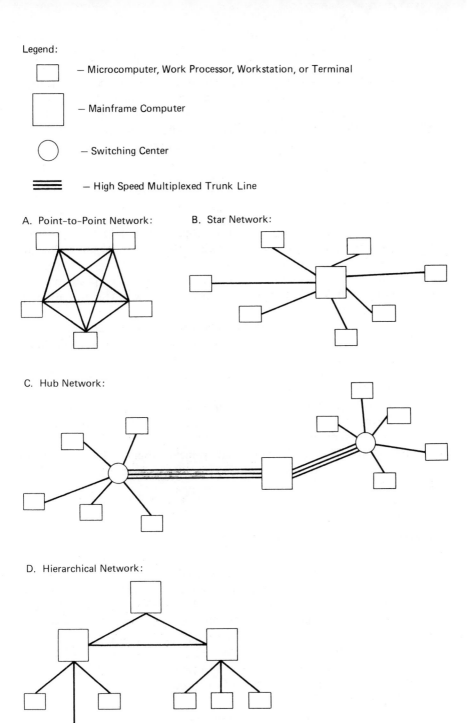

Legend:

☐ — Microcomputer, Work Processor, Workstation, or Terminal

☐ — Mainframe Computer

◯ — Switching Center

≡ — High Speed Multiplexed Trunk Line

A. Point-to-Point Network:

B. Star Network:

C. Hub Network:

D. Hierarchical Network:

Figure 5.3 Four network design architectures.

processing. The first advantage is relief from overloading problems in the main data center. The second is lower communications costs, since summarized data can be transmitted instead of raw data, because local minicomputers and micros are more self-sufficient. The various computers in the hierarchy may be used for processing, message switching, or concentrating data from a number of smaller systems.

5.2.5 Network Configuration

In determining whether to use a point-to-point, star, hub, or hierarchical network, the volume of traffic between each of the systems is more important than the number of systems. A direct link between only two offices may need a 9600-bps leased line if they both have sizable computer usage and communications. Nationwide links between 20 offices may have low traffic, which can be handled by inexpensive direct dial.

The next step is to specify the communications speed of each line. Again, the volume of traffic on a line is the determining factor: the higher the volume, the greater the speed. A strong movement toward faster communications speeds is taking place, however, as part of the development of more productive and user-friendly business systems.

To minimize costs, every line in a network should be chosen individually, based on the amount of traffic it carries. A large network can use a variety of kinds of lines (from direct dial through satellite links), each of them matched to the volume of traffic on it. Network management should include periodic or constant measurement of traffic volumes so that the kinds of lines used are adjusted to save money.

5.3 COMMUNICATIONS SPEEDS

While 300 bps was the communications speed for the first micros in the mid-1970s, few experienced users consider this a desirable speed today. In the past, low speeds were justified on inexpensive home micros because of low volumes of data traffic. Today, however, an increasing number of business users are moving to the highest speeds they can arrange, partly to save on-line charges but also to accomplish more work in less time.

On a micro or word processor, the information moves back and forth between the screen and the computer at a fast speed: 19,200 bps, or on a slower system, 9600 bps.

If a 300-bps modem is used to communicate with another system, the screen suddenly becomes a primitive environment, because it looks like it is slogging through glue. The user can actually see individual characters being written across the screen on one line at a time. Instead of whole files being transferred rapidly, communications becomes a trying ordeal that retards productivity, the opposite of what is wanted.

When 300 bps is accelerated four times, to 1200 bps, it is like driving the smallest economy car. Lines are painted across the screen, one after the other, in a steady march from top to bottom. The communications does not zip along, but users can get their work done if they have patience.

A speed of 2400 bps is like returning to the familiar environment of working within one's own workstation: screens of information start to appear one after the other, even though there might be thousands of miles between the local and remote computers. Users gain working-speed access to computers throughout a company: across town, in other states, or around the world.

If users like 2400 bps, speeds of 4800 bps and higher will spoil them for life. The feeling of separation between computers begins to dissolve, as if the user had one giant system. In some situations, immediate computer response is essential, and these are called real-time systems. Airlines, banks, and brokerage houses often have customers waiting for answers so that they can make a purchase, and immediate revenue transactions usually dictate the highest communications speeds, even if the remote computer is several time zones away.

5.4 USER REQUIREMENTS

As the network design emerges, the original feasibility study should be reviewed to make sure the network fits the organization's *business needs.* DP's technical expertise should not be expected to contribute the business side of communications planning. These business needs are the users' responsibility, and they are almost always more important in communications planning than the technical details of how systems are linked together.

In the end, users who are helping plan high-speed computer communications must also learn a basic lesson: Technical experts are essential. They can answer the complex questions of hardware and software selection, installation, and development of useful operating procedures. There are different ways to build networks, and some approaches are better than others.

Both users and DP staff are essential in planning, because together they know the company's business needs and technical systems. Three examples illustrate the critical relationship between business goals and communications planning. In most networks, *business goals should influence almost every planning decision made.*

5.4.1 Departmental Network

The same problems had been with the company for as long as anyone could remember. Every time the medical geniuses in Research and Development created a new pharmaceutical drug, the marketing department was expected to go out and sell it without understanding it fully. Furthermore, times had changed. The questions facing new wonder drugs were more skeptical, even after they had passed years of testing and FDA approval.

There just wasn't close enough contact between the medical researchers and the salesmen. Not only were their department headquarters located 20 miles apart, but the salesmen in the field had absolutely no way to get their customers' technical questions answered immediately, jeopardizing the big sales that would turn this hot new cure into a winner.

Jack knew his marketing department had to have closer liaison with R&D. He could cost-justify almost any solution that linked them effectively, but he didn't want to spend one penny more than needed. Launching a new product was expensive, and he needed every spare dollar he could scrape up.

Fortunately, the answer was much less expensive than Jack expected. He assigned Sherry, a key assistant, to the job. She contacted the computer department and they worked together in developing their solution.

Both the marketing and R&D departments had the systems they needed to communicate, and had only to add communications hardware, software, protocol conversion, several WATS lines, and one leased line. In marketing there was a nine-user shared-logic word processing system, while R&D had a minicomputer supporting about thirty terminals.

Since both the word processing vendor and the minicomputer vendor offered electronic mail systems, the slowest part of the decision was choosing the best electronic mail system for their needs. After considering the alternatives, the marketing department's system was selected, so that this system could be the focal point for nationwide communications with the field salesmen, as well as with R&D. See Figure 5.4.

Research and Development's computer was linked to the word processing system via a 4800-bps leased line, including modems and a protocol converter. Modems were added to the word processors and micros in field offices all over the country, and these joined the new electronic mail system at marketing by calling in on new incoming WATS lines.

The field offices gained more than fast answers for their questions. The R&D department was asked to prepare a summary of each week's questions and answers, along with the latest medical information on the product, and have it ready each Friday. On Friday morning this was turned into a brief electronic newsletter on the marketing department's word processor, reviewed, then sent nationwide to all the sales offices by the middle of the afternoon. In each office it was printed, photocopied, and distributed to each salesman by Monday.

The result was a better educated sales force with a stronger information base supporting them, and a faster takeoff for a helpful new drug.

5.4.2 Local Area Network

Paula is president of a small consulting firm that has four microcomputers that use only floppy disks. One system is on her desk and she has an Apple at

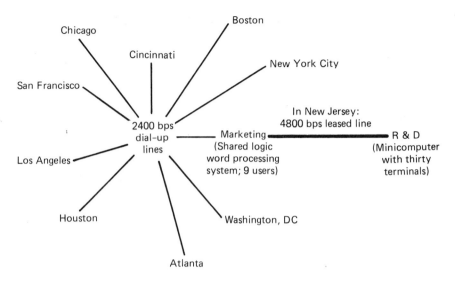

Figure 5.4 A point-to-point network met the business needs of a pharmaceutical company's marketing department, with a high-speed link to the R&D department, and medium-speed links to its sales offices.

home that she shares with her family. She has three long-term projects on which she spends most of her time: (1) purchasing systems at a large computer manufacturer, (2) cost containment studies in the manufacturing operations of a consumer products company, and (3) recommending improved systems for her city's Department of Welfare.

Each of her clients is steadily computerizing more of its daily activities, using both its mainframe computer systems and micros.

Paula has decided that she is in the same situation as many accountants, engineers, lawyers, and other professionals. Computers are becoming everyday business tools, and clients prefer professionals who are at home in more sophisticated networks of computers.

After completing her research, Paula determines that she can increase both the quality of her company's work and the value of her consulting services to her clients by doing three things:

1. Link her micro with her clients' computer systems, for faster turnaround at most stages of most projects. This reduces her estimated completion dates by 10 to 20 percent, plus providing immediate responses in time-critical situations.

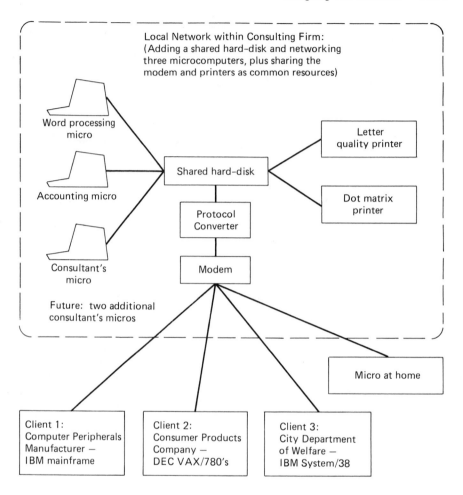

Figure 5.5 Adding a local area network to microcomputers, and linking the network with remote computer systems.

2. Create a local area network out of her consulting firm's micros, so they share the common resources of a modem, hard disk, printers, and software.

3. Use her firm's computer system from her Apple computer at home, so she can work at home more evenings, instead of staying late at the office.

Because she used several cost-cutting measures, Paula's network plans accomplish her goals at a low cost, and provide a base for extensive future growth. See Figure 5.5.

Since her firm's micros are all the same, a shared hard-disk local area network is purchased off the shelf. After this is installed, additional micros can be added to the network for less than $2000 each, because it is not necessary to buy printers, disk drives, or certain applications software—these are now common resources the micros share.

The modem Paula added also becomes a common resource, as does a protocol converter for communicating with her major clients' computers. No additional investments are needed for the firm's other two consultants to start using computer communications with their clients immediately.

By adding the same speed modem to her Apple computer at home, Paula works on either her firm's computer after hours (using the Apple as a remote terminal), or she works on the Apple directly and then sends her work to the office over phone lines.

For a low cost, Paula has added much faster ways to develop and move a larger volume of high-quality information, which is her basic professional product.

5.4.3 Corporate Network

Jeff frowned at his assistant director's latest report. He had spent nearly a decade as his company's director of data processing, and countless man-years had been spent creating the corporate data base. Now it was being turned into a shambles in a few years.

Departments all over the company kept buying microcomputers and justifying them as anything but computers. Then they picked dozens of incompatible software packages and stored their own local data in formats that couldn't be processed by the company's mainframe computer system.

Sure, the departments were sending in the same written reports as before, but more often than not the reports were prepared and printed on micros. Then data entry staff had to keyboard the same data into the mainframe computer, even though it was already computerized in the micros!

At least he wasn't alone, Jeff thought. If it was crazy to use stand-alone micros to run obsolete paper systems, then half the DP directors in the country had to be going crazy. Micros were unstoppable, and Jeff knew it was only a matter of time before he was cornered into the last step for someone in his position—accept them and open the company's communications network to micros, word processors, and workstations. This would be a nightmare of incompatibility if he didn't take a leadership role right away.

Three months later, Jeff reviewed his planning group's proposal for what seemed like the tenth time. On paper it seemed all right, linking large areas of the company to his mainframe computer.

A limited number of interfaces would handle about 95 percent of the systems. Each of the suggested protocol conversion solutions seemed sound. Each type of micro-to-mainframe link would be tested by DP staff, then proven on a small scale at carefully selected end-user sites. The test installations would be monitored for six-month periods, with monthly meetings both at the end-user sites and in the DP department, to discuss problems and develop growing access to the data base on the mainframe.

User needs in each office would be investigated carefully, and an overall plan for sharing business information would be developed for the company. This would then be reviewed and signed off by a special steering committee that would include users from major corporate divisions.

The types of hardware and software needed for communications by each department would be confirmed during the testing. After a department's needs were known and at least half the types of links needed had been tested and proven, that department's installations could begin. Large numbers of micros,

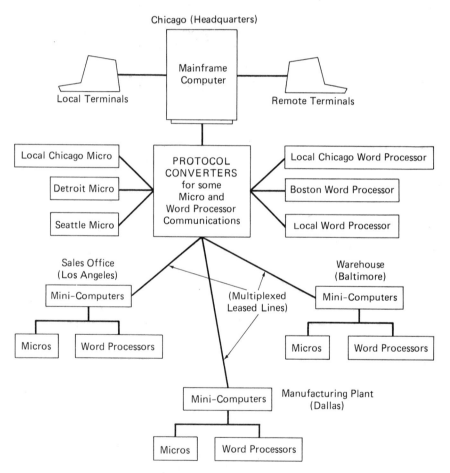

Figure 5.6   Linking a corporation's micros, word processors, and minicomputers to its mainframe computer, creating a national network for transferring files between any system. (Only a small number of representative systems are shown.)

workstations, and word processors could be linked quickly after the initial connections were developed. See Figure 5.6.

The lines linking all the systems were an expanded version of their present network, though larger-capacity multiplexers were used because more systems would be on the same lines at once. That was a clever touch, he thought, holding down communications costs by increasing the speed and volume of the multiplexed leased lines. He was glad that statistical multiplexers could mix signals that were different speeds and protocols, without interfering with each other.

The real political problems would come when he demanded changes in the software being run on the micros, limiting it to a reasonable number of tested and proven packages whose standardized data formats were compatible with the mainframe. There would be loud howls, but the cost-benefit figures said to buy or build reliable data bridges between the software on the different systems—and to begin doing so soon. The down-the-road costs from incompatible software kept climbing higher, and more micros were going in all the time. Without compatible data files, computer communications would soon reach a plateau and be unable to grow.

Surprisingly, the start-up "data bridges" didn't seem overly difficult. There were already several good micro software packages that could move data files between many of the popular micro applications, so most of the data bridge could be built around this. Other micro packages could rewrite data files so that they were compatible with the mainframe. It appeared that the micros offered the software needed to solve most of the data conversion problem they'd created.

5.5 IMPLEMENTATION ALTERNATIVES

Together, DP and users must become the architects of the new information, communications, and management structures emerging today. This must be a flexible future, since new opportunities will continually emerge in coming years, and both users and DP will want to take advantage of them. Business skills and technology are changing so quickly that this DP-user sharing may continue indefinitely.

Within the next communications architecture, appropriate micros, word processors, and workstations should not be islands, because they can link every office in a company closer and faster than ever before. When users and DP staff plan the network(s) together, the communications should be tailored to the business needs of each office involved.

As a network is planned and built one year at a time, the corporate-wide architecture of computing and communications should consider six main building blocks in each company (see Figure 5.7). The importance of each ele-

1. Horizontal Communications:

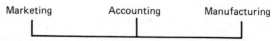

    Marketing   Accounting   Manufacturing

2. Vertical Communications:

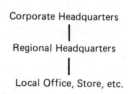

    Corporate Headquarters

    Regional Headquarters

    Local Office, Store, etc.

3. Intra-Division Communications:

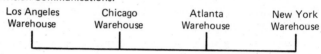

| Los Angeles Warehouse | Chicago Warehouse | Atlanta Warehouse | New York Warehouse |

4. Temporal Integration:

    Historical Business Data   Current Business Data   Future Business Data

5. Conglomerate Communications:

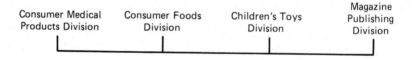

    Consumer Medical Products Division   Consumer Foods Division   Children's Toys Division   Magazine Publishing Division

6. External Communications:

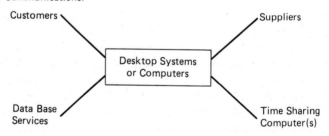

    Customers   Suppliers

    Desktop Systems or Computers

    Data Base Services   Time Sharing Computer(s)

Figure 5.7   Six types of electronic communications in a computerized corporation with multiple desktop systems and larger computers.

ment will differ between companies, and they will change in one company over several years:

1. Horizontal communications: between divisions like marketing, accounting, and manufacturing, each of which is a separate business function.
2. Vertical communications: spanning the hierarchy of a company, such as between a truck rental office in Iowa, its division headquarters in Chicago, and corporate headquarters in Miami.
3. Intradivision communications: to raise the performance of a division, such as between warehouses shipping the same products but located in different regions, so that items out of stock in one location can still be shipped rapidly from another warehouse.

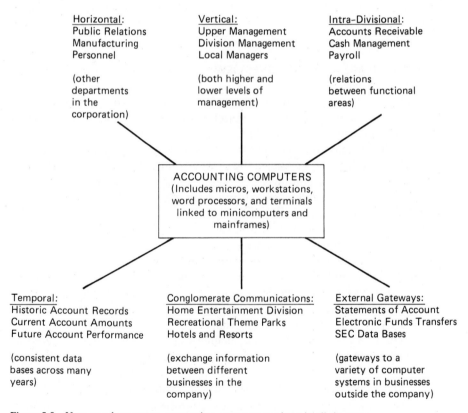

Figure 5.8 How one department, accounting, may communicate in all six areas.

4. Temporal integration: from one time period to the next, so that the business data in computers today remains compatible with the data in coming years.
5. Conglomerate communications: in companies where different kinds of businesses are under the same corporate umbrella, so that at least text files and relevant data files (usually financial) can be exchanged at high speeds.
6. External communications: to develop high-speed business with a company's customers, suppliers, time-sharing computers, or data base services, using its workstations or larger computers.

Each of these six areas may contribute to the overall computer communications of a company. Included in each of these areas are the data file formats; communications hardware, software, and protocols; and utilities that translate data files from one system's format to the next, when needed.

Some departments, such as accounting, require greater attention because they communicate in many of these areas at once. Accounting, for example, may expand its computer communications to include all six areas. See Figure 5.8.

5.6 HARDWARE AND COST OVERVIEW

At this point a network diagram should have been developed that includes the location of each office, lines that connect them, and *notes for each communications line* indicating if several systems share it with multiplexers, the expected volume of traffic on the line, and the communications speed of the line.

The next step is to make all the areas as similar to each other, and to the company's existing communications, as is reasonable. This supports easier management, repair, and training throughout the entire network. The speed of communications, for example, can be simplified by choosing two speeds that will be used throughout the network, such as 2400 bps for single lines and 9600 bps for high-speed multiplexed lines.

After the network has been planned and diagrammed, its hardware and software needs must be listed. End users may not know the best choice for each item, but they can make itemized lists of the quantity of each item needed, and offer informed suggestions to DP. This itemized list can accelerate the work of in-house DP or communications specialists.

This network summary should include six main areas, which are described below. The answers can be entered in a chart like Figure 5.9.

1. List the locations and systems that will be linked together.
2. Determine the level of reliability and "up-time" desired in the communications.

1. Overall network description:

   The number of locations that will be connected: _____

   Listed the locations and the number of systems to be connected in each, including the characteristics of each system (kind of system, synch. or asynch., and its standard protocol; use additional paper, if necessary):

Location:	Number of Systems:	Kind of Systems:
_____	_____	_____
_____	_____	_____
_____	_____	_____
_____	_____	_____

2. Reliability:

   A. Communications Availability (check one):

      _____ Total Availability
      _____ Almost All the Time
      _____ Most of the Time

   B. Data Integrity (check one):

      _____ Total Accuracy
      _____ High Accuracy
      _____ Tolerable Accuracy

3. Hardware required:

   Filling this out creates a purchase list. In a final purchase list, each item should show its communications speed and if local or remote diagnostics are needed. Vendors can provide price quotations from this list.   _____

   Total number of modems needed: _____
   (two modems per line)

   Total number of multiplexers needed: _____
   (two multiplexers per multiplexed line)

   Protocol conversion needed (Yes or No):   _____
       Number of hardware protocol converters: _____
       Number of software protocol conversion packages: _____
   Data encryption needed (Yes or No):   _____
       Number of hardware data encryption units: _____
       Number of software data encryption packages: _____
   Monitoring and control equipment needed (Yes or No):   _____
       Number of portable test sets: _____
       Communications management system needed (Yes or No): _____

Figure 5.9   Network itemizing form for end users and systems analysts, including comparative cost projections.

4. Additional Features: (check all that apply)

    A. General Features:

        _____ Full Duplex or Half Duplex (select one)
        _____ Synchronous or Asynchronous (select one)
        _____ Auto-Dial/Auto-Answer
        _____ Broad Protocol Compatability
        _____ Expandable for Network Management
        _____ Other (list items):

    B. Diagnostics:

        _____ Loopback Testing
        _____ Remotely Controlled Diagnostics
        _____ Compatible with a Network Management System
        _____ Other

---

5. Telecommunications Lines:
    This provides for a complete network inventory, though
    most leased lines are beyond the needs of end-user
    planners. They should consult DP specialists at
    corporate headquarters if leased lines are needed.
    They may still fill out this chart to provide
    their recommendations:

Low-speed lines — Single or multiple systems per line:

    Number of single-system lines: _____
    (with two modems per line)

    Number of multiple-system lines: _____
    (with two multiplexers and two modems per line)

    Speed of communications desired on low-speed lines: _____
    (in bits per second: 0 to 300 bps;
    all these lines should have the same speed)

    Type of low-speed lines: _____
    (DDD, WATS, leased lines, value-added carrier)

    Protocol conversion needed: _____
    (none or name protocols)

    Type of data security: _____
    (none or password protection or data encryption)

Medium-speed lines — Single system per line:

    Number of remote centers included: _____

    Number of medium-speed communications lines: _____
    (with two modems per line)

    Speed of communications desired on medium-speed lines: _____
    (in bits per second: 1200 bps or 2400 bps;
    all these lines should have the same speed)

Figure 5.9   Continued

5. Telecommunications Lines: (continued)

Type of medium–speed lines: _____
(DDD, WATS, leased lines, value-added carrier,
satellite channels)

Protocol conversion needed: _____
(none or name protocols)

Type of data security: _____
(none or password protection or data encryption)

Medium-speed lines — Multiple sysyems per line:

Number of major central or regional centers dialed into: _____

Number of medium-speed communications lines: _____
(with multiplexers, and multiple systems per line;
two modems needed on each multiplexed line)

Speed of communications desired on medium-speed lines: _____
(in bits per second: 1200 bps or 2400 bps;
all these lines should have the same speed)

Type of medium-speed lines: _____
(leased lines, value-added carrier, satellite channels)

Protocol conversion needed: _____
(none or name protocols)

Type of data security: _____
(none or password protection or data encryption)

High-speed lines — Multiple systems per line: _____

Number of major central or regional sites dialed into: _____

Number of high-speed communications lines: _____
(with multiplexers, and multiple systems per line;
two modems needed on each multiplexed line)

Speed of communications desired on multiplexed lines: _____
(in bits per second: 2400 bps, 4800 bps, or 9600 bps;
these lines generally have the same speed)

Type at high-speed lines: _____
(leased lines, satellite channels)

Protocol conversion needed: _____
(none or name protocols)

Type of data security: _____
(none or password protection or data encryption)

Figure 5.9 Continued

6.   Projected costs:

(Estimate costs for each vendor that bids. Subtract
differences, and compare this to problems encountered by
current users contacted from each vendor. Calculate net
value of different vendors' hardware <u>including</u> possible
problems, and the cost of problems to the organization.)

Installation (total start–up expense):
    Hardware   _____
    Software   _____
    Training   _____
    Consultants (if needed)   _____
    Other (list items and costs)   _____
    Total Start–up Cost: _____

Operating Expenses (per month):

    Personnel   _____
    Long Distance Telephone Charges _____
      (varies with speed of modems)
    Leased Line Charges   _____
    Outside services   _____
      (time sharing, data base, etc.)
    Supplies   _____
    Maintenance   _____
    Consultants (if needed)   _____
    Other (list items and cost)   _____

    Total per Month: _____

    Annual Cost: _____

Figure 5.9   Continued

3. Determine the communications hardware needed (the number of modems, multiplexers, protocol converters, etc.).
4. Determine the features needed in the equipment, such as diagnostics for discovering the source of any problems, or its expandability for future growth into network management.
5. Determine the communications speed(s) and lines in the network.
6. Determine the projected costs for both installing and operating the telecommunications system(s), and whether this fits projected budgets.

To answer these questions, first enter all known answers. Then handle the remaining questions. Revise the network design as more is learned, and fit the network to the organization's business needs and budget. The goal is a solid description of a network, along with its projected business benefits, start-up costs, and operating expenses.

Since the micros and word processors are already in place (or are being installed), the major costs are the communications hardware and software that connects the systems, and the new lines needed in the network. If excess capacity is used on an existing network, this may be included as a benefit, not a cost.

6

COMMUNICATIONS COMPATIBILITY

IN A CORPORATE ENVIRONMENT

Most companies already have a variety of types of systems in a diverse number of locations. The question of communications compatibility is a serious issue to many of these users. They are concerned that current systems and the new ones they purchase in the future work effectively with each other.

The 1980s is a decade of establishing and expanding communications links between microcomputers, word processors, workstations, minicomputers, and mainframes. It is a pipe dream to imagine every system working smoothly with every other system, no matter who made it and what operating system it uses. Total communications may always stay a dream, but exchanging information rapidly between many different kinds of systems is an expanding reality.

In practice, every link between two different systems must be developed carefully and tested even more carefully. Once a link is proven, however, the hardware and software that make it work are pushed into the background. Except when there is a problem, the end user will not see the complexities of communicating between different systems.

Increasingly, these links are being bought off the shelf from a rapidly growing number of vendors who sell products designed to help different systems communicate with each other. One of the fastest areas of growth is linking countless business micros and word processors to minicomputers and mainframe computers. New products are being developed for this market at an accelerating rate. See Figure 6.1.

How quickly can a new communications link be established? The best answer is one careful step at a time. After a new link is forged successfully, such as between a CP/M micro and an IBM mainframe, it can be duplicated reasonably

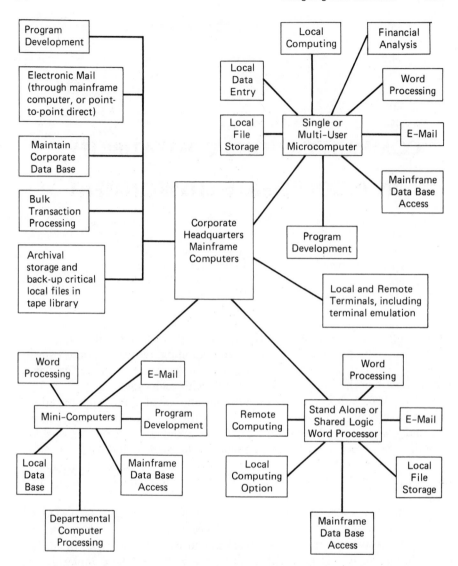

Figure 6.1 Types of communications compatibility possible in a major modern corporation.

rapidly throughout a company, for other CP/M micros. After three or four types of links are developed, the growth of entire networks can be accelerated.

Within the product lines of a few large software vendors, it is possible to run integrated software on local micros that is thoroughly linked to related applications on larger remote computers. These leading software companies are pouring enormous sums into creating and marketing these advanced computing environments.

In the typical company, however, these products are not available. Even where they are introduced, many applications will exist for years outside of the newly purchased, integrated communications environment. In general, there is a long way to go before users can move transparently and effortlessly between one application and the next, regardless of the local or remote system on which they run.

6.1 HARDWARE COMPATIBILITY PROBLEMS AND SOLUTIONS

Protocols are the rules that systems use to communicate with each other. For data to be sent by one system and understood by another, both must use the same protocol. If they do not, the receiving system hears only noise. Fortunately, many standard protocols are widely supported, and the processing power of computers is increasingly being used to bridge this gap and provide conversion between these standard protocols.

The two most common ways to build a bridge between different systems is either with hardware or with software that provides the protocol translation. The choices in hardware compatibility generally fall into three categories. These are add-ons to microcomputers, add-ons to mainframe computers, and the often simplest solution of buying all equipment from the same vendor.

6.1.1 Add-Ons to Microcomputers

There are several kinds of add-ons for micros. The first are protocol conversion boards that are inserted into the micro or separate, stand-alone protocol converters. These are designed to allow micros to emulate IBM 3270 terminals and access IBM mainframes. These peripherals are one of the largest single categories of communications add-ons to microcomputers. See Figure 6.2.

Careful investigation is required before purchasing, to select and test the appropriate terminal emulation for each company's systems and needs. Excellent solutions are available for links between IBM or DEC hosts and Apples, CP/M, and "industry standard" micros such as the IBM PC. The availability of these devices for linking many varieties of micros to Univac, Burroughs, NCR, and other mainframes is slower to arrive, but it is also emerging.

A second kind of microcomputer add-on turns a computer terminal into a microcomputer, while retaining the terminal's ability to directly access the mainframe computer. These are available both as retrofit boards that are inserted into the terminal and make it a microcomputer, or as an external box that may include floppy disks as well as the CPU chip and RAM memory.

Figure 6.2   The IRMA board plugs into the IBM Personal Computer and links it to IBM 3270 networks. It has been used in thousands of installations worldwide. Courtesy of Digital Communications Associates, Inc.

Often, this is a less expensive option than purchasing an entire new microcomputer system. Not including floppy disks, some retrofits are available for under one thousand dollars.

6.1.2 Add-Ons to Mainframe Computers

Peripherals added at the host computer site are the second approach to compatibility. These are like front-end processors that handle communications with a variety of micros, word processors, terminals, or even printers. They do not control the communications, however. Their main role is to convert the communications protocols so that information can be exchanged and mainframe computer applications can even be run from remote sites. See Figure 6.3.

Some of these units also support asynchronous to synchronous communications. Others allow inexpensive ASCII terminals to access IBM mainframes. Some converters support several micros or word processors at the same time. For a DP manager trying to develop compatible communications quickly, a few multifunction boxes at the main data center may prove an easier solution than a different software or hardware add-on for each workstation.

6.1.3 Purchasing from a Compatible Vendor

Minicomputer and mainframe manufacturers have moved into manufacturing micros forcefully: Most DEC micros are compatible with DEC minis, even with the VAX super-minis. The same is true for the micros and larger systems from Wang, Univac, NCR, Burroughs, Honeywell, Data General, and

Figure 6.3   This is one of a complete line of protocol converters from Protocol Computers. It handles communications between business micros and IBM's SNA/SDLC, including both terminal emulation and file transfers. Courtesy of Protocol Computers, Inc.

some of the other computer manufacturers. At the least, they want their established computer customers to choose their micros. At most, there are more than 100 manufacturers that would each like a 10 percent market share. See Figure 6.4.

IBM is also providing compatibility between its PC and its minicomputers and mainframes by developing a variety of methods that make the PC emulate terminals compatible with a variety of IBM systems. In addition, IBM is also introducing new microcomputer systems, such as the 3270-PC and the XT/370. The 3270-PC offers up to seven windows running simultaneous applications, with most of the applications being concurrent jobs on the mainframe. The XT/370 is a microcomputer version of the System 370 mainframe. It runs both the 370's operating system VM/CM, and PC DOS, the PC's operating system. The user can upload or download software and data from a System 370, and run it in the XT/370, essentially a mainframe on a desk.

Another cost-saving possibility has been introduced by some vendors of IBM-compatible terminals. They have introduced workstations that fit into IBM networks. These are usually called *multifunction terminals* instead of micros, but they are micros that already have built-in compatibility with IBM mainframes.

The disadvantage of purchasing from a compatible vendor is that a cost premium is often exacted for the simplicity of this solution. In the long run, however, this extra payment may be worth it. It eliminates the expense and time needed to research and install alternate methods of compatibility.

Figure 6.4 Data General's "Desktop Generation" microcomputers are compatible with its minicomputers and with most applications software that runs on its minis. Courtesy of Data General Corporation.

6.2 PROTOCOL CONVERSION SOFTWARE

Protocol conversion software is a type of communications package that is marketed as applications software. Many users prefer the hardware solution, however, because software consumes a great deal of a workstation's processing capacity. For example, if protocol conversion software temporarily takes up 100 percent of a workstation's capacity, this may be acceptable in a single-user system, because the user doesn't expect it to handle several jobs at once. If this user wants the micro to continue working on other things while conversion is taking place, the best answer may be to do protocol conversion by an external piece of hardware.

The same problem exists for a mainframe computer. A capacity crunch, with 20-second response times, can easily prevent even a one percent overhead for software protocol conversion. Hardware converters also offer greater capacity than a single software package. Some converters can handle sixteen or more remote micros, word processors, or terminals at one time.

If protocol conversion software is used, one desirable feature is command file capabilities, so that one command file can be set up once to link two types of systems. End users can perform the protocol conversion by using menus, so they don't have to understand the command files.

A single micro or word processor may need several protocol conversion programs to communicate with different systems. An Apple may need one package to communicate with IBM micros, one to communicate with DEC minis, and one to communicate with an IBM mainframe.

If this Apple has a hard disk and its communications are run by menus, command files, and automatic dialing, then the end user does not need to know that different protocol translation software is run for each system called. When the user selects any particular remote system, a simple menu choice is made. The Apple automatically dials the remote system. Command files dial the remote system and run the protocol conversion appropriate for it, so the user's concerns are minimized.

6.3 THIRD-PARTY NETWORK COMPATIBILITY

The most explosive growth in communications compatibility—and one real compatibility revolution of the 1980s—is being offered by an increasing number of third-party networks. The attraction of this solution is simple: Let IBM, Telenet, Tymnet, AT&T, RCA, or someone else be your network. One entry in this race even calls itself the "Freedom Network." These vendors generally promise simplified and compatible communications between the customer's systems, regardless of the type of systems connected. Some offer access to time-sharing computer services, remote data bases, and even international computer communications.

The biggest difference between a third-party network and going it alone is cost. With the third-party network, costs are on a "pay as you go" basis. This means that in any period costs can increase rapidly as usage goes up. In future years the price can also be increased.

When a company answers its own communications needs, the only outside service used is communications lines. If lines are leased, the monthly cost is fixed and limited to acceptable levels. The investment up front is not that much higher, but once the interfaces are established and paid for, down-the-road costs are lower.

For some companies however, outside networks offer strong advantages, including:

1. Creating a network with current staff. Only a small amount of knowledge is needed, compared to setting up compatible communications on one's own.

2. Linking different systems quickly. If a company has many kinds of systems that need to talk to each other, using a network offers viable connections right away. This is faster than making dozens of hardware and software purchase decisions, and then installing and testing each link.

3. Communication between companies. Outside networks offer immediate access to the outside world. Since many companies feel this is a valuable service or a competitive advantage, early availability of intercompany communications results.

4. One company-wide solution. Setting up integrated applications across a whole company is an ambitious project, and compatibility is one hurdle most planners would like to solve as easily as possible. If the goal is a single solution for an entire corporation, an outside network may be the best choice.

Before signing on with any third-party network, check to make sure that the compatibility of one's specific systems is really solved. "We can do it" is easy to say, but try to arrange a variety of tests between actual systems using the vendor's network, to prove the vendor's promises before the contract is signed.

6.4 A CORPORATION-WIDE COMMUNICATIONS ENVIRONMENT

Compared to the 1960s and 1970s, this is a booming decade for bridging the gaps between different kinds of micros, word processors, and workstations, and between them and larger computers. While there is a need for caution and guidance from those who have experience in these areas, there is an expanding range of solutions that have been used successfully time and again. For those who want a unified flow of information throughout their departments or companies, and many users want this now, there is a growing range of opportunities available today.

As a result, it is gradually becoming possible to build and extend a single communications environment throughout a corporation. Training, procedure manuals, maintenance, and end-user support can all be standardized. On-line help can also be built into the communications system, so users can answer "how-to" questions immediately, without having to track down a manual or a support specialist.

When properly developed, an integrated computer communications environment cradles as well as supports end users. For example, the same on-screen communications menus can be developed for use throughout a company. A menu program displays on the screen the actions that the system can take, and it allows users to select among the options with a minimum of keystrokes or operating knowledge.

Similar company-wide communications menus, with on-line help to answer typical questions, might allow users to link communicating systems quickly and easily. While it takes more work to set this up than leaving communications procedures up to end users, it allows employees throughout an entire company to enter an era of rapid communications between different types of systems with fewer errors and problems.

If a secretary in Denver has to send a standard business report to a corporate office in Los Angeles, the secretary can link into the Los Angeles computer during the first day on the job if a standard communications menu is available.

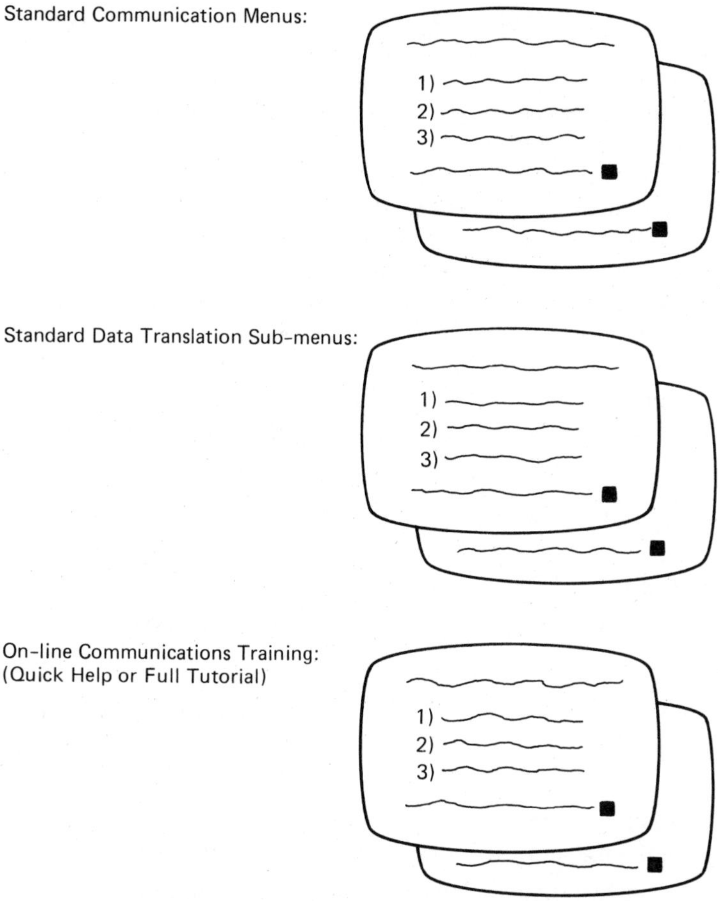

Standard Communication Menus:

Standard Data Translation Sub-menus:

On-line Communications Training:
(Quick Help or Full Tutorial)

Figure 6.5   Developing standard communications menus for users throughout a corporation.

Even though different menu software may be used, the same appearance for communications menus can be used on all the company's systems, including word processors, micros, workstations, and terminals linked to minis and mainframes. The communications paths and protocols required to link different systems are contained in instructions in the menu programs. Each set of these instructions may reside in a separate command file. It is on this level that the technical details of communicating between different systems are found—without users being aware of the differences. These menus and command files use the power of the computer to make it easy for users to move information rapidly throughout a company. See Figure 6.5.

If a standard communications environment is desired, it is best to start with the simple exchange of text between different kinds of systems. This allows the communications menus and simple command files to be created, tested, improved, and finalized. Users learn similar communications procedures, regardless of the system they are on. Once this is done, a common communications environment has been started, though it will take years to build successfully in most large corporations.

The next step is to add the automated conversion of applications data files needed by the software that runs on different systems. In the stage of software integration, communicating data files between the same applications on different systems should be added one at a time. A corporation's diverse software applications will probably never be completely linked, because the ways computers are used change more rapidly with each year.

If end users have purchased micros and word processors from only a limited number of vendors, and if offices can be brought on board one at a time, then the lessons learned and command files written in one office can be applied rapidly to other systems.

A tidal wave of new business information is being put on computers as micros, workstations, and word processors are introduced throughout a corporation. This information is initially stored in each office's local systems. This offers the advantage of matching the type of information stored locally with the use of each system, which supports fast information access throughout the company.

Beyond the start-up stage, building a standard communications environment around this tidal wave of computerized business information has several impacts:

1. Information available on communicating systems in each office can enhance the use and value of computer systems throughout the company.
2. Just as the company's business operations are not independent, micros, workstations, and word processors become part of interrelated company operations and contribute to its performance.
3. If uniform standards are developed for hardware, software, and the storage of business information, this creates a "building-block" approach to the growth and use of communicating systems. Each office can reconfigure its systems as needed, in small low-cost steps, while staying compatible with other systems.

When minicomputers were introduced, they were also stand-alone systems, but they soon evolved into processing alternatives as part of integrated computing environments. In many major companies, it won't take long before there is a movement to integrate powerful micros, workstations, and word processors with larger systems.

In building a nationwide communications environment, the activities of communicating systems are coordinated so that linked offices can transfer useful business information rapidly with related areas of the company. Higher performance comes from different departments working together at a faster pace. The result is an evolving concept of how a computerized corporation can operate. Each office gains high-speed access to information available throughout a company, and the company gains rapid access to that office and department's computerized information.

6.5 CORPORATE STANDARDS FOR COMMUNICATIONS

The ways end users will want to use communications are opportunistic. They must be adaptable to include a new business need or a helpful new software package. Since business conditions are far from peaceful, the ability to connect appropriate remote systems for new applications is critical.

This points to a need to limit exploding software and hardware choices to fit communications standards that support integrated computer communications. To do this, the DP department should contribute its technical experience in handling corporate data networks and systems. End users guide the creation of communications between their appropriate systems so that their business goals are achieved.

Seven elements offer a framework of communications standards that can be adapted to changing user communications needs. It offers users flexible local choices while linking them into a compatible corporate information environment.

This approach also minimizes the communications design and maintenance problem by defining once the communications "modules" used in the company. Dollar savings result because corporate purchasing can buy the communications hardware and software in larger volumes. The communications plan allows the company to supply systematic training and support for users in both the hardware and software commonly used throughout the company.

The specific corporate policy adopted can be explained to groups of end users in seminars developed by DP staff. These seminars may explain how end users can do their jobs better and faster by using computer communications. With a minimum number of standard skills, end users can achieve major results. This helps create a corporate environment in which the quality of business information and communications are improved systematically. See Figure 6.6.

The seven elements that are potential foundations for this policy include:

6.5.1 Hardware Standards

To give users compatible communications, hardware standards should include specific approved modems (or vendors), multiplexers, protocol translators, communications speeds, and communications lines vendors for end-user-

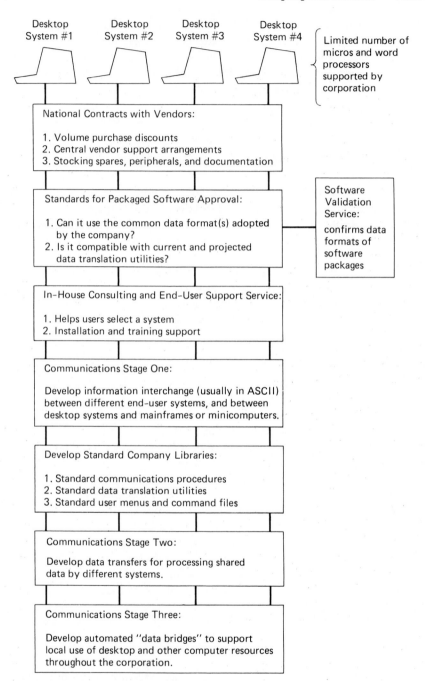

Figure 6.6   The facets of an integrated communications policy for corporation-wide communications.

controlled micros, workstations, word processors, and minicomputers. These standards will simplify end-user planning and allow them to make informed recommendations that can be evaluated by DP or data communications specialists.

6.5.2 Corporate Purchasing

After vendor selections have been made, the purchasing department can set up accounts with each vendor on a national contract basis. This offers the benefits of volume purchase discounts; centralized availability of spares, peripherals, and documentation; and stronger vendor support and responsiveness.

6.5.3 Software Standards

The two most important criteria for selecting communications software are first, the packages should be easy enough for users to learn and for appropriate staff to provide support when needed; second, a variety of file formats should be supported by the communications software, to allow data file transfers between many different systems. To exchange files, different communications software may use unique protocols. A small number of relevant protocols should be chosen as the company's standard for communications. Error checking is an essential communications software feature.

6.5.4 End-User Support

Develop an in-house consulting service to aid users in selecting the appropriate communications hardware and software for their workstations and to train and support new users when communications are installed. If any end users purchase hardware that is outside the corporate standard, they should be encouraged to run communications software that is compatible, so data transfers may still be possible.

6.5.5 Staged Development

The first communications priority should be moving text and information between different systems, and standardizing these procedures. Postpone integrating applications software on different systems until information interchange is routine. In developing any data conversion utilities needed, make maximum use of software packages that can be operated through command files run by menus. This gives the end user ways to get data from one system's applications software into the next system's applications software with a minimum of knowledge and training.

6.5.6 Data File Validation for New Software

Require software validation for all new applications software to ensure that the software's data files fit the company's standard data file formats. This can be a broad and flexible standard, since data conversion software is available or can be written. Still, limits exist, so that the data files can be communicated between appropriate systems in a company.

6.5.7 Communications Procedures

Interfaces between the communicating systems supported should be turned into a library of standard communications hardware, software, and procedures; data translation utilities; and command menus. Identify these *repetitive modules* by the type of system on which each runs, i.e., an IBM PC's communications module, or an Apple's module.

If a reasonable number of local systems are supported, only a limited number of modules need to be developed, documented, and maintained. When a new communicating system is added in an office, its communications module can be added quickly to put it on-line with relevant systems throughout the company.

Sophisticated guidance should offer a standardized framework that answers the corporation's needs for data integrity and communications compatibility. Within these standards, end users should receive both autonomy and independence. A department like finance, for example, may want to use certain decision support software on its local micros, and there should be no objection so long as the software meets established data file formats and corporate communications standards. With a wide range of powerful micros, word processors, workstations, and larger computers available, each company must work out its own balance between end-user flexibility and standardized controls.

7

MICRO-MAINFRAME
COMMUNICATIONS

Imagine having a Boeing 747 airliner flown and serviced by people who have only looked at planes from a distance, don't know anything about mechanics, and are just learning how to fly. Then stop imagining and think of a corporation's mainframe computer opened to links with first-time users of micros, word processors, and workstations.

New users need communications models and guidance. In most cases they've never used or managed a large computer before, yet they can't afford to stop. Personal computing linked to an advanced information environment or computerized information may well be the most important business advantage available today. More and more users are rushing to request this.

When users get high-speed communications and download data, many users analyze it with a spreadsheet and create private data bases. Soon, the information in these local data bases starts to differ in structure and content from the corporate data base in the mainframe computer. When reports are produced on these local office systems, and these reports are compared to the numbers from the main data center, an inevitable problem looms.

This leads to an understanding by users of the value of computer communications. The need to integrate fast-growing end-user data bases with the corporate information environment makes it critical for both DP managers and users to be involved in communications planning. Every department and office that has communicating micros, word processors, or workstations may become part of an overall approach to managing the company's information resources. The starting point is the changing role of the mainframe computer.

7.1 ADVANTAGES OF MAINFRAME COMPUTERS

To the company's computer department, the big mainframe computer may have been pushed out of the spotlight, but it is still the star. While workstations are winning over end users, the mainframe has been getting bigger, faster, and more able to do things that are impossible for today's minis and micros:

- Hard disks on mainframes can easily hold 600 million characters each. Even larger hard disks hold 2.5 billion characters. This allows the storage of the corporate data base on the mainframe, increasing its importance to the company.
- The capacity of mainframes is measured in MIPS (millions of instructions per second) and megabytes of RAM (millions of characters of internal processing memory). Mainframes are clearly the best systems to handle big jobs, like modeling a business environment, running a manufacturing line, or processing tens of thousands of transactions per day.
- Mainframes handle many terminals and users at one time, so a single nationwide system, like airline reservations, is realistic.
- Mainframes run different applications at one time for multiple users, like accounting, inventory, shipping, personnel, forecasting, corporate data bases, and management reporting.

The future of the mainframe computer is clear and strong, but it no longer dominates computing. The mainframe has become a bigger, faster computer that is best suited for some kinds of computing, while a personal desktop system is the best choice for others. Mainframes are like large trucks that haul big loads long distances, while a personal system is like a sports car that zips individuals quickly to nearby destinations, whenever they must get there. Just as roads allow trucks and cars to go everywhere, so do networks support the movement of business information throughout a company.

Among DP staff, business micros have lost their reputation as toys. DP increasingly advocates their use in data communication networks instead of intelligent terminals, because micros can do so much to process, store, and control local business information when they are not linked to remote computers. In some cases micro-mainframe links are established easily, because the micro is manufactured to be connected with a specific mainframe computer. In other cases, terminal emulation makes the micro look as if it were an intelligent or a dumb terminal to the mainframe.

Today, the users of both small and large systems feel that they are at the center of the computing world. All the computers in a company are like a single corporate highway system with thousands of cars and trucks. Every user with a communicating micro, workstation, or word processor thinks he or she is an independent driver sharing the same road network, just like every DP manager.

7.2 PRACTICAL BUSINESS INFORMATION SHARING

After many users get micros they want to look at their data in the mainframe computer. "What's my department's year-to-date numbers?" one asks. "How did Chicago do last week?" an executive wants to know. Questions like these are an opportunity for the DP department to introduce users to the idea of integrating the information on local workstations with the information in the main data center.

Today, it is becoming easier to send files between different kinds of computer systems at high speeds. This becomes increasingly important as desktop systems replace manual methods in many offices. Vast new computerized information resources are becoming available in many corporations. With an increasing percentage of current business information being put into rapidly transmitted electronic form, there are critical business reasons why available customer data should be instantly accessible by sales staffs. Or, for internal management, appropriate office production statistics should be immediately available to managers.

If the software used in local office systems offers accessible data file formats, extensive business information can be uploaded from local offices to a mainframe. Once there, it can be verified and massaged before being added to the corporate data base. Practical and effective sharing of business data can become a reality: Order entry in sales offices around the country may send new orders to the mainframe daily, so transactions can be handled swiftly. Desktop systems in other departments can access the new order information on the mainframe. Accounting produces invoices. Warehouses send out shipments. Purchasing orders new inventory. Marketing management tracks sales. See Figure 7.1.

Canned menus can be provided on the mainframe computer or on users' office systems, for uploading daily work files after local processing, or acquiring routinely needed data from the main data center. By allowing requests that appear simple to the end user (such as "Summary of Today's Shipments"), these canned choices extract the data needed from the local system and upload it to the main data center, or vice versa.

Available software packages for micros can form the backbone of part of this "data bridge" between mainframes and desktop systems. By using command files to answer standardized information requests, a library of translation utilities can support the conversion of data from files on desktop systems into some of the formats of files on mainframes and minicomputers. When needed, these software packages can be supplemented by custom-written data conversion software.

For example, among the microcomputer software available there are flexible and powerful report generators designed to be used on the data files of many popular microcomputer software packages. Run by users or by predefined command files, some of these report generators can read data files, reorganize them, peform requested computations, and write new files in new data formats, such as fixed-length fields or comma-delimited BASIC formats. Other programs offer EBCDIC conversion, so ASCII data files can be read by programs on some mainframes. See Figure 7.2.

Many of these programs can be run by command files, which may be called by menus. End users can execute them with one keystroke, letting the computer handle report generation and data conversion prior to transmission. A "report menu" selection could be as simple as:

```
4 = Prepare Weekly Sales Summary for Headquarters
```

When this item is selected, the report can be generated and the data file converted into the format needed by the mainframe. Although setting up these menus and command files is not as easy as an off the shelf purchase, personal

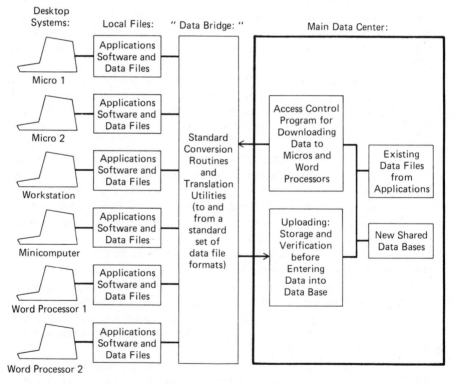

Figure 7.1 One possible strategy for developing data compatibility among different applications on desktop systems in related departments of a corporation.

1. One-Vendor Environment: Extensive (though not complete) software compatibility. Example vendors: Wang, DEC, and Data General

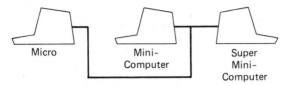

2. Multi-Vendor Environment: The typical situation in most companies.

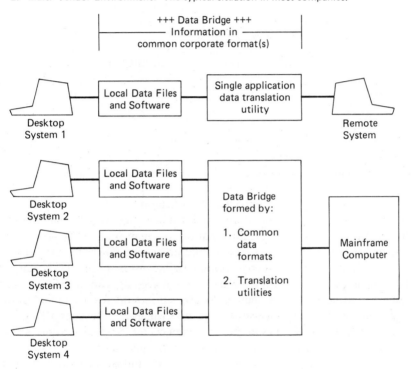

Figure 7.2 Two roads to achieving applications software compatibility among desktop systems, and between them and larger computers.

computing has arived at a level of maturity where these kinds of complex applications are within reach. See Figure 7.3.

Each company must decide how much information can be made available on its mainframe, depending on the organization of its data files and its ability to extract data from them. The introduction of new software packages that bridge the gap to micros, word processors, and workstations prompts user requests for an expanding information environment.

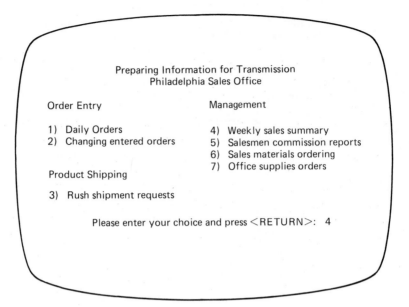

Preparing Information for Transmission
Philadelphia Sales Office

Order Entry   Management

1) Daily Orders   4) Weekly sales summary
2) Changing entered orders   5) Salesmen commission reports
                               6) Sales materials ordering
                               7) Office supplies orders
Product Shipping

3) Rush shipment requests

Please enter your choice and press <RETURN>:   4

Figure 7.3   Translation utility menu, for exchanging shared data files between different systems.

The most interesting impact of beneficial micro-mainframe links is predicted to be greater demand for mainframe computers. Each micro that downloads from and uploads information to a mainframe will need some tiny fraction of that mainframe's storage and processing power to support it.

With thousands of micros computerizing vast new amounts of corporate data, main data centers will have to expand to keep up with the proliferation of valuable business data on micros. As appropriate micros are linked to mainframes in corporations, the use of these links will grow. This may affect the size and number of mainframes in the main data center. Some data centers may be forced to grow in a ratio that will vary between companies—one mainframe for every 2000 new micros in one corporation, or a mainframe for every 400 micros in another. In requesting links to the mainframe, users are creating new horizons for expanding corporate data centers as well.

7.3 COMMUNICATIONS SUPPORT
POLICIES FOR WORKSTATIONS

Company-wide computer communications cannot exist without the support of the DP department. The essential element is a DP-user strategy to develop and follow effective communications hardware and software standards for micros, word processors, and workstations. Some elements to include:

1. Select and recommend "preferred communications vendors," including hardware, software, and types of communications lines for workstations.
2. Plan for an expanding volume of communications that mirrors the company's business needs, and work towards integrated operations between computer systems of many sizes that can move business information on demand. The goal is having rapid access to local business information regardless of where it is located, for faster transactions and improved decisions.
3. Users should not be restrained from adding communications to their local office systems if they use sound communications planning.
4. Establish a "help center" that offers users assistance in solving communications problems and provides training. This center can range from a single person who answers communications questions over the phone, a DP- or user-staffed support group, to part of a fully staffed information center.
5. Start one or more users' groups linked by instant communications. The groups can set up their own electronic mail or bulletin board systems so that users of communicating micros, word processors, or workstations can join even if they are thousands of miles away. By broadcasting newsletters, club mail, and users' group software, they gain telecommunications experience and informal networks for self-support.

Some DP departments start out with a voice in the purchase of local office systems by end users. But DP regains its central leadership role when it starts building an advanced information environment with communications. This expands the role of DP from data processing and puts it at the vanguard of the technological future of the company. If a centralized communications policy is adopted, special pricing can also be negotiated for the communications hardware and software needed on a company-wide basis.

With this approach DP managers can guide computer communications throughout the company. This gives DP a major new voice in helping to shape the corporate future.

7.4 COMMUNICATIONS OPTIONS

In the 1960s, communications architectures were built around mainframe computers and their remote terminals. In the 1970s this architecture expanded to accommodate distributed processing, with minicomputers revolving around one or more mainframes. The next architecture will include data networks that support micros, workstations, and word processors that can extract data from many other computers, process it, and send it on at electronic speeds. This is becoming possible at the rate that new communications software makes this possible.

A rapidly growing number of communications software choices are being sold. One example is VisiLink, the result of a collaboration between Data Resources, Inc., (DRI), a McGraw-Hill subsidiary, and VisiCorp, the former marketer of VisiCalc. Information requests are sent to DRI's data bank and data is downloaded into the micro. Since the data is sent in formats that fit VisiCalc templates, the end user can go off line to run spreadsheet analyses of the mainframe's data. Sample templates can also be downloaded from DRI.

Another product, from Accounting Systems, Ltd., downloads accounting data from General Electric Information Services Co.'s (GEISCO) Mark III time-sharing service. This converts accounting data to a format VisiCalc or Lotus 1-2-3 can read, so the end user can do what-if analysis and forecasting off line. Since spreadsheets can be converted to business graphs and can be stored in a local data base, end users can now manipulate mainframe data with unheard-of ease.

Management Science Associates (MSA) is still another vendor that is taking a leadership role in this area. Working with the microcomputer software vendor Peachtree Software, these two companies are building a bridge between MSA's accounting packages for mainframes, and Peachtree's applications for micros.

These are far from complete solutions, because they ignore the in-house software many companies have written. But they do answer the needs of some companies and some of their applications. As the computer industry's newspapers and magazines report in their headlines, ads, and stories, the possibilities expand steadily:

"Micro to Main Frame Links Bow"

"Microcomputer Networking Packages Debut"

"(Product) Completes the Micro to Mini to Mainframe Connection"

"The package is written in a user friendly language, which
managers can use without the intercession of the DP department."

"Four mainframe software vendors recently pre-announced products
that will allow microcomputer users to retrive, manipulate and,
in some cases, update information in mainframe-resident data bases."

A partial list of these products includes many of the largest and best known software vendors: ADR/Link (Applied Data Research), Rim and R:Base (Boeing Computer Services), PC204 (Computer Corporation of America), MBA (Context Management Systems), Goldengate (Cullinet Software), FCS-EPS (EPS, Inc.), IFPS Personal (Execucom Systems), PC-Focus (Information Builders), VisiAnswer (Informatics General and VisiCorp),

Express (Management Decision Systems), RAMIS II and RAM-PC/Link (Mathematica Products Group), PC Link (McCormack & Dodge), Executive Peachlink (MSA/Peachtree Software), Omnimicro and Omniquery (On-Line Software International), Oracle (Oracle Corp.), Sequitur (Pacific Software Manufacturing), and INGRES (Relational Technology).

Utility programs have been introduced specifically for broad communications use between micros and mainframes. One of these programs is the File Transfer Protocol from OBS Software, a division of On-Line Business Systems. This utility program includes a micro portion that can run on either the IBM Personal Computer, the Apple II, or CP/M micros, and a mainframe portion that runs on IBM mainframes running TSO or VM/CMS.

This type of software is exploding in availability, with recent product announcements from VM Personal Computing (Please and Relay, linking IBM PC to IBM mainframe) and Performance Software (Master-Link, which connects IBM environments with IBM PC's, CP/M, or UNIX systems). There are also offerings like Infoscope and Access 80, which are data management and report generators designed to manipulate and control data files. They give users extensive power to prepare business data for communications, regardless of the file formats.

As the years pass, vendors that are trying to make large sales to corporations are under pressure to expand the communications features and standards to match what is needed in corporate networks. Each computer show offers new products that allow micros to go on line more easily with large mainframe computers or other micros. Some of these new software products offer a completely integrated system. For example, a recent entry is an off-line order entry system for micros. This has the ability to put the micros on line with remote computers, to upload and download large batches of data, and also to serve as an on-line order entry terminal for priority orders.

When computer communications goes into wide use, the impact on corporate structure may be considerable. To some extent, the DP department and the corporation itself may merge and the DP-user partnership might become a leading force in shaping corporate operations.

8

INTEGRATING WORD PROCESSING
WITH COMPUTING AND
COMMUNICATIONS

Integration is the key word that describes moving information rapidly to all levels of a corporation. It is especially involved with word processors, because this device is often used by the secretaries or word processing staff of senior managers and executives.

Integration is a process of linking fundamentally different kinds of systems, the situation in which many of the largest organizations find themselves. Communications between word processors and other systems in a corporation is an essential but difficult element in linking appropriate systems throughout the organization.

8.1 COMMUNICATIONS AND DATA PROCESSING
WITH WORD PROCESSORS

Office automation was the ambitious name given to the word processor when it was first introduced. While this was premature, the word processor has been expanded repeatedly. Today, most quality word processors offer the options of communications and computing, so they can be advanced tools that really are an important part of office automation.

On the data processing side of this evolution, most business micros, workstations, minicomputers, and mainframe computers offer word processing and communications.

While these two lines of development are approaching each other, many large corporations are still buying dedicated word processors because their vendors offer more extensive training, detailed documentation, and ongoing end-user support than microcomputer vendors. These dedicated word processors can usually run micro software, so their role in the office is steadily growing beyond text capture, revision, and high-speed printing.

Two things set apart today's word processors from yesterday's. First, the microcomputer applications that can be run on word processors include spreadsheets, local data bases, business mathematics, project planning, and hundreds of other available software packages. This may satisfy an office's computing needs without requiring purchase of micros or a larger computer.

The second major advance is communications, both with other word processors and with computers. This is the real gateway for word processors to enter the world of communications, because they can:

- Communicate between the different office automation technologies a company uses. These links often include computers of all sizes, word processors, and the data networks of the company.
- Communicate at computer speeds between different offices, such as the headquarters of each subsidiary in a conglomerate.
- Communicate between different departments such as marketing, manufacturing, and management.

This is a substantial synthesis, and it is not built overnight. Communicating word processors can exchange documents at high speeds over telephone lines or by using a telecommunications network. At 2400 bps, it takes one minute to send ten typewritten pages (240 words each) from one word processor to another. Most communicating word processors have point-to-point communications. This means that the word processor will communicate with a specific remote word processor, micro, or larger computer on an as needed basis.

Word processors can also become terminals on mainframe computers, just like micros and workstations. This gives them the same access to the corporate data base as other small systems. This access also means that, like micros, some of the computing can be downloaded from the mainframe to the word processor, such as creating and managing mailing lists or preparing reports that include mathematics.

With an emerging corporate objective of allowing information that is entered on any keyboard in a company to be transferred at high speed to other systems in the company, word processors are an important part of this evolution: They excel at the high-volume capture of keystrokes. When a network has been created, information entered rapidly on word processors can be sent immediately to any other system.

8.2 WORD PROCESSOR COMMUNICATIONS FEATURES

When communications are added to an existing word processor, the only choices may well be those offered by its vendor. Sometimes, however, additional communications choices may be made from the microcomputer software that the word processor can run. The options available on each system should be evaluated carefully, based on the needs of its users.

When a new word processor is being purchased, however, the value of communications makes this a critical area for product evaluation. The most important criterion is that a word processor should have a growth path. System upgrades should be available so that sophisticated communications and integrated data and word processing can be added, as needed, without the purchase of a different word processor.

In reality, communications is a set of broadly based features that answer the question: Will the word processor be at home in the computerized corporation being built during the 1980s?

The first important feature is compatible communications with other word processors from at least the same vendor. This should also include one or more standard protocols for communicating with computers. If data processing is not available for the word processor, this allows it to use communications to resemble a terminal on a remote computer, and run DP applications from the word processor.

In many organizations it is essential to have a networking option available, so that the word processor can be linked to a local area network (LAN) when one is installed. A LAN gives word processors access to the communications between the interconnected systems in an office, so that all the systems can share the same business information in their work. Some word processors can only be attached to a single local area network, such as Ethernet. Others are more versatile.

An additional feature that helps communications is foreground-background operation. This means that the word processor may be able to receive files through communications at the same time that it is being used to do other work, such as text editing or printing.

The next most important set of features is the ability to add data processing applications to the word processor, such as by running a mainstream microcomputer operating system like CP/M. Check to make sure that the files created by word and data processing can be interchanged and merged into each other. This makes it possible for the operator to add numerical information generated by data processing into word processing, such as copying parts of a spreadsheet into a report. Since this is sometimes available in the different software applications from the word processor's vendor, single-source software purchasing may provide this function.

8.3 COMPATIBILITY SOLUTIONS FOR
WORD PROCESSOR COMMUNICATIONS

Some users think that *communicating word processor* means electronic mail. This has some truth to it, because the users of communicating word processors were the pioneers of electronic mail in many companies. In some organizations, entire networks have been set up using only communicating word processors, to speed the development and use of business information throughout the organization.

The biggest problem in word processor communications is that each word processor manufacturer uses a different text formatting protocol, with unique editing symbols and commands. While one word processor may communicate with systems from the same vendor, the first attempt to link that word processor with systems from other vendors is likely to prove frustrating.

A specialized type of protocol translator has been developed to link together different types of word processors. These translators usually also link word processors with mainframe computers, as shown in Figure 8.1.

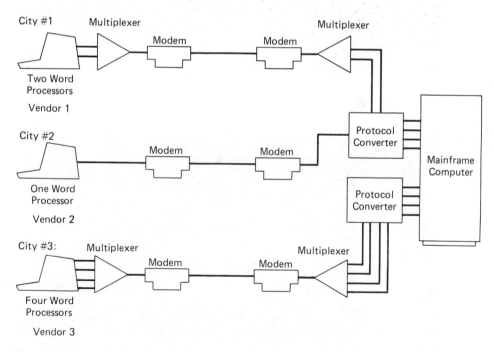

Figure 8.1 To coordinate communications, protocol translators are used to link a corporation's word processors with each other and with the mainframe computer.

In the Indian Self-Determination Act, for example, Congress instructed the Indian Health Service (IHS) to aid Indian tribes in operating their own health programs. An efficient communications system was needed immediately, to set up and monitor the many new contracts and grants with the tribes.

Creating a network of local word processors was the IHS's answer, because it helped solve the paperwork explosion that followed. This fast-track program almost derailed when the problem of incompatibility prevented telecommunications between the word processing systems at each location.

After investigating the available solutions, the IHS installed a protocol translator from Racal-Telesystems, at the main IHS computer center in Albuquerque, New Mexico. This worked well, so a second translator was purchased for IHS headquarters in Rockville, Maryland. Now, both key IHS centers have direct access to every word processor in the network, as well as access to the mainframe computer from word processors.

This protocol translator is part of a family of modern protocol translation hardware that provides protocol conversion and data network access for different types of word processors. These devices support both point-to-point links between two remote systems or communications with a central word processing system or computer.

A modern protocol translator for word processors performs high-speed translation between multiple protocols at rates up to 9600 bps, either under operator control or automatic software control. One box can link word processing systems such as Xerox, IBM, Wang, DEC, CPT, NBI, Lainer, Lexitron, etc., into a compatible network—*seventeen* protocols are available from at least one vendor. The same translator also links word processors to mainframe computers through either of two widely used protocols. See Figure 8.2.

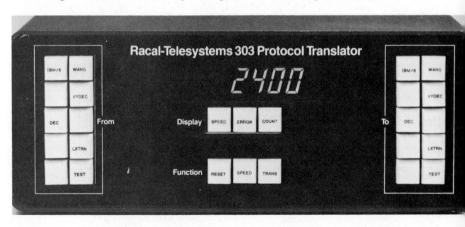

Figure 8.2 Protocol translation can be handled easily by word processor operators, by pressing an input button on the left and an output button on the right. Courtesy of Racal-Telesystems.

Another way to provide protocol translation is with a software package such as Soft-Switch. This software runs on a IBM mainframe, to which the word processors are linked. Different word processors communicate with each other by calling the mainframe and uploading the file to the mainframe. The mainframe provides the translation to the second system's protocol, along with store-and-forward transmission.

9

LOCAL AREA NETWORKS

Within an office, a local area network (LAN) is the high-tech "glue" that can link a range of separate micros, word processors, workstations, expensive peripherals, and larger computers into a single business information system. The main emphases are on providing access to shared data, file management, and saving money.

LANs can be thought of as a separate product, but this view makes this purchase a complicated decision requiring both technical sophistication and rigorous analysis. From a top-down approach, however, user objectives and business benefits come first.

9.1 ADVANTAGES OF LOCAL AREA NETWORKS

In an office with a number of workstations, why should each have its own floppy or hard disk drives, printer, and modem? These are expensive peripherals when every system has them. Instead, sharing these resources saves money and allows an office's workstations to communicate with each other at the same time. They can share business information as well as some hardware and software.

Even the most primitive local area network (LAN) offers advantages over stand-alone systems. First, a networked office can accomplish more peak-volume jobs with a smaller number of micros and word processors. For example, if a major pricing/profitability analysis is needed, a large number of local systems can be assigned to the job, if they can all use the same software and data files from a hard disk on the network. When this job is finished and annual budgeting must be done, a larger number of local systems might work on this during budgeting's peak demand period.

The second advantage is that flexible sharing is accomplished economically. A smaller number of letter-quality printers, high-speed dot matrix (or line) printers, modems, hard disk drives, and other peripherals may be shared under some local area networks, offering their usefulness to all the local systems. When hard disks are shared, this helps standardize information between users, as illustrated in Figure 9.1.

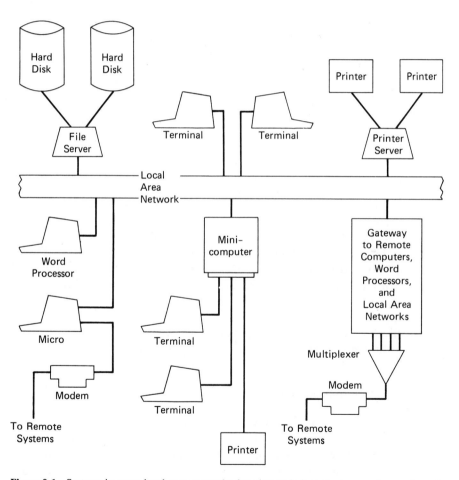

Figure 9.1 Systems in some local area networks function as independent computers and word processors, even though they might share peripherals like printers and modems.

Most LANs support systems from only a limited number of vendors. The LAN selected should be chosen for the kind of micros, workstations, and word processors in each office. The critical selection question is how the LAN will be used, because it should satisfy users both when it is installed and for years to come.

Purchasing and installing a local area network is usually a technical decision beyond the expertise of users of micros and word processors. A large LAN can handle literally dozens of buildings on a university campus, or an entire corporate headquarters with hundreds of workstations, word processors, and computers of all sizes. Even a small LAN forces a variety of technical questions to be answered. While some experienced users can handle these decisions, and then supervise the installation and management of a small LAN, these users are rare.

Data processing specialists are almost always needed to make the decisions involved in evaluating, planning, installing, and using a local area network. Cost/performance tradeoffs must be evaluated; vendors and products must be investigated; the connection to corporate data networks must be planned; and the compatibility of installed systems with alternative LANs must be tested.

9.2 TYPES OF LOCAL AREA NETWORKS

Before local area networks, the only way one office's users could share the same on-line data was by sharing the same computer system. The sizes of these computers ranged from large mainframes to small minis with a few users.

During the 1980s, many organizations will want to link a dozen or even hundreds of stand-alone systems in one office. Users will need to sit at their micros, word processors, or workstations and rapidly access the data files they need in their job, then have the updated file available for the next person to use. The value and performance of each local system is improved by connecting them together.

While there are a number of types of local area networks, they are all built from one of three kinds of links: point-to-point links, multipoint links, or PBX links.

9.2.1 Point-to-Point: Star Networks

A straight point-to-point network is impractical (see Figure 9.2) because this creates enormous wiring problems. When more than four or five systems need to be connected to each other, the situation becomes unreasonable. Adding one more node that must connect with all existing nodes is a major problem.

The only widely accepted use of point-to-point links is the star network. With this architecture, all the systems are linked through a central point, which.

Legend:

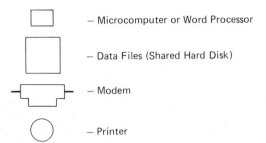

A. Point-to-Point Network:

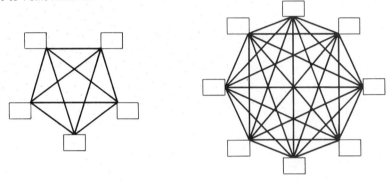

B. Star Network:

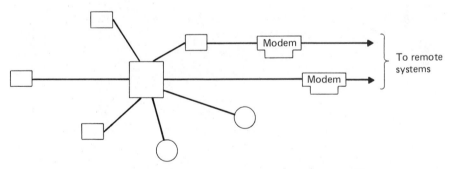

Figure 9.2   In the point-to-point network (a) wiring problems become immense when one tries to wire numerous systems directly to each other. The star network (b) is the only widely used form of the point-to-point network.

controls the network. All the information flows through the central point, which usually contains shared hard disks for common storage of software and data. When a new system is added, only one point-to-point line must be added, connecting it with the center.

Star networks work best when most of the communications traffic is between the center point and the attached systems. The typical example is a shared disk local network. The attached systems can access this common data base. The speed and capacity of the central controller determines the performance of the network. If users have high traffic levels with the central controller, they may find that it becomes overworked and slow to keep up. If this occurs, it is often possible to acquire a faster (and larger) central controller. A large minicomputer, such as a DEC VAX, is sometimes used when a higher-capacity central controller is needed.

The reliability of this network is directly related to the reliability of its central controller. If the central point fails, the network goes down. One or more peripherals can fail, however, without slowing the work of the remaining units on the network.

9.2.2 Multipoint: Ring and Bus Networks

The multipoint link is the second type of connection on which local area networks are built. This is a transmission path that is shared by all the systems and peripherals on the network. It is used in either a ring or a bus approach to design.

Figure 9.3 Colonial Penn uses Racal-Milgo's Planet (TM) Private Local Area Network to interconnect several departments and functions for real-time, intra-facility communications.

A number of ring networks are available from vendors (see Figure 9.3). These are popular for several reasons: They are reasonably easy to install, training is minimal, and they use a proven technology, which means less problems for the user.

Each system on the ring is attached to a node. Data travels around the ring from node to node. Each node is like the address of a house, and each message is like a letter with an address. When a "letter" arrives at a "house," if the address is correct, the "letter" is accepted. If the address is wrong, the data is sent to the next node.

On some ring systems, one intelligent node directs the operation of the entire ring. This can give a ring network both higher performance and helpful features, such as:

- Diagnostic tests of nodes and connecting cables on power up.
- Fail-safe reliability by automatically reconfiguring the network to isolate and bypass a failed node or cable.
- Providing information, such as network use statistics.
- Offering password protection to control access to the network or to selected peripherals.
- Bypassing a section of the network while new nodes or systems are added, so that users are not interrupted when the network is expanded.

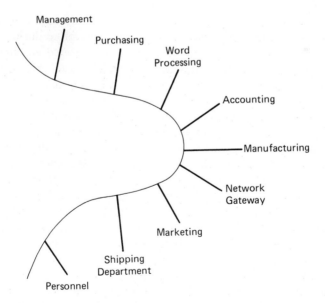

Figure 9.4   Unlike the ring, the bus network does not have to form a complete circle.

The bus architecture is the next kind of commonly used LAN. This is the same as the ring, except the circle can be broken, as in Figure 9.4. Data that is put on the bus is broadcast to all nodes. The nodes have to recognize their own address, as in the ring, to receive the data.

One of the best-known bus networks is Xerox's Ethernet, which also has a large number of proven installations. Ethernet supports a range of hardware and software. Though Ethernet offers wide compatibility, users should investigate which specific computers, micros, word processors, and workstations can be linked to this LAN when evaluating Ethernet for their offices.

The IEEE 802 Standard (based on Xerox's Ethernet) has been agreed to by more than 13 vendors, including DEC, Hewlett-Packard, Data General, and Intel. Some vendors of large LANs also offer gateways to the Ethernet standard, such as Interlan, Ungerman Bass, 3-Com, and Bridge Communications.

9.2.3 PBX Networks

Just as the multipoint LANs began to be widely used in customer sites, a new approach to LANs was anounced. This is now going into wide use, because it offers the advantage of using a company's "private branch exchange" (PBX) telephone system for handling both voice and data calls.

A PBX is a private telephone exchange, connected to the public telephone network, that is located on a customer's premises and operated by the customer's employees. It provides many advanced features, including the ability to transmit data between computers located throughout the area served by the PBX.

With a PBX phone/data network, both voice and data calls may take place at the same time. Voice calls can be placed or received during computer communications, and incoming data calls can be answered automatically or manually while a voice call continues. Modems are still used for remote communications with computers outside the PBX, either using the public telephone network or leased lines. The modems can be configured as either shared or dedicated resources for both inbound and outbound data calls.

PBXs are not for small companies or single offices, however. Data transmission through a PBX is usually included as a feature on digital PBXs, and these range in size from about 60 lines to well over 5000 lines.

For appropriately sized companies that need a new phone system, there may be cost savings in using a PBX for computer communications. The same wiring is used for both voice telephone calls and computerized data transmission. Local terminals or workstations still require an interface with the PBX system, however. In most cases this is not called a modem, but it is functionally similar to a modem.

On some digital PBXs, the phone system's convenience features can be used for data calls, including speed dialing, ring again (if a modem or computer is busy, the system notifies the user when it is available), and call forwarding.

The PBX is an attractive data choice, because its wiring is already installed throughout an office. It has several drawbacks, however, that may affect decision making. First, it is often slow compared to other LANs. Second, some PBX LANs are more, not less expensive than other LANs. Third, PBXs are engineered to optimize voice, not data, traffic, so extensive data use may tie it up.

Now that the PBX LAN is becoming an established product, some vendors are announcing the availability of fiber optic LANs. A single optical fiber carries 10,000 times the volume of information as copper wire, and 100 times more than coaxial cable. Fiber optic cable is light in weight (60 miles weighs only about five pounds) and secure from tapping or interception.

Since fiber optics offers a range of unique advantages, it already has its own wave of followers, such as AT&T, which has linked a fiber-optic LAN to its System 85 PBX.

In the coming years there will be a variety of ways to build effective LANs, and it will be up to each company to select its own cost-effective solution. If a company chooses several types of LANs for different offices around the country, it should test the links between the LANs before they are purchased.

9.3 LOCAL AREA NETWORKS FOR MICROCOMPUTERS

LANs for microcomputers offer many of the same advantages as larger LANs, but with one extra feature. They are inexpensive and affordable. Like the cost of micros, the price of this LAN hardware is also falling rapidly. Since expensive peripherals such as hard disks, letter-quality printers, and modems cost more than microcomputer LANs, they offer savings and performance advantages even if there are only three or four workstations in an office.

Two approaches to LANs for micros are available. First is with a LAN that supports several different kinds of micros. For example, 3-Com offers a LAN for micros based on the Ethernet standard. The vendors of these LANs are slowly adding compatibility with more micros (though they often stay with the most popular systems such as IBM-compatibles and Apple), so it is increasingly possible to buy one LAN that supports different micros in an office.

The second approach to LANs for micros is provided by individual microcomputer vendors such as Televideo, Altos, and Cromemco. Their main focus is resource sharing for the systems they sell. Basic network operations such as software and data file transfers, and control over printers and modems, are the main features provided today. This is all most users need. The network operating software on these small LANs is increasing in sophistication over time, however.

The communications protocols used on LANs for micros are generally nonstandard, which means that direct micro-LAN to larger-LAN links are often difficult, though links using modems are readily available. A few LANs for micros have interfaces to larger LANs, primarily through the Ethernet standard. This provides a bridge between some LANs, even if their internal communications are not compatible.

Perhaps the most important difference in LANs for micros is the speed at which they operate. While larger LANs offer speeds from 3 Mbits (one Mbit is one million bits per second) to 15 Mbits, the typical speed on micro LANs is from 250 Kbits (one Kbit is one thousand bits per second) to 1 Mbit. To a micro user, on a LAN with under a dozen workstations, the network usually seems reasonably fast and responsive. In general, this means that a LAN for micros can support a limited number of workstations and peripherals, while faster LANs handle hundreds of devices.

What impact does a LAN for micros have on an office? Consider the familiar case of several functions in one office, each of which uses micros. Right now, sales, order entry, bookkeeping, word processing, and administration each has its own files, often duplicating the data in another microcomputer. The growing problem this business faces is that the data on each system is different, even though it may apply to the same customer, product, or time period.

With a LAN linking the office, these files can be kept in one place, on hard disks, and the micros in each area can use compatible software to access the same files on the hard disk when they need the information.

Since each workstation has its own CPU chip and RAM memory, response time is fast. To each user there is little difference between a local floppy disk and a remote hard disk, except the remote one may have 40 megabytes of storage while the floppy disk only offers 400K, usually less than 1 percent of the LANs storage capacity. Additional micros can be added without buying disk storage or printers for them. The office's computing power can be expanded inexpensively and rapidly, whenever needed.

9.4 COMMUNICATING OUT OF OR INTO
A LOCAL AREA NETWORK

Most large companies are using data communications to link together their offices around the country and around the world. As more offices install LANs, gateways to remote computer systems and remote LANs become critical.

Within a local area network, transmission speeds are high, so users have reasonably fast response times, even with long documents. Once data must be sent outside a LAN, however, slower communications speeds are encountered. For remote communications, 9600 bps (bits per second) is considered fast, and 2400 bps is much more common. This is lower than the millions of bits per second typically found within LANs.

Within today's technology, it is difficult to link geographically separate LANs over many miles, directly to each other. Instead, there are three ways to link modems to a LAN for external communications, two of which are shown in Figure 9.5.

1. *A modem on a workstation or terminal.*   Individual workstations can be the gateways between a LAN and the rest of a company. This may be the best start-up approach since it reduces the number of people who must be trained to handle remote communications. A small number of gatekeepers control the trafic into and out of the LAN. This may be enough at the beginning, but it will prove confining when the use of communications grows.

2. *Modems on the LAN.*   Most LANs allow modems to be shared as a common resource. To use a modem, one user "captures" it, and then uses it as if it were attached to the user's system or terminal. Only two limits apply to capturing a modem: First, the modem must not be in use by another user. Second, in an "intelligent" LAN, the user must have authorized access to the modem.

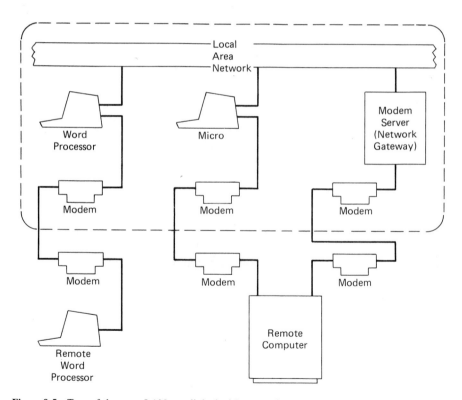

Figure 9.5   Two of the ways LANs are linked with external computers and word processors.

3. *Multiple Gateways.* A hybrid approach tailors the availability of modems to the needs of different users. Certain workers, such as order entry clerks, may each need a modem on their micro, workstation, or terminal. They may use frequent communications with a central computer to enter orders, verify customer credit, inventory availability, or shipping dates. This group may also snare a multiplexer and a leased line that directly links their local systems and the mainframe to reduce the line charges in calling that system.

A group of managers may share one secretary who handles their communications by using a modem on the secretary's micro or word processor. The secretary may communicate directly with any other system in the company.

A number of shared modems may also be attached directly to the LAN, so that messages can be sent and received, as needed, by everyone else who is authorized to use them.

Different companies will develop these options at different rates of speed, depending on their unique needs. For companies with the best planners and forward-thinking decision makers, local area networks already offer extensive computer resources and rapid information exchange at a lower cost per user. Productively shared computer peripherals and information resources are becoming available at the level of entire offices and companies, even if they are spread across nations and continents.

Part III
IMPLEMENTATION

10

AUTHORIZATION TO PROCEED

A new baseball season starts when the President throws out the first ball, and most new networks need just as clear-cut a beginning. Top management usually refuses to be bypassed when the way business is done in their company is being changed.

By authorizing a substantial increase in communications using micros, workstations, word processors, and computer terminals, management has the opportunity to make a far-reaching decision that will benefit corporate operations. At the same time, the planners who create the decision options have the opportunity to move into a high-visibility leadership role.

Still, dealing with senior management is often an area for caution. In all companies there are strong and weak managers. All people resent being pushed around or bypassed. A decision maker who is aware of his or her responsibilities may resent a less-than-thoroughly prepared proposal or presentation.

In selling a proposal, planners must understand the specific objectives of the program, including the benefits that will be received by the company and the decision maker's area of operations. For this to happen, the planners must be able to explain their proposal in English, not in computer jargon.

10.1 THE COMMUNICATIONS SYSTEM PROPOSAL

For senior management, verbal presentations of the feasibility study should follow the sequence in Figure 2.6. Since this presentation has been given repeatedly during planning meetings, it should be a polished performance. The wide range of questions asked in previous meetings should have helped refine the presentation prior to final approval requests.

In most corporations, a written proposal is also needed. Well written, clear reports add credibility to feasibility study recommendations and the work of planners.

If the objective is a decision to proceed that reflects a formal organizational commitment, this report assumes considerable importance. Its format might follow either of two approaches, depending on the one most appropriate for the project or organization. The report can range from five to more than fifty pages, depending on the size and complexity of the network proposed.

FORMAT 1:   LIMITED SCOPE AND TIME PROJECTS

Projects within one office or department, or
within a small organization, designed for
implementation within a short time horizon

1. Introduction

   The purpose of this program is. . . .

2. Summary

   The current situation is. . . .
   The recommended proposal is. . . .
   Alternative solutions are. . . .
   The compatibility with existing data networks is. . . .

3. Recommended Program

   An integrated view of the operating network includes. . . .
   (Provide work flowcharts, with communications across department
   boundaries.)
   Gantt Chart of Project Implementation
   The cost summary includes. . . .

4. Call to Action

   The specific decision requested is. . . .
   A decision is requested by (date). . . .

FORMAT 2:   LARGE AND LENGTHY PROGRAMS

Projects that span multiple offices or
departments, and require
lengthy implementation schedules

1. Introduction

   The purpose of this program is. . . .
   The action alternatives for management include. . . .
   (One-page summary of each solution; the first is recommended over the others.)

2. Feasibility Study

   The current situation is. . . .
   The sequence of steps and people consulted included. . . .

3. Recommended Program

   The specific benefits are projected to be. . . .
   The projected phases include. . . .
   A summary of the costs includes. . . .
   Gantt Chart of Project Implementation
   Special features (or problems) include. . . .
   The compatibility with current data networks is. . . .

4. Alternative Solutions Proposed

   Management may also want to review. . . .
   (For each proposed solution)
   Specific benefits are projected to be. . . .
   The projected phases include. . . .
   A summary of the costs includes. . . .
   Brief Gantt Chart of Project Implementation
   Special features (or problems) include. . . .
   The compatibility with current data networks is. . . .

5. Cost/Benefit Analysis

   A cost summary by fiscal periods is. . . .
   The financial and business benefits include. . . .

6. Call to Action

   The specific decision requested is. . . .
   A decision is requested by (date). . . .

A decision to proceed should be made by specific executives, either individually or in committee. A favorable decision should be put in writing, and should authorize a budget for a specific network. The decision should also include a time horizon for completion.

10.2 MANAGEMENT CONCERNS

If a software program has a bug in it, fixing it may take only a day. If an applications program is designed wrong, it may take up to a month to redesign it and finish the programming. If a mainframe computer system is planned poorly, it may take months and cost hundreds of thousands of dollars before it works properly.

Until now, this has been the largest mistake that could be made.

A threshold is crossed when micros, word processors, workstations, and terminals are turned into an advanced information environment that will eventually grow to span a whole company. The size of the potential problems, as well as the rewards, are multiplied by the number of systems linked together.

This triggers one of the greatest fears of a senior executive: What protection is there from approving a bad system, or from authorizing one that will soon become obsolete?

The perspective of top management is different, and those who plan communications systems must understand it. No matter how well a network is planned, it cannot be built without top management's approval. Planners who speak top management's language have a much greater chance of gaining approval than having their proposals fail.

In the same way that each company has its own personality, the words used to address top management should reflect that company's style. If appropriate for a particular company, the language can be highly professional, such as: "...an orderly, integrated growth path that is well conceived and will complement the goals of the organization." In another company, simple English serves the same purpose. Regardless of the company, however, a new network should never be described in purely technical terms, and computer jargon should be avoided.

The new communications systems recommended should also be described in the light of a company's business style, its organizational structure, and its methods of doing business, such as:

- Management should be reminded of its commitment to the project through its previous approval of the feasibility study.
- The plan was developed with the best suggestions of users, data processing specialists, and data communications specialists in the company.
- After the plan's development, it was reviewed with many line and staff business managers, and with additional DP department technicians. The reviews show that the proposed network is widely considered to be realistic and desirable.
- The network's plans were closely checked against the organization's business plans in the operating areas affected.

- The implementation schedule for adding communications to micros or word processors has been matched to the timetable of relevant business plans.
- The degree of compatibility of the new communications with the company's existing hardware and software is as high as can be achieved with current technology, given realistic cost limitations.
- The costs have been carefully considered, and expensive capital resources are being used wisely.
- Computer communications is projected to have measurable impacts on the organization's business (or on its business plan). It is possible to track the benefits of the new network, and to use this information when considering either network expansion or additional networks in the future.

10.3 MANAGEMENT EDUCATION

When communications is started among appropriate micros, word processors, workstations, and computer terminals, this is an ideal time to help educate senior executives about a company's business information resources. Management requires an understanding of how communications between workstations can help the company improve profits.

The computer specialty of information resource management views a company's information as one of its most valuable assets: Relevant, complete, and timely information can have a dramatic impact on the bottom line. One piece of information, sent to a key decision maker at the right time, can make millions of dollars for a company.

Since competition is becoming more sophisticated, the right kind of information can propel a company or its products ahead of its competitors. Information planning has a fundamental relationship to a company's management style. In a computer age, the way a company creates and uses its business information will help determine its future.

A generation of new computer users is now making micros, word processors, workstations, and larger computers into the major business information resource. Users are storing, calculating, and rapidly retrieving quantities of newly computerized information in offices all over the country.

Business information is not a static or stable resource. It changes quickly and reflects the current situation of an organization, its competitors, and the marketplace. When a company introduces a new product, builds a plant, or adds a new office, this changes the information it needs to manage its operations.

Once information is inside any communicating micro, word processor, workstation, or computer, it is easier and cheaper to move it from computer to computer at virtually instant speeds than to print it, mail it, and reenter it in another computer. Powerful local information resources can be retrieved and sent to other operating areas of a company in minutes instead of days or weeks.

Since computer communications is a new technology that can accelerate information's speed, reduce its dissemination cost, and help analyze it rapidly to highlight key decision factors, there are business advantages to be gained by making intelligent use of interlinked computers and word processors throughout organizations.

Adding communications to workstations becomes an effective way to improve a company's accessible information resources. Because more of a company's information is being put on micros and word processors, and since these systems are routinely used to analyze and structure the information, moving it at faster speeds and lower costs is an excellent way to improve corporate performance.

An important change takes place in the location of a company's information as computer communications spreads in a company. Ideally, this should parallel the way a company really does business: End users will store their information locally. Their local office systems will process and transmit it quickly to related corporate departments and decision makers, matching the information resources and computer power with the business needs of each office.

The goal is not an information deluge. It is specific policies and procedures that help make information more accurate, timely, and useful. An organization's flow of information links its operations, and these links can be accelerated to computer speeds where this contributes to the company's bottom line.

As computers and communications merge, it will become harder to separate the impact of these two technologies. Information that is stored in any size business system can be sent across the country faster than it can be delivered to executives in the same building via interoffice mail.

11

PRODUCT SELECTION
AND PURCHASING

The planner's best choice is purchasing the right communications hardware the first time, even if the planners happen to be end users making their first communications hardware purchase.

Imagine a corporate division whose computer communications goes down just when it must send key reports immediately to headquarters. Or picture the coordination problems when a warehouse that ships priority goods goes off-line from the company.

Once computer communications start, reliability is a necessity, not a luxury. The costs of downtime are much too high, especially when instant business communications becomes an everyday expectation. Even if a network is planned brilliantly, selection of a poor communications vendor can lead to continuing problems. See Figure 11.1.

11.1 REQUEST FOR PROPOSAL

The complete network, including both hardware and software required, should be included in the solicitation document. This gives each vendor a clear picture of the entire network, and how their products fit in. The vendors can reply to the user's real needs. This is sent with a reply date specified, so that vendor bids can be compared to each other.

While the document needs to be comprehensive, it also needs to be easy to understand. Four basic areas should be included, as shown in Figure 11.2.

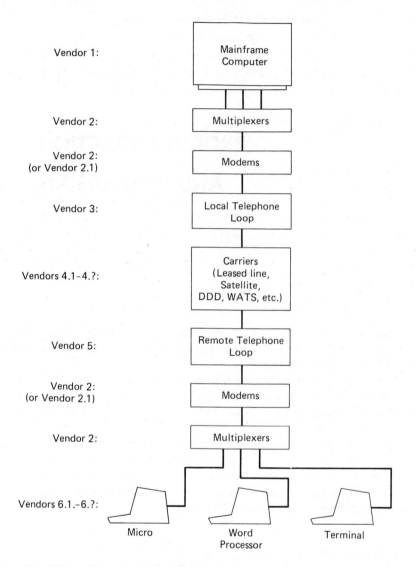

Figure 11.1 The normal network includes hardware and communication lines from multiple vendors (plus software that may come from still more vendors).

11.1.1 Instructions and Overview

The cover page contains a brief overview of the network, the vendor's reply deadline to the solicitation, key contact people, and the contents of the solicitation.

11.1.2 Purchase List and Related Items

This section includes (1) a list of the hardware and software required by the user, (2) projected dates when product delivery will be required, (3) a request for maintenance contract information, and (4) the purchaser's procedures for testing and accepting the products purchased.

11.1.3 Network Requirements

Next is a summary of the computer communications network being set up with a request that the vendor add any suggestions or product changes that may offer improved performance.

11.1.4 Unique Company Requirements

Last is a list of any unique requirements the purchaser has, such as equipment installation by the vendor in remote offices, special contract provisions that are standard in a corporation, or a request for payment options like leasing the hardware.

VENDOR SOLICITATION

SUMMARY: Trucking, Inc., is adding local networks to the microcomputers in twelve of its offices, and linking the offices to each other and the mainframe computer at its corporate headquarters. The first installations will be in the computer center (San Francisco) and one office (Chicago). After those installations are proven, the other offices will be added in four groups, each two months apart. After the first twelve cities are linked, more offices may be added later.

VENDOR'S REPLY DEADLINE: March 25, 198– (eight weeks)

ADDRESS REPLY TO: Mr. Carl Howard, Office Manager
(Authorized Negotiator) Trucking, Inc.
100 N. Belt Avenue
Chicago, Illinois 00000
Phone: (000) 000-0000

CONTENTS ENCLOSED: 1. Purchase List and Related Items
2. Network Summary
3. Special Requirements

Figure 11.2 A sample solicitation for the first phase of a private nationwide network, including local area networks, high-speed modems, protocol translator, and software.

I. PURCHASE LIST AND RELATED ITEMS

Vendor Instructions:

Vendors should reply by the date on the cover, or their proposal cannot be considered. If the vendor would like an explanation of anything in this solicitation, it should be requested promptly. Vendors should not expect reimbursement for any costs related to responding to this solicitation.

Vendor Products and Prices:

The hardware and software needed is listed below. Vendors should write "Yes" in the left-hand column for all items you sell, then enter its unit price on the right. The last column, "Total Price," should include volume discounts when multiple units are purchased.

Sell This Item (Y/N)	Quantity/Description	Unit Price	Discount (Amount or Percent)	Total Price
	Twelve Regional Offices:			
_____	12 Winchester hard disks (30–40 megabytes each)	$ ___.__	$ ___.__	$ ___.__
_____	12 local networks including all software (compatibility: 3 to 8 IBM Personal Computers per office with MS-DOS)	___.__	___.__	___.__
_____	12 high-speed tape cartridge backup units	___.__	___.__	___.__
_____	12 modems (2400 baud; will use dial-up WATS lines)	___.__	___.__	___.__
_____	12 copies communications software (see list of features needed)	___.__	___.__	___.__
	Headquarters Computer Center: (start-up quantities)			
_____	2 Modems (2400 baud; rack mount, with room for two more modems)	___.__	___.__	___.__
_____	1 Copy Communications Software (See list of features needed)	___.__	___.__	___.__
_____	1 Protocol Translator (IBM PC ≪–≫ IBM 3270)	___.__	___.__	___.__

Figure 11.2   continued

Volume Discounts:

Mr. Carl Howard, in Chicago, is Trucking, Inc.'s authorized negotiator for all questions on price. Mr. Howard will negotiate volume discounts with the vendor(s), based on the total being purchased from each vendor.

Projected Delivery Dates:

Delivery of everything required for the Chicago office will be expected 30 days after the purchase contract(s) are signed, including one hard disk, one local area network and software, one modem, and one copy of the communications software.

Delivery of everything required for initial communications at the Headquarters Computer Center (San Francisco) will be required at the same time (30 days after contract is signed). This includes one modem, one copy of the communications software, and the protocol translator.

Acceptance testing will be for a period of ninety days (see below). After the acceptance test has been completed successfully, the remaining hardware and software will be shipped to three offices at a time, with shipments to take place every two months, until all offices have been supplied. The last shipment will be to two offices, since there is an odd number of offices.

Maintenance Contract(s):

Trucking, Inc., plans to purchase a maintenance contract for critical system components, with the items covered to be decided by Trucking, Inc. Vendors are requested to supply complete information on the costs of their maintenance services for all of their products covered by this solicitation. This should include all their services, such as local installation, local stocking of replacement parts, on-site response time they will contract to provide, a map (or list) of cities where local maintenance is provided, etc.

If the vendor does not provide maintenance service covering all locations, the vendor should provide the name and phone number of a third-party maintenance service that provides service at all office locations. On-site hardware maintenance is of the essence of this solicitation.

All installations will be done by the vendor or the service organization.

Product Performance and Acceptance:

Prior to the signing of any purchase contract, the buyer must (1) see an existing installation where the communications software is working properly with the modems that will be purchased, or (2) have the compatibility of the modem and software tested and shown to be working properly in the way Trucking, Inc., plans to use it (see below). If possible, this installation or test should include a shared-disk local network (or a multi-user microcomputer) that resembles the buyer's planned installation.

The buyer's acceptance period will begin when installation is completed in the Headquarters Computer Center and the Chicago office. The acceptance period will end when the equipment has performed with 75% availability for the first thirty days, and 90% availability for the second thirty days, and 97% availability for the third 30 days.

The availability of the local networks and hard disks will be computed on a time basis (hours of downtime divided by hours of operational use time). The availability of remote communications will be computed on a number of calls basis (number of calls that failed from hardware problems or had substantial errors in transmission, divided by the number of calls that went through successfully). It is the responsibility of Trucking, Inc., to keep daily logs sufficient to record the above events. Downtime starts when the proper service organization is notified of a problem according to its normal notification procedures, and ends when normal service is restored.

For acceptance purposes, remote communications shall be considered separately from the "shared hard-disk local networks." If either of these systems fails to meet the above standard of performance, the acceptance test period shall continue up to a

Figure 11.2   continued

maximum of 150 days. If the acceptance test has not been passed in 150 days, the buyer may request replacement or a refund and, at the buyer's option, the order for the remaining components may be cancelled.

Communications Software Features:

Trucking, Inc., has purchased Menu software that automatically executes a string of commands when a single keystroke is pressed. If this particular program should be replaced with another menu program that works better with the communications software, Trucking, Inc., will purchase it.

Regardless of which menu program is used, the user should see a Menu similar to the following when he or she wants to communicate with another computer:

COMPUTER COMMUNICATIONS

11 = San Francisco	17 = Cincinnati
12 = Los Angeles	18 = Boston
13 = San Diego	19 = New York
14 = Seattle	20 = Washington, D.C.
15 = Chicago	21 = Atlanta
16 = Dallas	22 = Miami

Please enter your choice and press <RETURN>:

The Menu software then executes the modem software automatically. All special instructions to control the modem (such as telephone numbers, capture to memory, etc.) must be handled within command files run by user-friendly menus, so they are invisible to the user. Automatic dialing of a specific remote computer is required, as is automatic answering without operator intervention.

Error checking is required in the communications software, for reliable data transmission.

Figure 11.2 continued

II. NETWORK SUMMARY

Trucking, Inc., has 43 offices nationwide, so there is considerable room for future growth in this network.

The initial network includes the following cities. While the transmission lines below show communications with the mainframe computer in San Francisco, this will evolve into a point-to-point network where any office may call every other office directly, as needed. All offices will initially have an outgoing WATS line to place data calls, or an incoming WATS line to receive calls, depending on their expected calling pattern.

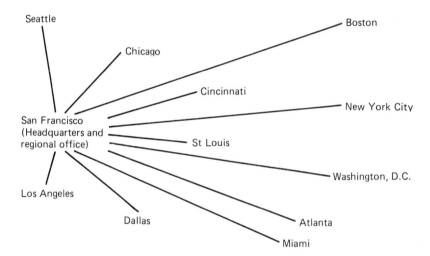

Trucking, Inc., has programs that run on the IBM Personal Computer for entering, storing, sorting, and transmitting most of the paper documents required for shipping freight by truck. By using protocol translation, the data formats are compatible with the company's mainframe computer, so the data base can be updated daily, easing the tracking of shipments.

According to its volume of shipments, each local office will have a varying number of IBM PCs, with the maximum number projected to be eight in one office. The typical office will share a hard disk, a modem, and two printers, with the planned addition of high-speed tape backup. The offices will be set up as follows:

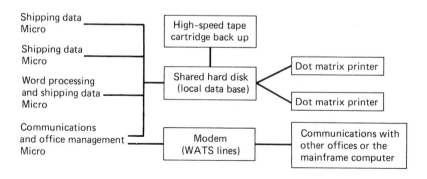

Figure 11.2   continued

III. SPECIAL REQUIREMENTS

Installation:

As soon as the purchase contract is signed, Trucking, Inc., requires that it be notified in writing of any special installation conditions needed, such as the power requirements of each component (dedicated lines, electrical grounding, anti-static protection, etc.), maximum cabling length between components, temperature and humidity requirements, etc.

Documentation:

One extra copy of all documentation should be provided in each office, to be held in reserve for any future maintenance needs. Each reserve set of documentation should include all pertinent technical manuals that may be required for hardware maintenance, software modification, etc.

Two complete extra sets of documentation should be provided for the corporate computer center's use. The cost of extra documentation should be added to vendor's estimated prices, in the reply to this solicitation.

Source Code:

One copy of the source code for all software should be provided for the corporate computer center's archiving. If there is an extra charge for source code, this should be listed in the vendor's proposal. Trucking, Inc., will sign a non-disclosure agreement, and use password protection to restrict access to software source codes. If source code is not available, this should be clearly stated.

Figure 11.2   continued

11.2 VENDOR SELECTION PROCEDURES

It is wise to know the stages in a formal purchasing cycle, though this should be adapted to each company's situation:

11.2.1 Vendor Identification

One of the best ways to create a starting list of vendors is to include the company's communications experts in the purchasing. They know who the best vendors are, and this can save an enormous amount of work.

Another way to build a list of acceptable vendors is to include the ones that can provide the level of local service the network will need when there is a problem at any of its remote sites.

It is rare to have requirements that only a single vendor can meet, so several vendors should be contacted and evaluated using a systematic checklist like the one in Figure 11.3.

Vendor Evaluation	Vendor A	Vendor B	Vendor C
References:			
Strong recommendations from current users?	_____	_____	_____
High ratings by national surveys (Datapro, etc.)?	_____	_____	_____
Recommended by staff or leaders of national data communications organizations?	_____	_____	_____
Product Features:			
Are diagnostics included?	_____	_____	_____
Remote diagnostics?	_____	_____	_____
Compatible with network management system?	_____	_____	_____
Quality documentation?	_____	_____	_____
Is the hardware as reliable as needed?	_____	_____	_____
Services:			
Local maintenance at all sites?	_____	_____	_____
Rapid service at all sites?	_____	_____	_____
Payment:			
Is hardware leasing available?	_____	_____	_____
Can purchases be financed?	_____	_____	_____
Customer Assistance:			
Communications planning help?	_____	_____	_____
Local installation available?	_____	_____	_____
User training available at local sites?	_____	_____	_____

Figure 11.3   Vendor evaluation checklist.

11.2.2 Vendor Solicitation

The only way to compare the vendors' products and services one on one against each other is to give them the same Request for Proposal (RFP). The more detail vendors receive about the network wanted, the better they can match their products to its needs.

The hardware specifications may change as a result of vendor selection, because more is learned about what can and cannot be done by each vendor's products and service organization.

11.2.3 Selecting Appropriate Vendors

Vendors who appear to fit projected needs should be noted, and a file should be started on each of them.

Research these vendors in depth, and focus on their ability to meet long-term needs. If the company will gradually build a nationwide network, some vendors offer network management and control systems that will be required when extensive communication becomes commonplace. If the company wants local area networks that will eventually be linked together into a large national net, specific vendors are working to fill those needs. If many different kinds of communications hardware are needed, vendors with wider product lines are desirable. If a specific capability is essential, such as point-to-point high-speed satellite links, that will also influence vendor selection.

When this research is done, the field should be narrowed to a small number of appropriate vendors.

11.2.4 Interviewing Vendor Representatives

There is no substitute for face-to-face contact. Since the caliber of people and corporate ability differs from company to company, there needs to be a high confidence level so that when there is a problem, reliable service will be provided by the vendor. Ultimately, does the vendor appear able to help keep the network up and running dependably no matter where the offices are located, especially if they are spread all over the country or the world?

11.2.5 Price Considerations

Performance is more important than price when one is choosing a communications vendor, even though costs are always a question in sound business planning. With computer communications, the penalties from problems can be so severe that four things come before price: product performance, vendor support, maintenance availability, and overall reliability. Be forewarned by the lesson some first-time purchasers learn when they create a network: The less expensive choice today is often the most expensive choice tomorrow.

Should the hardware be leased or bought? Some vendors offer only products for sale, and this locks users into a single network design for years at a time when communications technology is advancing rapidly.

Some vendors who offer leases allow users to respond to rapidly changing communications technology. These leases have lease-to-lease upgrading of individual pieces of hardware at any time. This allows the network to be upgraded whenever new technology provides more powerful products at lower prices.

11.2.6 Maintenance Availability

When computer communications is important enough to be used, the availability of rapid nationwide service is not an "extra." The question, "Who is available to fix any problems?" should be central to purchasing decisions.

Many large companies do some in-house maintenance, but this makes sense only when all the systems are located in one metropolitan area. Since computer communications links offices scattered over thousands of miles, these networks cannot be maintained by an in-house staff.

Most companies take advantage of the field maintenance contract that their communications vendor offers. At the sites serviced this may include installation, technical support, repair, and network expansion.

Some vendors offer service organizations that cover both individual countries and the world. One phone call brings fast service, whether in Atlanta or Amsterdam, Boston or Buenos Aires, Chicago or Calcutta. Since long-standing customers call the same local service engineers, personal relationships can be forged that yield in-depth responses to sudden problems almost anywhere in the world.

Another way to secure repair and maintenance services is with a maintenance contract from a third-party maintenance company. These companies often deal with multivendor networks, and users must make sure that a particular service organization will handle their unique mix of hardware and locations. Since this is a younger branch of the industry, few independent service vendors provide worldwide multivendor repair service, though a limited number offer nationwide service support.

While both options are effective, most communications networks are supported by maintenance contracts with vendors. When the maintenance decision is made, vendor differences in service quality should be evaluated and matched to the unique needs of the user.

11.2.7 Customer References

After the search has identified the few best vendors, always review customer references. If possible, the customers should have offices in a nearby city, so they can be visited easily, and the people who use the hardware should be personally interviewed. If this isn't possible, spend some time on the phone, contacting customers and evaluating their satisfaction.

If possible, customers should be asked about five key areas: (1) the reliability of the hardware and communications, (2) how easy it was to install, (3) the speed and quality of maintenance service, (4) the diagnostic abilities of the hardware, and (5) the customers' satisfaction with the vendor's overall performance—would they choose the same vendor if they could make their decision again?

11.2.8 Final Vendor Selection

At this point, one or two vendors should stand out as the best choice. For the final evaluation, look at the corporate history and customer reputation of each vendor. Based on their track records, which one has most of the needed products already developed and can be expected to provide the products and services required during the coming years?

12

INSTALLATION AND TESTING

From the user's viewpoint, installation isn't complicated. The modems are brought in on a scheduled date and installed. The new communications software is loaded into the local micros, word processors, or workstations. Since the communications were pretested, everything should work properly within a short time. After going on-line with several remote systems, and sending and receiving test files with each of them, a thoroughly pretrained staff person starts training the staff who will use the communications. In a few days, if all goes well, the installation is finished.

In reality, however, installation introduces nontechnical employees to the latest data communications hardware and software, new communications techniques, and accelerated business procedures. When an installation is problem-free, its success is due to preparation that started long before the installation date. A testing and installation schedule is prepared in advance, and followed. Thorough tests are completed before the first trial installations. After the test sites are proved, a phased rollout to other offices can be started.

12.1 TEST SELECTED HARDWARE AND SOFTWARE

Acquire test hardware and software, and run all relevant tests, including testing actual applications and interfacing the systems that will be used by end users. The objective is to prove the communications systems before installing them in end-user sites. Three kinds of tests are relevant at the start. See Figure 12.1.

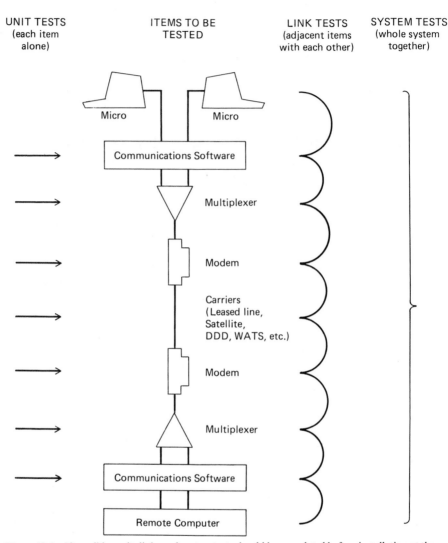

UNIT TESTS   ITEMS TO BE   LINK TESTS   SYSTEM TESTS
(each item   TESTED   (adjacent items   (whole system
alone)   with each other)   together)

Figure 12.1   If possible, unit, link, and system tests should be completed before installation at the first site.

12.1.1 Unit Tests

Unit tests check each hardware and software element separately to make sure that each works to the standard(s) expected—modems, multiplexers, communications software and applications software, communications lines, and so on—all are checked individually.

12.1.2 Link Tests

Link tests check the linkage between related elements, to make sure that each works properly with the next element: micro to communications software to modem to communications line to modem to remote computer. If applications software should work together, run transaction tests between the applications software in the micro and the applications software in the remote computer. Move data files in both directions between the systems, and test their running under typical end-user situations. If possible, use sample live data.

12.1.3 System Tests

System tests take in the whole communications system. These include end-user menus and procedures, sending and receiving test files, rechecking password security procedures, using test data and copies of live data to trace the interfacing of applications in simulated production runs, verifying restart and recovery procedures after potential problems, adding any on-line user help desired, etc.

12.2 PROCEDURE MANUALS

Prepare an end-user procedure manual. While this is described in a later chapter, remember to involve end users in preparing and reviewing the manual. Plan to rewrite sections of the manual based on user suggestions.

12.3 DATA CONVERSION

Develop and test automated data conversion bridges, if needed. The data files used by specific applications software may need conversion between the file formats used by micros, word processors, or workstations, and the file formats used for the same business data in a remote mainframe or minicomputer. A rapidly growing number of hardware and software solutions are available to do this conversion automatically, using user-friendly command files. Once each data conversion method is developed, it should be thoroughly tested before installation, documented, and promoted as a standard companywide solution for moving business data between the specific file formats.

12.4 PERFORMANCE APPROVAL

Before the first live test installation, review the above steps to confirm their satisfactory completion. The date for the first live communications test should be announced only when the above steps have been completed successfully and everything runs properly. All problems before this point are development work, while problems after this point are viewed as mistakes. Make sure everything runs properly before turning it over to end users, even at the first test site.

12.5 INSTALLATION AT TEST SITE, WITH TRAINING

Install communications in one or two end-user test sites. Select sites that are small and have interested users. Schedule the installation for a Thursday or Friday. If there are problems, the weekend offers time to solve them. End users should be informed that problems are normal in the first live test installation, so problems may not be seen as mistakes in case they occur.

Any site preparation needed should be planned when the contract is signed to purchase the communications hardware. Special requirements should be listed by the vendor(s) and planners, and arrangements should be made to meet them before the installation date. These may include items like power line filters, dedicated phone lines, etc.

When the hardware is delivered, every component should be tested before it is plugged into any computer system, to make sure that it wasn't damaged in shipping and is operating properly.

The steps to be taken during the first days of installation should be scheduled in advance according to the tests needed, allowing for some time slippage. Responsibilities for support and repair should be decided before the installation date, and all key individuals should be notified of the critical dates, so that they can be available on short notice.

Phase in the first test installations by starting one kind of actual communications at a time. Repeat the full system test between the initial test sites to insure that all planned communications are running properly, including expected peak load conditions.

Acceptance testing by end users may well be the most important test. For the first time, computer communications is being added to users' normal jobs. It will benefit them in the long run, but how do they see it after the first week or month?

In the event the system doesn't work, contingency plans should be prepared for handling both partial and total failures. If the system works as expected, normal maintenance and support start as soon as the communications are up and running.

12.6 END-USER TRAINING, PARALLEL RUNNING, AND CUTOVER
TO NEW SYSTEM

If the communications have been planned by end users, then the individuals responsible for end-user training are likely to be on site and ready to start immediate training. If the planners are not on site, training may have to be arranged.

Several approaches are possible, such as bringing selected users to the central site for classes, sending an in-house or outside trainer into the field to give classes, or relying on a manual with back-up phone support.

Initially, parallel running should be used. Parallel running means starting the new communications on live data, while checking to make sure that the data went through after each call—and being prepared to go back to the old system immediately, if the computer communications has problems. For a few selected applications, a cutover to computer communications begins at the time of installation, since this is so much faster than the mail or overnight courier. It doesn't make sense to continue an old system that is much slower, but it is necessary to make sure that all communications actually go through before relying fully on computer communications.

Operate the new computer communications for at least three weeks (two months is recommended) to confirm that everything runs properly. If an older mail-in/data entry system is shut down, make sure that performance logs and problem reports from the test sites are maintained faithfully, so the evaluation of the test can proceed smoothly.

12.7 INSTALLATION AT ADDITIONAL SITES

After the first test installations have been completed successfully, start installing communications at additional end-user sites. Schedule only one group of sites at a time. Make sure that each group of sites is operating properly before adding the next group.

Even if computer communications works flawlessly, end users may have problems in changing their procedures or adding new technology. Since the number of people providing end-user support is limited, the number of sites added in each group should match the amount of training and support available. If too many sites are put on-line at one time, it may be impossible to solve normal startup problems quickly. This adds to business costs, and it risks both end-user and management acceptance of computer communications.

Before every installation inform end users that solving startup problems is normal. They should notify designated individuals to help fix any problems that occur, then be patient while the problems are corrected.

Start with small sites, work carefully, and be sure to produce successful early results to build credibility. By developing a positive track record, both productivity and specific benefits can be proved at an early stage. Starting small identifies areas of concern on a small scale and provides a learning curve for improved installation performance. Offices and departments with the most complex requirements for communications should be the last ones added.

Successful installations accelerate feasibility studies and network planning in other areas of a company. Proved links between micros, word processors, workstations, and larger computers can be copied. Costs and time

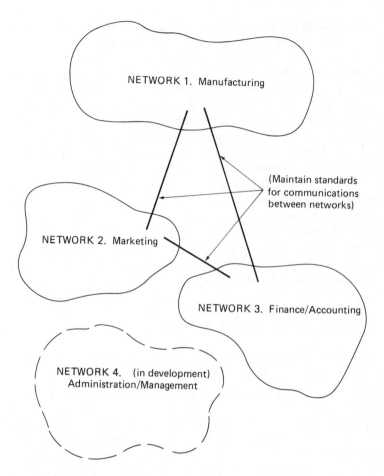

Figure 12.2 After one division sets up a successful network, other divisions can use their model to add a network quickly.

requirements are known. Procedures have been developed for all phases of planning, management approval, purchasing, and installation. In the same time it took to do the first feasibility study, a second network can be planned and its hardware and software installed. After one network is in place and running, a second network can usually be added with even smoother results. See Figure 12.2.

13

TRAINING END USERS

An essential part of every installation is the training that users receive. Effective high-speed business communications requires more than reliable communications hardware and software, even though the quality of the communications systems affects the speed at which employees learn to use them. In most cases, however, people, not technology, decide the success or failure of communications.

"We're getting computer communications!"

To some users this sounds interesting and exciting. For other users, the same situation evokes fear and anxiety. If Murphy's Law holds true, these scared people will have to run at least one critical part of the new communications. During installation, everyone is likely to cooperate and everything should work well. The problems won't begin until users are on their own.

The individuals responsible for end-user training are likely to be on site and ready to start training end users if the communications have been planned by end users. Another training approach will have to be used if the planners are not on site, which will usually be the case. Several approaches are available, including an in-house or outside trainer who travels to the site, bringing selected users to the central site for classes, or relying on a manual with backup phone support.

Training offers benefits besides solving end-user problems. It improves short-term performance during the period when communications is first evaluated. This alone may justify the training effort, because this may be the test period when the costs and benefits of communications are reviewed by management.

The potential for long-term acceptance is also boosted, because users feel more comfortable with new systems they understand. In the communications area alone, a new world is entering the office: modems, multiplexers, electronic mail, remote computers, system compatibility—these are some of the new words employees will hear and use.

13.1 USER ORIENTATION

The benefits from instant computer-to-computer communications cannot be denied, and users should understand them. It is easy to paint a picture for each employee: Their communicating micros, word processors, workstations, and terminals are linked to company's main data center, or with similar small systems in other departments. This replaces the exchange of specific types of business information in printed form via the mail. In minutes, their information can be sent to a second office. There, it can be called up on a screen, worked with, then sent instantly to a third office—even if the three offices are thousands of miles apart.

Sending and receiving information are easy when the communications system is designed well. As outlined in previous chapters, several keystrokes can connect any two computer systems—this is as easy as dialing a phone. A secret password is entered. Then a few more keystrokes send information or request it. See Figure 13.1.

As a company builds an advanced information environment using communicating micros, word processors, workstations, and terminals, the work flows much faster from department to department. Instead of products taking one to two weeks between sales orders and shipping and billing, turnaround time shrinks to days. The quality of the jobs also rises. Instant communications frees employees from repetitive keyboard entry and proofreading the same data in each department, so they can focus on the company's real business. If job satisfaction can be raised, error rates may be lowered.

Within the space of a few fast years, a new way of doing business is emerging. In many industries, business leadership is said to be swinging toward companies that use more computers to manage and run their business. By linking the appropriate systems in a company, a powerful network for rapid and flexible information processing is being built.

In most companies, the business systems being computerized with personal workstations used to be department specific. That is, the managers in each department devised their own ways to structure their information. Very little consideration was needed for standardized information throughout a company. When reports were needed across department lines, manual methods were used because faster and better choices were not available.

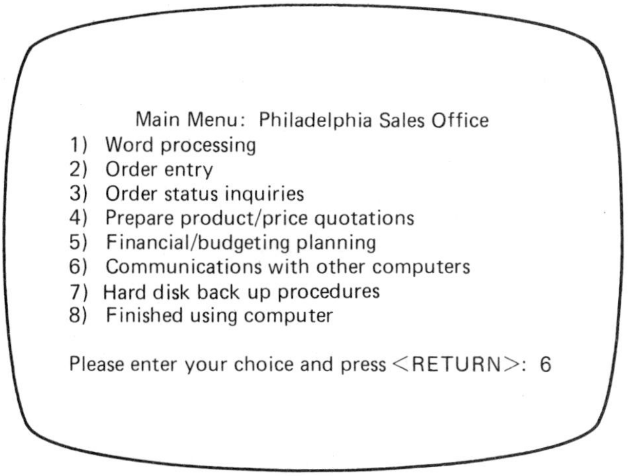

```
        Main Menu:  Philadelphia Sales Office
   1)  Word processing
   2)  Order entry
   3)  Order status inquiries
   4)  Prepare product/price quotations
   5)  Financial/budgeting planning
   6)  Communications with other computers
   7)  Hard disk back up procedures
   8)  Finished using computer

   Please enter your choice and press <RETURN>:  6
```

Figure 13.1   A user selects communications from the main menu of a hard-disk-based microcomputer system.

Now that micros, word processors, workstations, and terminals are being used widely, the software chosen generally offers most of the functions of the older manual methods. With communications, however, greater productivity results from standardizing the structure of the information. It can then be sent and used rapidly throughout the company.

For any employee to have rapid access to even one bit of business information on another system, communications are essential. Few "knowledge workers" will be able to get by without it.

13.2 PROCEDURES MANUAL

People, not technology, determine the success of computer communications in each company. A good procedures manual offers the benefits of improved performance, in addition to solving end-user problems.

The first step is knowing what to put in the manual. Simply put, the manual should include everything users need to handle communications without having to refer to any other person or document. The instructions should be easy to follow and written clearly, so that a user who has virtually no computer experience can communicate without difficulty.

It may seem that every computer manual is in a three-ring binder, and this should not be an exception. If possible, it should be a one-inch binder with the manual's name printed on the spine so that it is both attractive and easy to locate on a shelf. The value of a snap-open binder becomes obvious the first time different procedures must be added for a particular micro or word processor. New instruction sections can be added quickly, as needed in each office.

To make sure that everything is in the manual that should be there, the following sections should be considered:

13.2.1 Introduction and Table of Contents

The table of contents should be clear and detailed enough that users can quickly find any topic they may need when they have a problem. If desired, the introduction may motivate the user by explaining why computer communications helps the user do his or her job better.

A diagram of the complete communications network can be used, along with an explanation of it. If the user sees the "big picture" of how the organization is helped and how people can do their jobs faster, he or she will be more likely to appreciate its value.

13.2.2 Call Descriptions

A master list should be prepared that shows the types of calls made routinely in an office with computer communications. This master list should be listed in one section, with a brief (one-paragraph) description of each type of call.

13.2.3 Operating Instructions

The instructions for each call should be put in a separate section of the manual, separated by tabbed dividers so that each is easy to find. The manual in a regional sales office, for example, might have four sections: (1) Daily Order Entry, (2) Weekly Sales Summaries, (3) Weekly Supplies Orders, and (4) Electronic Mail. Figure 13.2 shows a standard call description form, suitable for these areas.

The instructions for each call should be placed directly behind each call description form. These are not data entry instructions, which belong in a separate manual.

To improve its clarity, the instructions should be written in a style that is best suited for each company's needs. The simplest format is a numbered list. This standard arrangement is in Figure 13.3.

When there is more interaction between the user and remote computer systems, it may be helpful to identify each person and system and what is done during a call. This method is commonly called the "script" style, because it resembles a standard script whose characters play different roles. Each script

Standard Computer Communications   Date: revised 8/12/8-

Disk File: send-ord   Disk: Order Entry

JOB NAME	Daily order entry
COMMAND FILE NAME	REGION (calls remote computer)
PURPOSE	Send in daily orders
DESTINATION	New York office
FREQUENCY	Monday through Friday
TIME OF DAY	Between 4:10 PM and 4:40 PM
AVERAGE LENGTH OF CALL	3-10 minutes
JOB INPUTS	Filename: DEO508.ORD ("DEtroit Office", "date—5/8," "ORDers") Sample source document attached
JOB OUTPUTS	Various. See samples on the following pages.
CONFIRMATION	Daily order entry log must be filled in and signed after each day's orders have been sent.

Figure 13.2 Sample call description form for routine communications. Form is in capital letters. Information to be entered is in lowercase.

SENDING IN DAILY ORDERS

1. Complete all the day's orders (see the Order Entry Manual).

2. Type CALL REGION <CR>.
   If you are not connected to the Regional Order Entry computer within 30 seconds, try again. If this fails a second time, refer to Section 6 of this manual:

   "IF YOU HAVE A PROBLEM, LOOK HERE."

3. When the Order Entry computer answers. . .

Figure 13.3 The simplest style for presenting instructions is to number them and list them in order.

identifies both the person (or computer) that takes each step, and the instructions that each follows.

There should be one script for each job. The same instructions (with slight variations) could apply to any number of different micros or word processors in different offices, all calling one central computer.See Figure 13.4.

If desired, a "quick reference" sheet can be written for frequent routine calls. Condense the instructions for a call to fit on one side of one page. Trained users can photocopy the pages they need and keep them at their workstations, using the manual for detailed reference if a problem arises.

SENDING IN DAILY ORDERS

ORDER ENTRY CLERK: 1. Complete the day's work on order entry. Refer to the Order Entry Manual if you have a question.

2. Your file names should follow the naming convention described in the Order Entry Manual, as follows:

XX   = Your city's alphabetic code
         For example, Kansas City is KS
9999 = Today's date in the form MODA
         For example, May 8th is 0508
.YYY = A file extension, telling us this is one
         of four kinds of files:
         .ORD = ORDers being placed today
         .CHA = CHAnges to previous orders
         .STA = STAtus inquiries on orders
         .MSG = MeSsaGes for order entry (this file
                   is created by a secretary, using
                   word processing)

3. Example: a complete set of files for Kansas City on May 8th:

KS0508.ORD
KS0508.CHA
KS0508.STA
KS0508.MSG

COMMUNICATIONS
SECRETARY: 4. Type CALL REGION <CR>.
                        If you are not connected to the Regional Order Entry computer within 30 seconds, try again. If this fails a second time, refer to Section 6 of this manual: "IF YOU HAVE A PROBLEM, LOOK HERE."

ORDER ENTRY
COMPUTER: 5. The Order Entry computer displays:

LOGON:
PASSWORD:

COMMUNICATIONS
SECRETARY: 6. Type in your User ID name, followed by <RETURN>. Then type your password, followed by <RETURN>. You should now be logged on to the computer.

Figure 13.4 An example of script style instructions, showing the role of each participant in transferring files.

ORDER ENTRY
COMPUTER: 7. The Order Entry computer displays a menu of
                                 choices. Hit the key that corresponds to your
                                 choice, followed by a carriage return. After
                                 transmitting each file, you can make another
                                 choice, until you are finished:

                                 1 = Place daily orders
                                     (send ".ORD" file)

                                 2 = Make changes to previously entered orders
                                     (send ".CHA" file)

                                 3 = Request status of particular orders
                                     (send ".STA" file)

                                 4 = Messages for Order Entry Department
                                     (send ".MSG" file)

                                 5 = Receive daily reply files from Order Entry
                                     (receive all files at once)

                                 6 = Log off Order Entry computer

COMMUNICATIONS
SECRETARY: 8. A separate instruction page is in this section for
                                 each choice above, giving instructions for sending
                                 each type of file. If you are a new user, please
                                 enter your choice, turn to the correct page, and
                                 follow its instructions.

                             9. Before logging off, request item 5, and all files
                                 you need to receive will be sent to you. A
                                 distribution list of individuals who should receive
                                 printed copies will be on the first screen of each
                                 file you receive.

                            10. To log off the Order Entry computer, enter choice 6
                                 at the main menu, followed by a carriage return.

Figure 13.4   Continued

13.2.4 Receiving Communications

Many workstations can receive high-speed messages and data files under
program control if they are set up with auto-answer modems and software. For
users, this is even easier than sending files, since the workstation's software
handles the communications with the remote system.

Users need procedures so that they know that incoming files have arrived,
however. With some workstations it is possible to alert a user. One such

prompt, typical in Unix-type systems, is the phrase, "You have mail." In other systems, directories where incoming files are left will have to be checked periodically, just as any mailbox has to be opened to see if mail is in it.

13.2.5 Error Messages and Problem Solutions

The manual should have a special section that helps users solve common problems, and informs them whom to call for various kinds of problems if their troubleshooting doesn't work.

The opening of this section might remind users of the old computer saying, "When something doesn't work, read the manual. If that doesn't work, *follow* the manual." If the communications hardware and software have been bought and installed properly, the solution to at least 90 percent of users' problems will be in the manual.

Most of the remaining problems can be grouped into the following categories:

1. Data is scrambled because of poor line quality.

   Phone numbers should be provided so that the user can notify an appropriate person to check the line and take corrective action.

2. A transmission is cut off by a disconnect.

   The user should reestablish the connection, and follow specific procedures to determine which files have been sent properly, and what remains to be transmitted. These procedures will vary for different computer systems, so explicit instructions should be given for the specific remote computer system(s) being called.

3. Users may accidentally hit a function key.

   This may erase part of the screen or cause other unexpected results, such as when a "page erase" key is pressed. Special instructions should be given for these occurrences, based on the operation of each workstation.

4. Computers sometimes do not work smoothly.

   If a floppy disk has a flaw, for example, the user may receive an error message such as, "Write Error, Drive A, Track XX, Sector YY, Status = ZZ." A list of the most likely error messages should be included, with instructions on what to do for each one.

If many different kinds of computers and word processors must be called, it may be clearer to divide this section into specific procedures for each kind of call that is made, and put a short problem-solving section into each call's instructions, instead of in a separate chapter of the manual.

13.3 TRAINING OBJECTIVES

The goal of training is more effective business performance. Since some departments set the pace and others are much slower, end-user training is the best way to equalize the differences. Then each installation can reach planned operating levels within projected deadlines.

There are three groups to whom training can be offered, and each has its own requirements. These groups are managers, end users, and technical support staff.

13.3.1 Executives and Managers

Two kinds of managers need training. The first is responsible for approving the creation of the networks, and accepting their performance. These managers need to understand how to send and receive information, and more. They must be given a conceptual understanding of what is being achieved by setting up the network(s), their projected impact on the company, and any changes in work flows needed for instant communications to succeed.

Most of this information is presented systematically to these managers during the planning, approval, and purchasing stages. It should not require much repetition at the installation stage—by now these managers are looking for reports about results, not plans.

Managers who will use instant communications in their work need another kind of training. These managers should be trained with the same tools used for other end users, though this should take place in a private office, behind closed doors. They should never appear to be lowered or unskilled in the eyes of their subordinates.

While it may not be necessary to train every manager personally, it is usually a good idea to spend at least 15 to 30 minutes with appropriate ones who are geographically accessible, and show them the routine steps their employees will use. While this is set up as a training meeting, its "hidden agenda" is to confirm their support for the use of instant communications within their department.

This training should also emphasize the self-teaching nature of computer communications, so that managers can learn how to use it later, if they need it. This also frees them from responsibility for having to teach or learn from their subordinates.

13.3.2 End Users

The next group that may need training is the largest, both in numbers and the amount of training needed—the end users who will use instant communications every day.

Middle managers, secretaries, clerical staff, and others using micros, word processors, workstations, and terminals will work in an environment of increasingly frequent communications between computers. Once networks are in place, the old pattern of receiving days-old information on paper will be replaced by sitting in an office, dialing other computers, and receiving timely information for early attention. This kind of job is more challenging and useful, because it combines the information resources of a mainframe computer, or systems in other departments, with the flexibility of personal computers and word processors. It may be a status symbol to use computers in these advanced ways, because it provides faster personal growth.

13.3.3 Communications Support Staff

The last group that needs training is the technical staff who supports the communications. These will sometimes be outside vendors, service organizations, and the employees who might be assigned to technical support. In other cases, employees will provide end-user support.

Support staff will receive a steady stream of phone calls from users. They may need additional training to keep pace with the new applications put on the network. These employees need at least a minimum of ongoing training to bring the network(s) up to optimum operation, help develop new applications, and introduce them to end users.

The technical staff needs a special kind of training, and it is usually not available in-house. Instead, these people should attend outside seminars and classes. Before reservations are made, both the subjects covered and the level of technical detail planned should be reviewed to make sure that a particular seminar is the right one. If it seems promising, any special company needs can be discussed with those giving the seminar to see if they can modify the content to include those areas. It is often possible to have the seminar given in-house and customized to one company's requirements. Finally, references of previous attendees with similar backgrounds should be requested, and they may be phoned briefly to make sure that they were helped.

13.4 TRAINING METHODS

There isn't any one best way to train end users. Each company must develop the mix of techniques that serves its needs. More than other areas of office automation, instant communications is moving ahead so rapidly that it has outrun the off-the-shelf educational tools available. Yet secretaries, clerks, middle managers, and others who will use instant communications need to learn it quickly. A variety of choices are available, including in-house staff, manuals, audiovisual courses, external training services, and on-line help.

13.4.1 In-House Staff

A traditional method of training can be applied. This is assigning a continuing responsibility for communications training to an existing training individual or staff. These people should be expected to offer training only to end users, not to technical support staff. For companies with ongoing training programs, this may be the best solution. This responsibility should be assigned early, however. Courses do not exist in this area, and they will have to be prepared and written, and support materials must be printed before they can be taught.

13.4.2 Documentation

Since users should turn to the procedures manual first when they have a question, the quality of the manual may affect the quality of communications.

Vendor documentation is also available for both the communications hardware and software being used. It is often helpful if the vendor's user manuals are understood by more experienced end users. This allows them to answer more complex questions within the office, and to add a new communication application without relying on someone else to create it for them.

Vendor manuals should not be considered training materials, though some users will treat them that way because they offer a growth path beyond the procedures manual.

13.4.3 Audiovisual Courses

A few of the largest companies create their own audiovisual courses or have outside consultants prepare them. While this takes longer than only preparing a class, it offers several advantages: First, it offers cost savings by reducing travel expenses. Second, multiple copies of the course can be made, so a larger quantity of training can be provided without difficulty. Third, the on-screen course can be keyed to an actual on-line session at a terminal (see Section 13.4.5, "On-line Help and Training"), so that it is a learning by *doing* method.

The major disadvantage of an audiovisual course is the absence of an instructor. There isn't any opportunity to respond to even the simplest questions, or to offer suggestions, if a user is confused.

13.4.4 External Training Services

There are two outside sources where training services can be purchased. This option saves a company continuing staff costs, while bringing in qualified trainers who are prepared to offer assistance on short notice.

The first source may be the vendor who sold the communications hardware. Unfortunately, local vendors may not be able to supply training in other cities, or in more than one location at a time. National vendors are better able to meet these needs, because they have the personnel and geographic base to match a major customer's needs.

Another source may be a communications or training consultant who creates and teaches a custom training program that matches a corporation's specific schedule.

With either of these sources, it may be possible to arrange for continuing training on an as-needed basis, to train appropriate new employees when they start computer communications.

13.4.5 On-Line Help and Training

Most workstations have ample power to help educate the end user. The buzzword for this is *computer aided instruction* or CAI, and there are several software packages that can be used. An easy way to visualize how this works is through the example of an airplane simulator: A pilot doesn't have to fly a passenger airliner to be trained on it. He or she climbs into a simulator, and "takes off" without ever leaving the ground.

In the same way, new end users can be taught computer communications, as indicated in options 4 and 5 of Figure 13.5.

Communications Menu: Philadelphia Sales Office

1) Communicate with other computers or
   word processors in the company

2) Electronic mail

3) Communicate with computers outside of the company
   (data base services, information utilities, etc.)

4) On-line help: quick answers to quick questions

5) On-line training in computer communications

Please enter your choice and press <RETURN>: 5

Figure 13.5   A new user selects on-line training in menu-driven computer communications.

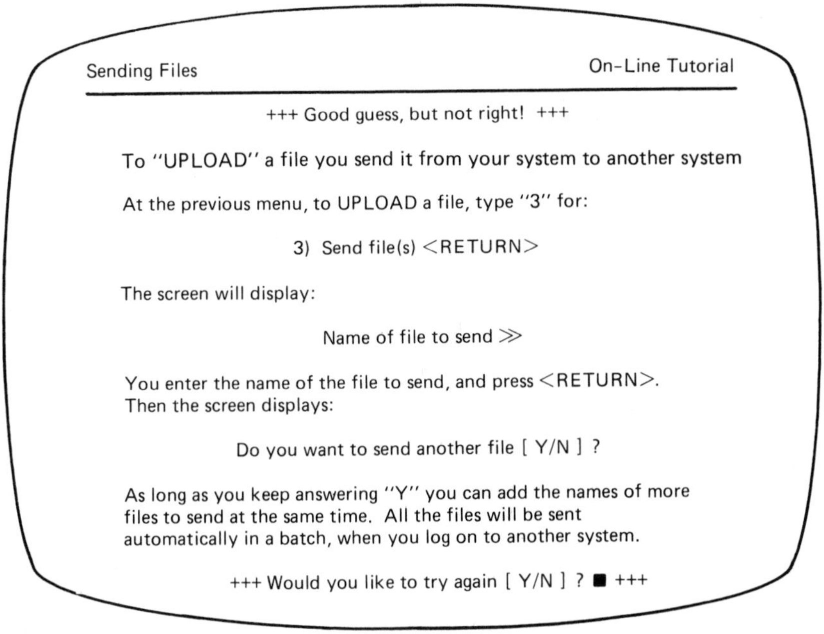

```
Sending Files                                          On-Line Tutorial
                +++ Good guess, but not right!  +++

     To "UPLOAD" a file you send it from your system to another system

     At the previous menu, to UPLOAD a file, type "3" for:

                    3)  Send file(s) <RETURN>

     The screen will display:

                     Name of file to send ≫

     You enter the name of the file to send, and press <RETURN>.
     Then the screen displays:

               Do you want to send another file [ Y/N ] ?

     As long as you keep answering "Y" you can add the names of more
     files to send at the same time.  All the files will be sent
     automatically in a batch, when you log on to another system.

           +++ Would you like to try again [ Y/N ] ? ■ +++
```

Figure 13.6   The on-line tutorial traps user errors, explains the procedure, and gives the user a chance to do it correctly.

When users select on-line training, their computer can take them through simulated communications where everything happens as if they were on-line with another computer. When the user makes a choice, the screen can simulate the same response the user would see during actual communications.

New users can run this simulation as many times as they want until they've mastered it, as illustrated in Figure 13.6. They can also return to it any time their skills need practice.

14

FUNCTIONAL COMPONENTS OF

COMMUNICATIONS MANAGEMENT

Long-term communications management begins as soon as the first test installation is turned over to its users without a communications specialist present in their office. End users should not be responsible for managing their data communications alone, even if they are only linking a small number of micros with modems.

If guidance and support are available, end users can run reasonably sophisticated communications. Ideally, this support should include the DP department, because the main data center will eventually be tapped by end users. If a communications department, an information center, or an OA (office automation) group are in the company, they should also be part of the team that guides (or has input to) network management.

In some companies, the pace at which micros, workstations, word processors, and terminals linked to larger computers are being added to their data network surpasses the organization's ability to keep up. In other companies the pace is so slow that dozens or hundreds of users would like modern communicating systems, so that they can have immediate access to business information throughout the organization.

Without communications understanding and management that matches the requirements of each organization, less than superior performance may be expected within a short time-horizon. The best business results and lowest communications costs can be achieved only if networks are managed properly.

Except in a few areas, network management is not excessively technical. Some nontechnical questions include: How can communications be managed effectively to build an advanced information environment that can include local systems in offices all over the country? Who supports new communication users in every local office, answers their questions, and solves their problems? Most important, how can costs be kept in line and money saved?

The nontechnical issues of communication management include end-user support, cost control, network administration, operations management, and planned growth.

14.1 END-USER SUPPORT

To most end users, their keyboard and screen are all they want to know about their company's data network. They don't have the desire to learn about how their communications are managed, if two basic questions offer them reliable answers: How easy is it to access the information they need in remote computers? Is the network transparent to them, or does it get in the way during communications (such as being overloaded for several hours each day)?

Some user problems are inevitable, however, especially during the early stages of building and supporting a network. There are five kinds of problems that end users will generally encounter.

First are errors by new users, which are normal because they do not have any experience with computers. This is why it is suggested that simple and direct menus be used to run computer communications and hide its inner workings in command files. New users will be a constant experience for many years to come, so simple communications menus may prove helpful for some time.

Some of the most common user errors include typing the letter O instead of the number 0. The same is true for the letter l and the number 1. Passwords must also be typed carefully, or else unseen mistakes will be made, because passwords do not print on the screen. Users may also put their local system into a mode that is different from the network without realizing it. For example, if they are in half duplex while the communications is full duplex, the terminal will display twice every character typed:

```
RREEQQUUEESSTT BBUUDDGGEETT
```

User problems are generally solved by reading the manual or by phoning for support.

The second type of problem is the communications lines. In survey after survey, users report that this is the most common technical problem encountered.

If the remote computer is down or not ready to receive the particular commands sent to it, this yields the third kind of problem. Unlike most minicomputers and mainframes, most micros, workstations, or word processors may not be configured to send a message automatically, saying that the system is unavailable.

The fastest way to confirm availability is to phone the remote system and listen for a carrier tone from its modem. If there is a tone, a technical problem may be present. If a tone is not heard, the remote system user should be called to request that the system be put back on-line. Often, more than one computer system can be called in the remote office, so if one is down, try another, If the remote office has a local area network, it can transfer the files easily from one system to the other.

The fourth type of problem comes from the communications hardware. If modems have a full range of diagnostic tests, problems can be traced to their source. In some companies, the network management center will have modems or network management systems that can test modems and line connections throughout the network, without local assistance at each site. In this case, it is easiest to call the management center and have its staff determine the source of the problem.

The fifth type of problem occurs in the local micro, workstation, or word processor, or in its connection to its modem. The origin of these problems is often the settings of switches on one piece of hardware or another, or the settings in a command file running one particular kind of call or another. One fast way to see if the problem is in the line or in a particular local system is to try using another system to make the call, if one is available. If not, the switch settings can be confirmed by checking the appropriate manual, and advice can be received by phoning the network management center.

Before reporting a problem, the local user should follow standard procedures to try to solve it. These should be outlined clearly in the communications procedures manual under a special section devoted to solving problems. If a local solution doesn't work, the network management staff should follow an escalation procedure that has three stages:

1. The management center should work with the user over the phone to try to fix the problem. The management center should fill out a trouble ticket for each problem reported to it. These records form the basis for network problem analysis and planned improvements.

2. If the problem still remains, the management center uses remote diagnostic tests (or guides the user in local diagnostic tests) to isolate the problem. Once determined, if it can be fixed with the tools available to the network's managers, the problem is assigned to the appropriate staff person.

3. If there is no other way to fix it, the problem is handed off to the appropriate specialists or service organization. The diagnosis and other relevant information should be given to the service organization when it is called, so that technicians can bring appropriate spare parts for the service call.

14.2 COST CONTROL

Since it costs less than first-class postage to send a one-page memo at either 1200 bps or 2400 bps over a WATS line, the volume of communications on workstations can be expected to grow rapidly in some companies. Where phone line connections are pay-by-time, costs can be expected to climb. If leased lines are used, however, these costs are fixed until the network's capacity is saturated and additional lines must be added.

During the 1970s, the cost of telecommunications rose faster than the price of gasoline. Obviously, a tight lid must be kept on costs, while true savings should be developed wherever possible.

The industry-standard rule of thumb is to spend 3 to 6 percent of the total communications expenditure on managing it. The ultimate administrators are usually the DP department, an office automation group, or data communications managers. With clear procedures and backup help from DP or data communications managers, knowledgeable end users can also provide some assistance. This reduces the number of high-salaried technical specialists needed to support a large volume of end-user communications.

Aid from end users offers several short-term returns:

- The business needs of end users receive higher priority. Computer communications is more a business tool, not a goal in itself.

- Most of the day-to-day questions asked by users can be answered by trained end users. This avoids the expense of putting highly trained communications specialists into this role.

- Trained end users can identify and help solve real problems on the network by verifying problems and directing specialists toward the areas where technical expertise is needed. See Figure 14.1.

- End users who provide support may also serve as a training team at new installations. Who can teach computer communications better than the people who field questions about it every day?

A second way to cut costs is to use a set of standard control procedures that are followed at planned intervals. A periodic monitoring and analysis survey will determine the volume of traffic and will lead to appropriate cost control adjustments.

For example, three target months may be selected in each year for monitoring. One of these months is a peak communications month, one is an average month, and one a low month. The resulting information shows both an average figure and the variation between high demand periods and low ones.

Everyone who pays any communications bills related to the network can send in a copy during the three target months and the month after each of them.

Users	End-user Network Assistance Staff	DP Dept. or Communications Specialists	Outside Technical Services	Impact on Network
Communications using micros and word processors	Training; Phone support; Writing some documentation	Reviews documentation, training, and phone support programs or materials		Improved on-line serives
Users report operating problems	Telephone counseling; Preliminary diagnostic testing	Trouble-shooting, if needed; stocking of some spares	Local repair or replacement services nationwide	Solves operating problems on the network
Desire new applications	Evaluation, planning, design, and testing	Confirm plans; Review tests; Add elements beyond users		Downloaded to end-users through the network
Start up additional users; Ongoing growth; New applications	New installations; Plan purchases; Prepare communication menus	Prepare, confirm, manage, or review each stage of development	Perfom some local installation; hardware trouble shooting	Download menus and menu fixes through the network
	Traffic and cost tracking; Analysis	Confirms tracking and analysis procedures; Plan network adjustments		Periodic adjustment and reconfiguration of lines

Figure 14.1   An activity matrix for end-user network assistance.

If a bill contains multiple items, communications charges may be circled for easy identification. As copies of the bills are received, a secretary or clerk files them for each location on the network and by each communicating micro, word processor, workstation, or computer terminal at that location.

While the data is arriving, a spreadsheet or a data base can be created on a micro or on a larger system if its capacity is needed. A data base takes longer to develop, but it offers long-term storage of all data for future trend-line analysis and more flexible reporting, as information needs evolve. A spreadsheet offers faster preparation time and faster analysis of each survey's results. With either method, a basic report can be designed like the one in Figure 14.2.

Month . . . . :   November
Period . . . . :   Peak Month
Includes. . . . . :   micros, minis, and word processors
Date done . . . . :   2/19/8–

S.E. Region	(1) Communi- cation Lines Costs	(2) Other Expenses	Total Costs	(1) Total Hours Spent Communi- cating	Cost per Hour	(1) Estimated Number of Messages	Cost per Message	Percent Variation from Regional Average
Atlanta . . . . . :								
Birmingham. . :								
Charlotte. . . . :								
–(Office)– . . . :								
–(Office)– . . . :								
–(Office)– . . . :								
–(etc.)– . . . . :								
Tampa. . . . . . :								
Total Region. . . . . :								
Average Office . . . . . :								

Notes:
(1) Includes local calls
(2) See supporting documents

Figure 14.2   Network cost analysis can be done by using a spreadsheet or "calc" software on a micro, or by setting up a data base on a micro.

If one location is put on each of the report's rows, then a single report will contain the essential summary information for the entire network. While it is possible to develop more detailed analyses, this initial report identifies key areas that need attention.

The right-hand columns on the report pinpoint high-priority areas. Each company should select measures that are meaningful to its management for this column. These measures may include (1) percentage variance from the average cost of communications by location or by cost per message, (2) the ratio of total communications cost to the sales volume (or manufacturing volume, or product shipments) at each location, (3) a ratio of communications costs to the number of employees at a location, etc. In each case, the highest figures are targeted for attention and the lowest considered for investigation.

Long-range management is aided by these ratios, since they permit trend analysis of communications use and costs for each location over time.

Another important figure on the report is the hourly cost of communications, compared with the number of hours in which communications is done at each location throughout the month. There are specific break points where leasing higher-volume communications lines should be considered, or lower-cost line alternatives reviewed. Since these lines are leased under long-term arrangements, it may be necessary to gather the data from more than one month before a change is made.

The total cost figures are also meaningful, both for each location and for the network. Are the costs within projected levels? If not, does this mean that there are unexpected problems like poor transmission lines? Or have users developed greater volumes of communications? Are tighter management controls needed, or are new savings and business benefits disguised by the cost figures?

COMMUNICATIONS HARDWARE/SOFTWARE   Date: 9/16/8–

(Include significant items only)   File: BUFFALO.COM   Disk: NE–NET

OFFICE: Buffalo, New York
                                           Local Sales/Service Office

CONTACT: Cheryl Parsons; Phone (716) 999–9999

COMPUTER SYSTEM: Vector Graphic 5532
                                           8-bit, Z80, CP/M, micro
                                           3 Users, 32 megabyte hard disk

MODEM: Racal–Vadic VA3451PA
                                           auto–dial/auto–answer

MODEM SPEED(S):   1200 bps and 300 bps

PROTOCOL(S):   Bell 103 and Bell 212A compatible
                                           Racal–Vadic 3400 compatible

CERTIFICATION: FCC Certified

AUTOMATIC DIALING: Built–in feature

DIAGNOSTICS: Complete range of diagnostics is
                                           built into the modem.

MODEM SOFTWARE: Crosstalk (for Vadic modem)

SOFTWARE COMMAND FILES: Yes: unlimited number of files

PROTOCOL CONVERSION ADDED: CP/M <====> DEC

SECURITY PROCEDURES: Computer system phone # is unlisted;
                                           Standard password logon;
                                           System cannot be used by remote users;
                                           Set up for file transfers only.

SPECIAL REQUIREMENTS: TEST ALL NEW STANDARD CALLS:
                                           Confirm that file transfers can be
                                           done while in multi–user mode

COMMENTS: Minor customization, but it works fine

Figure 14.3   Hardware and software description for each system on a network.

14.3 NETWORK ADMINISTRATION

The foundation for effective control is keeping ongoing records. An inventory of communications hardware and software is essential. Managing this may be facilitated by using a form like the one in Figure 14.3.

These records do not have to be complicated. They should describe the current configuration of the communications hardware and software for each micro, workstation word processor, or computer terminal in the organization.

Imagine what happens when 500 local systems are in a network and 50 new micros and 10 word processors are added to it. If an inventory is not available, it will be difficult to link the new systems to specific existing systems, since the details of the existing systems are not known. If "quick and dirty" links are thrown together to add the new systems, and they are not documented, the person who adds the next batch of local systems will have an even bigger headache. At some point, the network will become unmanageable.

14.4 OPERATIONS MANAGEMENT

Next month, your company is opening a new branch office in the Midwest. Six of the new office's micros will need regular communications with eight other offices or computers throughout the company. How is the new branch office going to set up a menu for those new systems, so that they automatically call the other eight systems? Who at each of the eight locations is going to change their communications menus (or command files) to include the new branch office?

The best way to set up computer communications for end users is to develop and test it at an operations management office. The appropriate menus or command files can be downloaded to each office's system(s) over phone lines. Local users should try each menu option on each major type of system used to make sure that the calls are correct and that the on-line connections are established automatically. Since excellent menu software is available as an off-the-shelf product, setting up these communications menus may be done rapidly at a central location.

In larger corporations, at least one center will have most of the standard micros, workstations, and word processors used throughout the company. They can store the master copy of the communications menus and command files on their systems. Then, when a remote office's communications menu must be changed, that menu can be called up on the appropriate system, the new command files written, and the changed menus tested quickly.

When a change is made, it should be documented. This is the heart of guiding a company's computer communications from a central site. At a minimum, two forms are needed for documentation:

1. Hardware/software description form. As illustrated in Figure 14.3, this form itemizes one computer or word processor on the network, the kind of communications hardware and software it uses, and other significant information.

2. Command file listing. Each routine call made by every system has its own command file, as illustrated in Figure 14.4.

Any number of command files like REGION can be prewritten for end users. They can have city names like CHICAGO or DALLAS. They can be named by product groups (BABYOIL), by a department in a company (SHIPPING), or by a person's name (EDWARDS).

To protect computer security, passwords should *never* be put into command files. Since command files can be accessed or copied (in local offices, in a network management center, or by dial-up access), corporatewide computer se-

---

COMMUNICATIONS COMMAND FILE   Date: 9/16/8–

Location: BOSTON   Command Fiel: REGION   Master Copy on Disk: NE–NET

PURPOSE OF FILE: Automatically dials regional
                                headquarters in New York City

DESTINATION SYSTEM: Cromemco CS-3; 8-bit Z-80 (CP/M) and
                                16-bit, 68000, UNIX'7 users, 96
                                megabyte hard disk

SENDOR'S SOFTWARE: "MODEM" (Christiansen protocol)
                                (set up for batch file transfers)

SECURITY LEVEL: Standard password procedures to
                                log on and Unix protected access
                                within the New York system

PROTOCOL CONVERSION NEEDED: None

BACKUP REQUIREMENTS: Extra copy of communications software
                                and all command files kept on separate
                                backup floppy disk in Boston; update
                                with new software or command files
                                when changes are made

UPDATE PROCEDURES: Boston has an excellent in-house
                                user who handles the communications
                                updates; he can be contacted for
                                help with other communications
                                problems on micros

                                Contact: Jim Fregosi in Boston office

Figure 14.4 Command file listing form for each command file on a network.

curity will be Swiss cheese if passwords are put in command files. The command file should automatically dial a remote system and stop at the prompt that says,

```
LOGIN:
PASSWORD:
```

At this point users should enter their own password at the keyboard. They will then enter the remote computer at the security level assigned to them, with access only to the areas they are permitted to use.

14.5 PLANNING AND MANAGING NETWORK GROWTH

Steadily falling prices of communications hardware lead to its installation on more systems and help cost-justify the increasing use of instant communications. As computer communications develops, users become aware of what instant business communications can contribute. Applications development steadily expands. When the volume of traffic reaches substantial levels, early approaches to network management will not be enough to handle the expected needs.

When this happens, a network growth plan is required. This plan should be developed in the same way as the original feasibility study. The network management group is an appropriate team to undertake this planning, in conjunction with DP and users, because both technical analyses and projected user requirements are needed. A substantial planning voice should be given to users, since they will be experienced in computer communications, and it is their business needs that are being planned.

For doing technical projections, network planning software has been developed that runs on micros. This software focuses on the major technical decisions, including (1) predicting network performance, (2) optimizing network topology, (3) the effects of grouping lines into trunks, (4) the impact of network control, and (5) other general network management needs.

Because microcomputers are used, this software usually handles only 200 to 500 nodes at a time, depending on the software and the size of the system on which it is run. Larger networks must therefore be tackled as separate regions or groups that are each optimized.

This software supports "what if" questions, and it offers answers within minutes for questions like the effect on response times from changes in the traffic flow, or adding multiple on-line applications. Protocol changes can also be studied, as well as the effects of other transmission speeds, message structures, and mixed types of traffic.

Since the Bell system has been deregulated, there are increased responsibilities for each company to plan and develop its network on its own. Managing a network involves both specialists and users in working together to provide the most cost-effective solutions to increasing needs for communications by microcomputer, workstation, word processor, and computer terminal users.

Part IV
APPLICATIONS

15

COMMUNICATIONS EXAMPLES

Planning, installing, and managing reliable communications are not as complex as the larger performance opportunities created. Once an organization's local systems are linked to other local systems and the data center, a years-long process begins. From this time forward, communications has become an always available, cost-justified business tool.

The next question is more significant. How can an organization take full advantage of the wealth of computerized information and accelerated access to it that are always a few keystrokes away?

Microcomputers and other small systems have turned out to be much easier for users than computer professionals expected. These personal systems also match the needs of users whose situation swiftly evolves from week to week and year to year. When a mainframe can't respond right away, this is exactly what personal computing does best.

Establishing standards for accessible data and setting up user-friendly communications provides users the remote information they need when they need it. This is a self-generating process, much like a pebble that rolls down a mountain and grows into a snowball. When the first network is well planned and then is installed successfully, communications results in an advanced information environment that works for end users. Since most of the custom design and programming has been completed, additional networks can be added more rapidly than expected.

In the early 1980s, microcomputers offered a revolution in the speed with which organizations and executives could reach their goals. This same scale of progress is available again today with microcomputer, word processor, and workstation communications with just as dramatic results. Right now, advanced information environments are being built and used productively in many companies and industries.

More than anything else, organizations communicate. Internally, they send business data, memos, and transaction information. Externally, they place and receive orders, and send documents and letters about every imaginable business need. When these communications are accelerated to computer speed, the impact is much larger than "the automated office."

An expanding legion of micros, word processors, workstations, and computer terminals stand waiting for communications to link them into modern business information environments. Already, they are strategically dispersed throughout many organizations.

15.1 ORGANIZATIONS, CORPORATIONS, AND GOVERNMENT

The following aren't pie-in-the-sky stories, because some of these organizations are handling real problems during their first years in development. Still, these real-life examples are having a far-reaching impact. Other organizations can learn from these examples, and can accelerate their returns from existing investments in micros, word processors, workstations, and computer terminals linked to minicomputers and mainframes.

15.1.1 Libraries

Libraries are not known for having high-budget DP centers or even one full-time DP professional on their staff. In fact, since most libraries are supported by taxes, their budgets have been slimmed steadily during the 1970s and 1980s, while the costs of books and magazine subscriptions have skyrocketed. In 1972, for example, the average cost of a hardcover book was $12.99, while a decade later, in 1982, it was $30.34.

Without large DP staffs or sizable DP budgets, thousands of libraries have turned to computer communications and computers of all sizes and types to become interdependent with each other. This has given them new ways to cope with the quadruple whammy of rising prices, tax revolts, recessions, and tighter book-buying budgets.

More than 3300 libraries are now linked to the Online Computer Library Center (OCLC), which was founded in 1979. This network of American and foreign libraries offers libraries and their patrons access to computerized lists of many of the books, magazines, and other holdings of the member libraries.

One of this network's main benefits is that libraries can borrow from other libraries the books that they do not have. Each library no longer has to think of itself as an island of knowledge that must hold five to ten million books to have a complete collection. Instead, computer communications allow rapid resource sharing between libraries around both the country and the world.

A library user in Finland can use OCLC to discover books on karate in a high school library in Illinois. The high school library may or may not want to send its karate books overseas, but their collection's list is already accessible from member libraries in other countries, as well as from libraries all over America.

Librarians have been stereotyped as meek and retiring, but they have built not one but a number of computer communications networks without the in-house computer expertise most corporate users take for granted. A second network, the Research Libraries Group, is based in Stanford, California, and it includes libraries both around the country and multiple institutions in one city, such as the libraries at Columbia University, New York University, and the New York Public Library.

A main goal of the Research Libraries Group is to insure that at least one member library holds a complete collection in every field to preserve our intellectual heritage. In this way, even the largest libraries can cope with tighter budgets by becoming specialists in certain areas of knowledge, and relying on other libraries to specialize in other fields.

Many library patrons are rapidly climbing their personal learning curves into this new era of shared intellectual resources. In OCLC's first 70 months, more than four million volumes were requested for interlibrary loans. The relevant number, however, is that 25 percent (or one million) of this total were requested during the latest eight months alone.

It is clear that thousands of keys are being turned in new electronic doors by librarians, offering a view of a growing worldwide knowledge environment. It is also clear that the hands on the keys are librarians', who are new end users themselves. They are successfully using computer communications between systems of all sizes to launch this new era for libraries, while enduring tighter budgets and less DP support than most corporate end users will ever face.

15.1.2 A Large Corporation

A major revolution has been brewing in one of technology's groundbreaking leaders, the Travelers Insurance Co. At this point, more than 5000 micros are being used throughout the company.

The forecast is for thousands more micros to be installed throughout Travelers within the near future.

This systematic program was originally built by two primary operating groups. The first is an in-house Personal Computing Center that combines "showroom" displays of microcomputers with four kinds of user services: a user support service, a technical laboratory that analyzes microcomputer hardware, a microcomputing resource center, and a software applications lending library.

Four micro systems have been selected by Travelers for their employees, though others are being considered. These are Apple, IBM, Radio Shack, and Hewlett-Packard.

The week the Center opened, over a thousand Travelers employees visited it. Now, on an average day, 20 to 25 people visit. Some are trying to decide if a micro can help them. Others have a micro and are investigating additional uses. All want to learn more about how micros can help them.

To receive a microcomputer, the user has to justify its acquisition and use. After this is done, the Personal Computing Center provides the system and charges the expense back to the user's department. This helps provide tight control over the spread of these systems—up to $5000 of company money is a lot to spend needlessly, but only a little if productive benefits result.

While the staff at the Center works closely with users in analyzing their needs and selecting a system, they recommend one system over others only if there are clear reasons why it benefits the user. If any of two or three systems will do the job, they let the user decide.

Once the user receives a micro, extensive support comes with it. The most obvious source is from additional visits to the Personal Computing Center.

Equally important is the second operating area involved in building this new computerized corporation: direct support from the Systems Division of Traveler's DP Department. Each line area of the Systems Division has a personal computing coordinator who works with users. With this kind of close coordination, DP employees overcame their initial concern over both central and local computing occurring at the same time.

The micros are typically used in one of two modes at Travelers. In their stand-alone mode, they are independent single-user systems. Since micros can do double duty as terminals on Traveler's minicomputers and mainframes, protocol translation has been added by the DP Department to allow the micros to operate as local workstations that are linked as distributed processors to the minis and mainframes.

Besides these in-house activities, hundreds of Travelers field agents are using micros they bought on their own, to provide customized quotations for Travelers products like home and automobile insurance. Travelers is now using its in-house expertise to build an available network for rapid computer communications with its field agents all over the country, to make their micros as helpful as possible.

15.1.3 Education

Statewide networks, including thousands of computers of all sizes, are now being developed in a number of states, years ahead of when most business and DP managers expect these types of networks to be built in their own companies. Three of these stages include Texas, West Virginia, and Florida.

The North Texas Multi-Region Processing Center has grown out of a DP center established in 1970 to process payrolls, grades, accounting, and other tasks for two school districts on its mainframe computers. It recently saved $500,000 while expanding its services to 214 school districts in 44 counties. The savings were produced by adding communications hardware that allows mini-computers and inexpensive ASCII terminals to link the school districts to the data center. Smaller districts have upgraded from manual to computerized procedures, and larger districts have also improved their access by adding more terminals and micros to their existing installed terminals.

West Virginia's microcomputer network will eventually link every school in the state. The network is built around a scholastic bulletin board operated out of a state educational department central library. Micros in each of the state's 1134 school microcomputer labs, including elementary schools, will be able to dial into the bulletin board. This will serve as an educational news and message center, and a statewide calendar for educational activities and meetings. Students and teachers will also be able to use their computers at home to hook into the computer labs at many of the schools. Adults are included, too, since an active and successful adult education program in computer literacy is taught in the evenings at the computer labs of many schools.

The targeted completion date for the Florida Information Resource Network (FIRN) is years away, though parts of it have reached testing stages. At that time, the public education system in this state will be linked electronically, from large university computer centers through school districts and public schools down to the elementary school level, including:

- Microcomputers at 2345 colleges, high schools, junior high schools, and elementary schools.
- Microcomputers at 67 school districts.
- Minicomputers at twenty regional data centers and large school districts.
- Large mainframe computers at nine state universities.

FIRN depends on taking advantage of existing in-place computer systems in schools all over the state. By building on these resources, about 75 percent of the schools have the hardware they need. This comprehensive network has two main responsibilities: educational data processing and shared-resource network communications.

The first area is educational DP, and it has three purposes. Student processing is designed to simplify the routine work of teachers and administrators by tracking student grades, class schedules, attendance, educational records, and per-student state funding reporting. Staff processing focuses on employees, personnel records, payroll, and skills records. Financial processing includes revenues, budgeting, general ledger, purchasing, and accounts payable.

In a smaller educational system, these would be standard educational DP functions. FIRN, however, is linking 67 school districts that employ 90,000 teachers and educate 1.5 million students, plus a higher education system of junior colleges and universities.

When a student enters Florida's school system, his or her basic information will be collected and passed with the student electronically to every new school in the state, like paper records, except faster and at a lower cost. When this student enters a higher school or transfers to another district, teachers will no longer be burdened with collecting information on the student and filling out standard forms listing items like name, sex, birth date, and ethnic background. If the student applies to a state university or junior college, his or her transcript will be available electronically to admissions officers.

FIRN's second major responsibility is expanding local educators' access to mainframe computing resources across the entire state. In 1977, the first year in which computing resources were shared statewide, $3.5 million was saved in computing costs. This will transform the computing capabilities of many local schools and small school districts where microcomputers are located. The terminals and microcomputers in FIRN will be given on-line access to the state's nine mainframe educational computing centers. Neighborhood schools throughout the state will have dial-up access to mainframe computing power and techniques.

15.1.4 Medicine

The American Medical Association has joined GTE Telenet in developing a breakthrough medical computer network that can be accessed by any computer or terminal that is connected to a telephone line.

With microcomputers entering doctors' offices and hospitals at a rapid rate, the systems required to access the new AMA network are becoming available all over the country.

GTE's Telenet can be accessed by placing a local phone call in over 250 major cities, and with a long distance call to a nearby city everywhere else. In seconds, the latest medical information available will be displayed on the screen. To simplify use, the system provides the medical data in easily accessible and usable formats. For example, this system offers universal access to the latest drug-related information that might be needed by a physician for determining the best treatment for a patient.

The AMA has always used a variety of journals and publications to provide physicians useful information. This new medical network not only brings doctors the best information in seconds, it also helps the AMA track the information requested most often, so it can develop those areas faster.

Doctors can also use their microcomputers to access other remote medical services that are rapidly becoming available from providers besides the AMA. For example, an on-line Infection Control Program is now available, so that medical professionals can track and analyze the progress of infections in patients, at a cost of about 15 cents per patient per day. Offered by Shared Medical Systems, this software package helps doctors compile microbiological data, infection data, and invasive procedures.

The day may be nearing when doctors consider putting microcomputers in an examining room. A quick consultation with the AMA network or an analytical computer program can become part of a doctor's more complicated diagnoses and treatments.

After all, the computer's encyclopedic memory can't forget even the most obscure symptom or detail. It would be the perfect doctor's helper, if it could only fill a foursome for golf on Wednesday afternoons.

15.1.5 Purchasing

How far off is the day when products can be ordered through your micro or word processor, and the order sent into the supplier's computer?

How close is the nearest micro or word processor that is linked to the phone lines? That's the distance to Ordernet, a computer-to-computer purchasing network available today.

How good are Ordernet's services? The fourth trade association to officially endorse Ordernet is the National Association of Service Merchandising (NASM).

Run by the Management Systems Division of Informatics General, Ordernet is an on-line central clearinghouse for purchase orders and related documents transmitted between buyers and sellers.

To send a purchase order, the buyer's system simply calls up Ordernet, and Ordernet in turn calls the seller's computer. By providing the essential technical linkage between different and incompatible computer systems, Ordernet links buyers and sellers today.

Other specialized services are also available from Ordernet, such as drug chargebacks in the National Wholesale Druggist Association (NWDA) format. These give pharmaceutical drug wholesalers additional price discounts on their volume sales to hospitals. In the past, wholesalers had to process these credits manually with each drug manufacturer. Now wholesalers can send Ordernet large batches of these credit chargebacks directly from their computers, and Ordernet transmits them into the computers of many drug companies—at a cost of one cent per record sent or received.

Using computers to handle high-speed purchasing offers a variety of benefits. The most obvious ones are standard benefits from data communications: immediate transmission instead of slower mail services, faster response times, and reduced errors, since operators don't have to rekey ordered items, shipping addresses, and other data into the destination computers.

The last benefit is financial, contributing directly to the bottom line. Efficient distributors and buyers can use shorter order lead times and data management to reduce their overall inventory investments and increase their rate of inventory turnover and profitability. After all, anyone who increases profits by using immediate on-line communications has just found another way to get more returns from a smaller capital investment. Cutting the cost of money is one key to business success today.

15.1.6 Government

Microcomputers and word processors are networking the U.S. House of Representatives in Washington, both within itself, and with the nation.

Within an individual representative's office, for example, a microcomputer network has been set up by the Chairman of the House's Policy Group on Information and Computers, Congressman Charlie Rose.

Seven Z-80 microcomputers are connected by shielded twisted-pair wiring that operates at 19.2K bps. The network's shared peripherals include a 20-megabyte hard disk, two letter-quality printers, and an auto-dial/auto-answer modem. By using dial-up lines, "Rosenet," as Congressman Rose's network is called, is linked to his North Carolina state headquarters and to his employees' home computers.

Throughout the House of Representatives informal links between the numerous stand-alone word processors and microcomputers have evolved into the House Information System (HIS), a broadband coaxial cable network linking at least 150 offices. This network offers direct access from the individual offices to:

- Local electronic mail throughout all connected systems.
- The Library of Congress, for research and information requests.
- Congressional data bases on the House's two Amdahl computers.
- Nationwide data networks with automatic dialing from directories maintained on the HIS network.

The systems in many congressmen's Washington offices are already used to transmit text and data to their home district office(s), providing high-speed text communications. Since the same modems that link home offices to the Capitol can be used to receive electronic mail from the voters and local companies, instant electronic lobbying is potentially available to anyone with a home or office system linked to a phone line.

Congressman James Coyne has started electronic mail with voters in his Pennsylvania home district using the electronic mail services provided by outside vendors such as CompuServe and the Source. He finds the time savings especially helpful for solving constituents' problems, such as when a Social Security check is late. Since his office can communicate electronically with the Social

Security Administration, still more time is saved in getting his constituent that late check.

Clearly, a new age of instant internal and external communications is dawning on the House of Representatives. All too soon, voters may be able to flood their congressmen with instant electronic mail, and representatives will be able to answer in the same way—the identical process that goes on today, but with the potential for thousands of computer-generated electronic messages sent in hours, just before critical votes.

15.2 THE TELEPHONE NETWORK

Everyday electronic communications have taken a giant step forward in Canada. Alberta Government Telephones (AGT), Canada's third largest phone company, recently completed a three-year trial in which it offered universal electronic mail between word processor users over its telephone network. (While AGT did not promote electronic mail for microcomputer and workstation users, their concepts can also be applied to micros.)

The program ended only when a Canada-wide electronic mail effort was launched. AGT joined the nationwide system so that its customers could take advantage of the wider communications opportunities.

During AGT's three-year trial it took only six seconds and 17 cents to send one page at 2400 bps between any two cities in the province of Alberta. Since sending additional pages cost six cents per page, a four-page management report could be sent for only 35 cents over the telephone network—and it took only 24 seconds to get it to its destination.

But AGT's charge was only for long distance. If that same four-page report were sent within the limits of a *local* telephone call (where unlimited free local calls exist), there wasn't any charge. *With local unlimited free phone calls, instant electronic mail was totally without charge.*

Furthermore, AGT offered a protocol translation service to provide incompatible word processing systems with compatible communications.

In short, AGT was stimulating four revolutions at once:

- Speed. They made text communications between any users virtually instantaneous.
- Reliability. They increased the reliability of the mail to the level of a normal telephone call.
- Universal access. They made electronic mail nearly universal by adding protocol translation to the phone network.
- Cost. They reduced entry and operating costs to low levels for both new and current users.

Between Calgary and Edmonton, Alberta Province, Canada:
(100 pages sent one page at a time at different times)

NUMBER OF PAGES	CWP: 2400 BAUD	CWP: 1200 BAUD	TELEX 66 WPM	FAX: 2 MIN/ PAGE	FAX: 4 MIN/ PAGE	FAX: 6 MIN/ PAGE	COURIER HAND DELIVERY
100	$17.00	21.00	107.00	120.00	230.00	340.00	685.00

(Percentage cost increase over CWP at 2400 baud)

	N/A	24%	529%	606%	1253%	1900%	3929%

Between Alberta and Houston, Texas:
(100 pages sent one page at a time at different times)

NUMBER OF PAGES	CWP: 2400 or 1200 BAUD	TELEX 66 WPM	FAX: 2 MIN/ PAGE	FAX: 4 MIN/ PAGE	FAX: 6 MIN/ PAGE	COURIER HAND DELIVERY
100	$90.00	386.00	170.00	330.00	490.00	4000.00

(Percentage cost increase over CWP at 2400 baud)

	N/A	329%	89%	267%	444%	4344%

Figure 15.1 Cost comparisons within Alberta Province, Canada, and between Alberta and Houston, Texas, for various methods of transmission between word processors with electronic mail features. It is for 100 pages sent one page at a time at different times. CWP = communicating word processor. One page = 240 words.

When AGT's electronic mail service is compared to the costs of existing alternatives (see Figure 15.1), it virtually creates a new "text communications rule of thumb": Where communicating word processors are installed, AGT-style electronic mail shows one way to develop fast, cheap, and reliable communications.

Of course, the same type of service is available *today* outside of AGT. In the United States, for example, WATS-line timing and billing are done on a six-second basis, so it can be argued that AGT-style billing is already available in America. (If the average length of calls on a WATS line is shorter than one minute, however, AT&T rebills the calls on a one-minute-per-call basis.)

15.2.1 Achievement with Existing Equipment

AGT called its universal electronic mail service the "Communicating Word Processor Network (CWPN)." Its originator was Don Brandon, a senior *business planner* at AGT. He developed the CWPN by assembling only four normal, existing elements to create this new service:

1. AGT's telephone network provided universal dial-up linkage between word processing systems.

2. Compatibility between over 90 percent of Alberta's communicating word processing systems was achieved with a commercially available protocol translator.

3. Word processor (long-distance) communications were billed in six-second blocks, instead of whole minutes, using standard long-distance timing equipment.

4. A special directory of CWPN users listed the phone numbers of word processors that could be dialed directly, instead of people.

According to Brandon, these four elements are all that any telephone services vendor or user needs to start low-cost electronic mail. A long-distance telephone company, alternative telephone carrier (such as MCI or ITT), or WATS-line reseller (like U.S. Telephone) could provide this type of universal, low-cost electronic mail over the phone network. New low-cost services like MCI Mail are being introduced to take advantage of these potentials. Some vendors can offer this without needing regulatory approval, cutting their entry time to a minimum.

In AGT's view, their CWPN was the key to changing the growing base of installed word processors, throughout Alberta Province, into an advanced electronic communications network. New users joined the CWPN easily, by calling AGT and having a CWPN line installed for six-second long-distance electronic mail billing. it took AGT a maximum of 20 days to install a CWPN line, anywhere in the province.

In countries throughout the world, similar services can be directed at changing the growing base of microcomputers, word processors, workstations, and computers into a modern information environment. This can be done privately, within one organization; throughout a nation; or eventually on a larger scale.

15.2.2 Solving the Incompatibility Problem

Until the late 1970s, a universal service like AGT's CWPN was impossible. Word processor users faced insurmountable obstacles in communicating between systems from different vendors, because of the different protocols used by the vendors.

AGT's CWPN took advantage of an advanced generation of protocol translators to provide the essential links between different systems, and they used a Protocol Translator from Racal-Telesystems. This provided automated translation between multiple protocols at rates up to 9600 bps. Although AGT used it in a store-and-forward mode as a peripheral to a Wang word processor, this device can be configured in the field in a variety of ways, which enables word processors to communicate directly with other vendors' word processors, computers, and intelligent printers over hard-wired or unconditioned voice grade lines in either half or full duplex.

The protocols AGT installed in their translator covered 90 percent of their market, and included Wang, AES (Lanier), Micom, IBM OS/6, Lexitron, and Xerox. Since AGT was trying to stimulate universal electronic mail, protocol translation had the central job of helping the CWPN mature into a universal network.

In the United States, most communication carriers are only starting to offer translation services. (Telenet, Tymnet, and AT&T Information Services are nationwide carriers that offer these services.) As a result, many corporations use privately owned protocol translators to realize within their own organizations the same kind of advantages AGT introduced.

15.2.3 User Benefits

The critical advantage of AGT's CWPN was that users needed only to add a modem (AGT recommended 2400 bps) and communications software, and they could start electronic mail without delay, using their CWPN line for six-second long-distance billing. That word processor could immediately make inexpensive calls to other communicating word processors in Alberta. This flexibility means that users began by determining the range and timing of their applications.

This is different from a centralized electronic mail system where a mainframe computer is its backbone. Involving a major computer center means centralized control over how and when the computer is used, who has access to it, and DP placement of the terminals.

When the phone system is the network's backbone, everything is decentralized. Wherever there is a word processor, microcomputer, workstation, or communicating terminal, whoever runs the local device can begin electronic mail at once. This allows users to select, test, and develop new applications on an as-needed basis. AGT itself was an example of this gradual expansion. In addition to its internal electronic mail, it added two regular uses of the CWPN with outside firms.

First was typesetting. AGT prepared their CWPN User Directory—a quarterly publication—on a word processor, and then sent it over the phone lines to a typesetter. The same procedure was followed in preparing AGT's annual report, and there were at least five phototypesetters on-line with the CWPN.

AGT's Inter-Carrier Regulatory Affairs Group often communicated with its outside law firm, concerning inquiries over regulatory matters. They transmitted from 20 to 200 pages per month, and found this extremely valuable on cutting down the working time. During a typical regulatory inquiry, for example, the typical two-week preparation of a reply was cut to as little as two days. Documents sent over the phone were automatically stored on disk. The searching capabilities of the word processor were then used to find key sections immediately and edit them quickly.

Companies that used the CWPN were released from the burdens of setting up, administering, and maintaining a computer-based electronic mail network. Diagnosis, testing, and maintenance of the network were supplied by AGT. This eliminated the users' need for technical personnel and hardware to control network performance. Any hardware-related problems within the user's word processor were solved by the vendor's service technicians.

A "cost of service" record system was provided to users by monthly phone bills on the CWPN line. The bills provided itemized tracking of CWPN long-distance use, both in the level of costs and the pattern of usage. Since local CWPN calls were free, they were not recorded on the monthly bill. Independent record keeping was required if local use needed to be monitored.

AGT's three-year trial showed that the phone system can be a network that routinely carries both voice and text, proving that any telephone service has the potential to offer this.

In the United States and some other countries, WATS lines and similar services offer six-second billing today. A private CWPN can literally be started by anyone by adding protocol translation using a hardware device or a third-party communications carrier. The critical factor is business planning, just as AGT's CWPN was started by a business planner. This is one contribution users can make by working with specialists in the DP department.

15.3 NEWSPAPERS

Most major newspapers are linked by an electronic network that resembles the computerized corporation of tomorrow. Reporters write stories using terminals at their desks, whether their department is business news, sports, local or national news, features, or another area. This is like a local network in a corporate headquarters.

External links include stories transmitted immediately by reporters who are in the newspaper's offices in other cities and around the world. Stories are also contributed by reporters working for other newspapers owned by the same newspaper chain, by editorial syndication services, or by UPI (United Press International) or AP (Associated Press) bureaus anywhere in the world.

Inside a newspaper's network appropriate users can create, review, and transmit stories whether they are writers, editors, or people who add typesetting codes for printing. In fact, most newspaper pages are composed on computers, and computers run the huge presses that print the papers.

In cities all across the nation a daily newspaper is published that has many of the same national news and feature stories written at different newspapers all over the country. The information in these newspapers is gathered, written, and printed competitively on tight daily deadlines using thousands of computer systems that are linked in networks that literally circle the globe.

This flow of instant communications, from city to city and desk to desk, includes three levels: the internal systems of individual newspapers, the worldwide networks of newspaper chains, and external news services like UPI and Associated Press. All this computerized communications has the purpose of transmitting the current in-depth news to millions of newspaper readers. Most major papers print several editions a day. Reporters who are following key stories may update them every few hours for their paper's latest edition.

Our society already depends on hundreds of high-speed communications networks in the fast-paced newspaper field for gathering and reporting significant information from all over the world within hours.

16

ELECTRONIC MAIL AND
MESSAGE SYSTEMS

Perhaps the widest application of instant computerized communications—and one that immediately saves enormous overnight courier expenses—is electronic mail.

From a purely technical view, micros, word processors, and workstations can be among the most advanced text communications devices in the world. If the communications has been designed so that many systems in the company can be called by pressing a few keys, then rapid text communications may await only the addition of electronic mail software. This is increasingly available for systems of all types and sizes, often with an array of sophisticated features.

Figure 16.1 illustrates the three minimum elements needed to set up electronic mail: various types of computers or word processors, modems, and a connecting medium.

This turns the public telephone network, or a corporation's private data network, into a delivery system that transmits computerized business information on demand for a company. The advantages are obvious: accelerated access to detailed business information throughout a corporation, reducing some text communication costs, instant delivery, ending "telephone tag" where it takes several tries to reach someone, potentially increased management and secretarial productivity, and a growing list of electronic mail software packages that are designed to run on end-user workstations.

Already, the technology available for some micros, workstations, word processors, and larger computers is far ahead of the people who might use it. Because of this gap, electronic mail can be developed at a slow or rapid pace, depending on the needs of users.

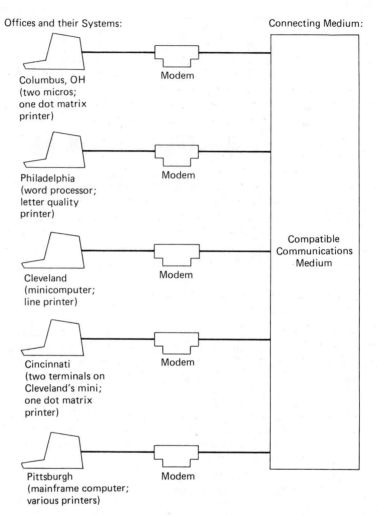

Offices and their Systems: Connecting Medium:

Columbus, OH
(two micros;
one dot matrix
printer)

Modem

Philadelphia
(word processor;
letter quality
printer)

Modem

Cleveland
(minicomputer;
line printer)

Modem

Compatible
Communications
Medium

Cincinnati
(two terminals on
Cleveland's mini;
one dot matrix
printer)

Modem

Pittsburgh
(mainframe computer;
various printers)

Modem

Figure 16.1   The minimum parts of an electronic mail system are various types of computers or word processors, modems, and a connecting medium.

For example, the first drafts of ten of this book's chapters were dictated, transcribed by a word processing service, and downloaded over phone lines into a co-author's multiuser microcomputer. There wasn't any communications cost, because free local phone calls were used to transfer the text. In the same way, businesses may rapidly solve many kinds of communications needs, including documents, business transactions, and reports of all kinds.

When set up carefully for the end user, electronic mail is as easy as sending a letter, except that the process is managed by pressing a few keys at the keyboard. See Figure 16.2.

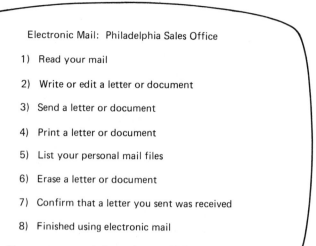

Figure 16.2   A secretary prepares to send a routine message to another corporate office.

A few managers may seize electronic mail and race ahead with it, setting up at least one local office system so that callers can dial in and exchange files and messages quickly. For example, a powerful capability is evolving with multiuser and multitasking operating systems, now available for an expanding number of micros, and some word processors. These allow a system to receive a call and exchange files with another computer while its local users continue working without interruption. Some of these multiuser operating systems offer security access on the level of each individual name and password, so callers from both inside and outside a company can be supported.

16.1 USES FOR ELECTRONIC MAIL

When electronic mail is made available and introduced successfully, it solves business problems that stand-alone systems cannot answer. A small number of communicating systems can provide high-speed communications throughout a company in offices where these systems are already in place. Electronic mail can be made available quickly by adding compatible software to handle it.

New applications of electronic mail should be added on a one-at-a-time basis in each department. Some sample uses include:

- *Accounting.*   Transmitting monthly, quarterly, and annual analyses and one-time business reports, such as cost-cutting studies, where information is requested from various parts of the corporation.

- *Marketing.* Sending marketing plans, new product strategies, sales fore-casts, and sales leads to appropriate offices; rapidly tracking current sales to a company's largest customers; running promotions and contests; distributing nationwide product information broadcasts.

- *Public relations.* Accelerating internal reviews of press releases, bro-chure copy, newsletters, corporate correspondence, product catalogs, data sheets, and bulletins.

- *Personnel.* Transmitting employee reviews, affirmative action summa-ries, broadcasting policy memos, open job lists.

- *Operations.* Sending training and procedures manuals, inventory, back order requests, product shipment requests.

- *Purchasing.* Rapid communications with purchasing, including pur-chase requests, developing vendor solicitations, confirming specs, track-ing vendor deliveries, and analyzing vendor performance.

- *Law.* Requests for legal opinions or advice; legal planning or internal documents such as contracts, pension plans, acquisitions, profit sharing, and other corporate activities.

16.2 ACCELERATING PAPER MAIL

Effective electronic mail is one way to accelerate the speed at which a modern corporation operates. While most companies are increasingly automated, they still move information internally by using the post office or in-house mail, then file the paper copy or use data entry to type the information from one computer into the next. As the use of electronic mail grows within a company, fast con-nections between two systems replaces slow, hand-carried letters and memos.

For most new users, the best starting point is to consider electronic mail as a faster version of the paper mail system they already know. In this way, elec-tronic mail does not disrupt or change accepted procedures. Instead, it fits into the daily routine in the same way that paper mail does—it is a tool for written communications.

The difference, of course, is that the mail is delivered in minutes or hours, not in days. Jobs can be done faster, because days are no longer wasted waiting for information to reach the person who needs it. Many activities can be started and completed right away, even if thousands of miles lie between people.

The most common misunderstanding about electronic mail is the thought that a terminal must be put on every desk. In fact, in years to come this will not happen. Instead, electronic mail will be sent between micros, word processors, workstations, larger computers, and terminals that are installed for other busi-ness reasons.

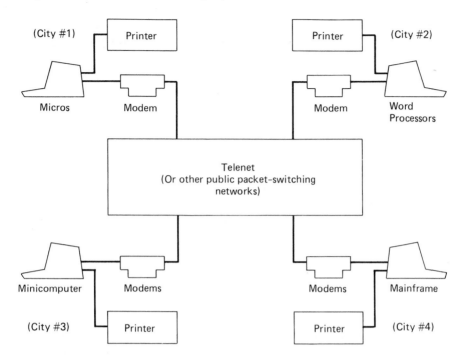

Figure 16.3   To begin widely compatible electronic mail quickly, a corporation uses a value-added network (Telenet) as a flexible medium with ASCII text as a protocol connecting many different kinds of systems right away.

In the beginning, most messages will follow this pattern (see Figure 16.3):

- Electronic mail uses whatever communicating micros, workstations, word processors, or terminals are available. Messages are created and revised on the local system, which speeds up their preparation and lowers on-line costs.
- The real power of electronic mail enters when the messages are sent and received immediately. Depending on the carrier used, this may be for a surprisingly low cost.
- At their destination, the messages might be read on a screen, but it is more likely that they will be printed on paper and given to the persons who need to receive them.

When used in this way, electronic mail simulates paper mail, though it speeds it up considerably. Consider five everyday situations, each of which represents a class of businesses or professionals that can transform their communications, regardless of whether they use word processors or micros.

1. The headquarters of a large corporation can start in-house electronic mail between micros or word processing systems in the headquarters offices. There aren't any per-message communication charges if the calls are made on a local area network or over the company's internal phone system. The time savings replaces comparatively slow in-house mail with a delivery time of seconds per page.

2. Lawyers and local clients can send legal briefs and other documents back and forth without charge, if they are using local calls in cities that do not charge "message units." If lawyers are located in state capitals or in Washington, D.C., they may be able to start electronic mail with government agencies. This saves days compared to first-class mail, or a large expense compared to using a courier service.

3. An engineering firm supervising the construction of a new manufacturing plant (or an architect or contractor) can send progress reports across the country to appropriate supervisors at their corporate client. Overnight courier charges would be saved on each report, or several days' wait if the mail were being relied on—critical time if one is building under normally tight deadlines.

4. A national business management network can be set up within a corporation where the national headquarters receives local data every day or week. Since the reports can be sent as data files into one headquarters system, regional and national reports can be consolidated within hours, and problem areas can be flagged, by using available microcomputer spreadsheets.

5. Routine business transactions can be sent from one department in a company directly to any other department in the same company. Since most internal business communications are transaction-related, this accelerates the most important information flow for most companies.

16.3 ELECTRONIC MAIL SYSTEMS

There are four basic ways to set up an electronic mail system. All focus on the key point that electronic mail is an add-on feature to the existing hardware and software used for communications. The types of equipment that a company installs for computing and word processing may well determine the design of the electronic mail system.

16.3.1 Point-to-Point Electronic Mail

The first type of electronic mail system, between micros, word processors, workstations, and other computers, may well be the choice of companies who use only a few compatible types of systems. Here the sender may use one system

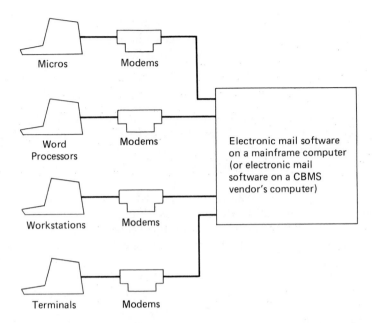

Figure 16.4   Computer Based Message Systems (CBMS) are among the most sophisticated electronic mail systems available, and the easiest to set up if a corporation's local office systems can emulate terminals on a mainframe computer.

to directly call any other system. This offers flexible communications directly between the users on both ends. The higher the communications speed, the lower the cost of each message.

16.3.2 Computer Based Message System

A second way to develop electronic mail involves the DP department in setting up a Computer Based Message System (CBMS) on a computer system at headquarters. Setting up a CBMS is a quick way to get electronic mail going on a companywide basis. The only requirement is that all the micros and word processors be able to call into the CBMS computer as if they were a dumb or an intelligent terminal on the system. See Figure 16.4.

CBMS software usually offers simple menus, or it prompts users on how to set up a personal or office post office box in the central computer where mail can be sent. Users regularly dial into their "mailboxes" to see what messages are waiting for them. Each of these boxes is usually password-protected so that only the recipient (or an authorized person with the password) can download his or her mail to a local micro, workstation, word processor, or terminal.

At present, CBMSs offer more features than electronic mail software that runs on small local systems, such as checking the status of whether a particular message has been received. New and more sophisticated software for small systems is being written all the time, and the most important features are migrating to electronic mail software for smaller local systems.

16.3.3 Third-Party Electronic Mail

A third method of electronic mail is to use a CBMS system on an outside vendor's computer. These range from public services on The Source or Compuserve to a private CBMS system from companies that sell CBMS systems and also lease a secure version of their system on their own computer for users in many companies.

This choice has the advantages of a proved, in-place system that is maintained by a professional staff. Because access through Telenet, Tymnet, or another value-added network handles the protocol conversion, this offers instant compatible communications both throughout a company and with others outside a company.

Even electronic mail on The Source or Compuserve can link most microcomputers, workstations, terminals, and word processors today. They also offer the most important features of large CBMS systems, such as password protection, store-and-forward delivery at preset times, and automatic delivery of single messages to more than one user at a time.

16.3.4 Western Union's Access System

The fourth way to set up electronic mail is by using a different kind of outside vendor. This is Western Union "Access System," which makes immediate hard-copy transmission and reception available to everyone through WU's mainframe computers. This system is available to send mailgrams, telex messages, electronic mail, international cablegrams, and other kinds of priority messages. It is available to any micro, word processor, or terminal that can communicate with Western Union, and Western Union offers protocol translation for most workstations.

Western Union's monthly charges are kept low for these high-priority services. Like other vendor-supplied electronic mail services, it can help businesses to link together incompatible systems quickly and can handle electronic mail both within a company and with outsiders.

16.4 RUNNING AN ELECTRONIC MAIL PILOT PROJECT

What would happen if every division in a large corporation set up a different kind of electronic mail system? Obviously, the divisions would soon find it impossible to communicate with each other by electronic mail.

When one part of a company wants to set up an electronic mail system, it is time to start involving other areas of the company, with the goal of choosing an overall corporate direction. The DP department, communications managers, and office automation specialists should be included.

Every division should still set its own goals for using electronic mail. The way in which the hardware and software are selected needs central coordination, however, so that a compatible companywide approach is used. This is what shrinks companywide communications to minutes or hours.

Electronic mail should be started in a pilot project. Even if the world's best electronic mail system were discovered, each company would use it differently and would find a basic feature that still might be wanted. The best place to start a pilot project is a department where users have many word processors, micros, terminals, and workstations in use, spread out through several offices. The steps in a typical pilot project include:

1. Select and install electronic mail software, including helpful menus and prompts that assist end users.
2. Experiment with sending short test files between various systems. Make sure that these are received successfully when sent in either direction by checking them for accuracy. If there are any up-front problems, the hardware or software vendor should be called for support.
3. Start live testing, using sample documents that are normally communicated on paper. On the receiving end, the documents can be printed and reinserted into the work flow. Again, manually confirm the accuracy of the communications at the receiving end.
4. Ease into using electronic mail for one application for several weeks. Document everything that happens, especially any problems that occur. This test should point out improvements needed in the menus and commands that run the electronic mail.
5. After fixing the menus, retest the system. This sequence should yield a good starting system that is easy for end users. Introduce this for a real application, run it for a month, and evaluate the results. Since the users will find the speed of this work flow faster than their other communications, the application should be selected carefully so that it is not disruptive.
6. Before cutting over to the normal use of electronic mail, carefully analyze the test. Make sure that users have learned how to use electronic mail properly. If they have started thinking about new uses that hadn't occurred to them before, this is a good sign that they may expand its use on their own after they have mastered the basics.

Every year, new electronic mail software arrives for small personal systems, offering more features at low costs. The best electronic mail software now available for some micros and word processors include features like sending one message to multiple recipients, password protection of messages to prevent unauthorized access, and message status (whether the message has been received).

When users can easily link two systems and exchange files quickly, the largest impact from electronic mail comes into view. This emerges from one simple fact about computers. Once business information is computerized, it is easier and cheaper to move it from computer to computer at virtually instant speeds than to print it, mail it, and reenter it in another computer.

16.5 INTERNATIONAL ELECTRONIC MAIL

Because international communications have been deregulated, it is possible to use micros, word processors, and workstations to call remote systems in some foreign countries as easily as dialing one in another city.

Until 1982, only a few authorized International Record Carriers (IRCs) could offer international computer communications. With deregulation, the IRC "club" has been opened to new companies that want to provide international communications. Telenet, for example, has been approved, and one of its offerings is service to Great Britain. This typically costs 20 to 25 dollars per hour, which is far less than the previous 100 dollars per hour for a voice-grade dial-up circuit. Telenet's service also includes end-to-end error correction, which phone lines do not. Tymnet and Satellite Business Systems (SBS) are two more companies that also offer international communications.

The real reason for deregulation is satellites. The old IRCs were created as an exclusive club during a time when only a limited number of undersea cables were available. With satellites offering tremendous volumes of high-speed communications, today's situation is totally different from that of decades ago. See Figure 16.5.

Communication through a Telex room can be a problem in a large corporation, because the turnaround time may be poor. When an executive has a message typed and says, "Send this to Paris," it is put in the outgoing mailbox. After interoffice mail picks it up, it is carried to the Telex room, where it must be prepared on the tape, then transmitted.

In contrast, if the original message is typed on a word processor, micro, or workstation, it can be sent to an international destination without any delay at all.

A process of document evolution accompanies decentralization from a Telex room to communicating local systems. Preparing that message becomes just like any other word processing: Memos, letters, even management reports are easily sent. The word volume of messages skyrockets compared to the average Telex message, which is only a couple of lines.

When executives have communicating systems, they gain the ability to send and receive information instantly around the world. Their systems become windows into a potentially new kind of international corporation.

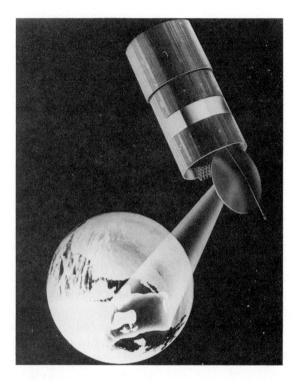

Figure 16.5   This Satellite Business Systems (SBS) communications satellite has ten transponders, each of which can transmit 48 Mbps (48 million bits per second). The minimum capacity of an SBS earth station is 12 Mbps. Courtesy of Satellite Business Systems.

17

SECURITY

Security is the one immediate application that includes every communicating system, regardless of its size. The secrets of using computers are being mastered by millions more new users every year. The mystery of data processing is vanishing quickly. Seemingly everyone is starting to speak the language of computers.

In most of the publicized computer crime cases, a mainframe computer was involved. Mainframe computers usually mean a range of standard security procedures, including limited physical access, password protection of software and data, enforced work rules, and audited data center policies.

In spite of careful security, the cost of mainframe computer fraud, theft, misuse of resources, and other losses are estimated to exceed $300 million per year.

What happens next, when direct communications opens links to millions of micros, word processors, and workstations, and attaches them to each other and to larger computers in the main data center?

17.1 COMMUNICATIONS SECURITY ON MICROCOMPUTERS AND WORD PROCESSORS

If computer crime succeeds in the carefully protected world of mainframe computers, small local systems are a ripe plum, indeed. The need for computer security will explode in the 1980s, as a system-to-system access becomes widespread.

There are two main reasons for protecting micros, workstations, and word processors. First are the links between mainframe computers and workstations, to protect the financial data and software in the main data center. Second is the astonishing value of the information in today's local systems.

Many local systems, especially those with hard disks, are being used to store large amounts of business information on-line. This includes daily transactions, financial projections, sales forecasts, product and parts inventories, detailed business performance reports, and other trade secrets.

If the files are named clearly, as they should be, these easily retrieved files hold the exact kind of business information that should *never* be available to unhappy employees, business competitors, legal adversaries, investors looking for inside information, political extremists, or anyone else who may have a micro with a modem:

- The names of customers with whom a company does business, what is ordered, and how much is paid.
- The current condition of the corporation and its weaknesses.
- Detailed descriptions of new products before they are introduced.
- The business plans that spell out where growth or corporate acquisitions will be pushed for the future.
- The memos that describe a company's internal position on controversial issues.

In our increasingly computerized age, a company's private information is becoming its real wealth. Where keys, combination locks, and safes protected the treasures of an earlier age, new types of security are needed today.

In most companies, communications security is either loose or nonexistent. The typical word processor transmission doesn't use any kind of protection, even if critical corporate data is sent. In some remote terminal installations, employees are allowed to log on to the mainframe, and then to leave their office without logging off the system. In other companies, when unauthorized accesses occur or are suspected, they usually go unreported. In fact, most computer crimes are discovered by accident.

To start reasonable protection, the first step may well be learning how easy it is to steal or change important information in micros, word processors, workstations, and perhaps in the main data center.

17.2 CONDUCTING A SECURITY REVIEW

Top and middle management do not usually realize the importance of security for small local systems. Without solid information, they may even reject the idea of any security protection at all.

A security review determines the kind of security needed to (1) protect these communications, and (2) limit access to stored information. When the review is completed, appropriate managers should be given documented security recommendations.

While a security review for micros, workstations, and word processors may be done by a company's computer department, the job will probably be done sooner if experienced end users are assigned the task. For a small number of offices, the review will generally take from 20 to 30 hours, spread over one to two weeks, if it is done by users familiar with the systems being evaluated.

A security review includes the following steps which should be adapted to each office's needs. Systems that have hard disks and communicate accounting data, strategic business plans, and other critical information should receive more attention.

17.2.1 Information Resources and Controls

The starting point is to learn how the microcomputers, word processors, and workstations are used. What information is stored on them? What operating controls guide and limit their users? Are employee instructions documented? Is the documentation effective? Is it followed by users, or is discipline lacking?

17.2.2 Value of Information

The risk level is determined by assigning dollar values to the information stored on-line in each system. Managers may have to be interviewed to determine these values.

If the files are stored on hard disks, this may allow easy unobserved access by outsiders. If the files are kept on floppy disks, this is a physical barrier to on-line access, since most of the data will not be on-line if an unauthorized access is made.

17.2.3 Current Security Policy

What defenses protect the information? Are passwords required to prevent remote access to data files or software through the phone lines?

What software controls keep employees working in their assigned areas when they are using a micro, word processor, workstation, or a terminal linked to a large computer? Can a critical application like accounting be run by anyone who sits at a keyboard, whether local or remote?

17.2.4 Security Penetrations

When security checks are being made, surreptitious penetration should not be attempted without *confidential written clearance from appropriate managers.* This authorization should explain all steps to be taken, and the approximate dates and times on which penetration will be attempted. To prevent after-the-fact problems, the authorization should be followed scrupulously.

After clearance is received, the target systems should be tested with *unannounced* attempts to penetrate and misuse micros, workstations, or word processors (on the remote office level) or the main data center (only if clearly authorized), with a remote micro or word processor being used as the access device.

Various scenarios can be tested. First is an outsider who wants to acquire private company information. Second is an unhappy employee who has some knowledge of the computer system, access to one or a few passwords, and wants to destroy files outside the offices where he or she works.

These tests must be done so that the data, existing security defenses, and other system components are *immediately restored following the tests.*

17.2.5 Wiretapping

Perhaps the most dangerous risk is an outsider who wants to tap messages sent over phone lines between computers. Since this requires specialized skills, phone taps may be simulated: It may be assumed that a successful tap was placed on an office phone line used to communicate between the office and other systems in the company, including the main data center. This tap has yielded a list of passwords and access procedures used by the employees of the office during a typical two- to three-week period. An attempted penetration of the mainframe computer and other remote computers called can then be done, using these passwords and procedures.

In this key area, virtually no security will exist at all. Consider Washington, D.C., the home of the security-conscious Federal Government. Hundreds of thousands of electronic messages are sent daily between the government's communicating word processors, micros, and other computers. Very few of these messages have any kind of protection from unauthorized tapping, recording, and use of the valid passwords and procedures sent over phone lines. See Figure 17.1.

What is the greatest crime that can be committed with authorized passwords? Is it stealing key information, erasing it, or altering it?

The same situation is common for most business communications. Most commonly used transmission media are easily tapped or picked up with an antenna, whether they are telephone lines, dedicated computer lines, microwave links, or earth stations that bounce signals off satellites. Some value-added networks do offer excellent security, but the phone lines from users into those networks are not secure.

CLEAR TEXT – NO ENCRYPTION

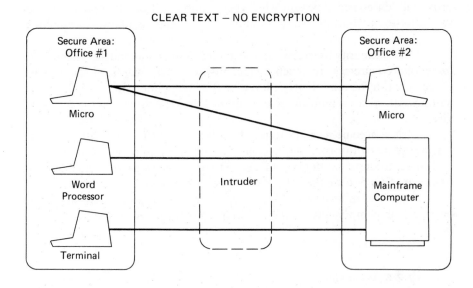

ENCRYPTED MESSAGES

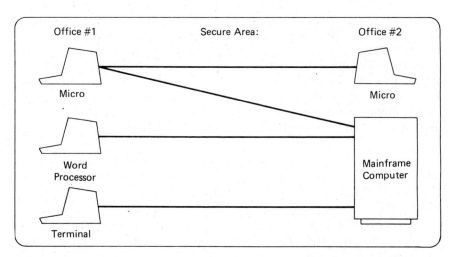

Figure 17.1   Effective security comes from encryption, not from any transmission media.

17.2.6 Charting Weaknesses and Strengths

The weaknesses and strengths of communications security should be charted carefully, to make sure that (1) the vulnerabilities are known, and (2) the business risks are estimated. The estimate can be done based on the types of information stored, the dollar value of the information, or both.

17.2.7 Report to Management

At this point, it is up to management to determine the appropriate course of action. The security review may penetrate some micros and word processors, and perhaps even the mainframe. It may show that security procedures are weak, or that they aren't being followed as planned.

Appropriate managers should receive a confidential copy of the final report. It should summarize each of the steps in the security review. Clear recommendations should be made if vulnerabilities are found.

Senior executives are usually aware that the mainframe computer holds the company's most sensitive financial information. Mainframe computer security has been "sold" to most executives. In almost every case, they have authorized a level of security for the mainframe computer that they believe fits their company. While their main interest is protecting financial data, managers also recognize the value of other kinds of business information.

The argument for mainframe computer security is well established:

- Computers are valuable corporate resources that provide key business services. It is a good business practice to know who uses these corporate resources, and for what purposes.

- The data in the computers are critical corporate assets. Who can access these assets? Who can alter the assets? Who can add to them or erase them?

- Basic business principles demand that key corporate information be properly controlled. This is the essence of accurate information for corporate operations.

- Protecting assets and resources is an essential management goal. Internal accounting rules, computer audit procedures, and Federal laws require an adequate level of security to safeguard significant corporate assets, including corporate data resources.

The same logic is true for micros, word processors, workstations, and minicomputers. This is especially true if a company's financial data and critical business plans are shared among a variety of systems in an advanced information environment. In this case, the argument for security on all appropriate systems exactly parallels the logic used for the mainframe computer.

17.3 COMMUNICATIONS SECURITY PROCEDURES

There are five ways to protect communications on micros, word processors, and workstations to complement existing security for terminals linked to larger computers. These procedures can often be implemented by knowledgeable end users or DP staff.

17.3.1 Physical Protection

Communications protection is needed in the smallest workstations only when they are hooked up to the phone lines and valuable information is on a floppy disk in a disk drive. With most floppy disk systems, this is not usually a problem.

The addition of auto-answer/auto-dial modems, hard disk storage, or multiuser micros or word processors changes this. When powerful on-line workstations are introduced, micros and word processors are as vulnerable as any other computer.

Some physical security is still possible, however. An executive may have a marketing plan on the hard disk of a micro and may want to prevent dial-up access. Unplugging the modem from the phone line prevents remote access. A security barrier is erected that is as strong as locking the office door. Of course, this method does not work if this micro needs to be on-line to receive messages throughout the day if it is connected to a local area network. But with some personal systems, unplugging the modem is both simple and effective.

17.3.2 Passwords

Passwords are a system's first line of defense, because they permit only authorized users into a system. In some micros, such as those with a Unix-type operating system, passwords also control the software that people can use and which files can be read by each user.

With both micros and mainframes, passwords should be used to limit who can log on, whenever someone dials into a computer from a remote location. This means that the first message anyone sees when the system is called should be

```
LOGON:
PASSWORD:
```

All passwords should be changed regularly. Passwords should not be common names or shared between users. When an employee leaves, that password should be cancelled immediately. Rules should keep an employee from writing down his or her password and taping it to the terminal, or leaving it in the desk.

Automatic computer logs are available in an increasing number of microcomputer operating systems. When a password is entered, the system keeps a record of the date and time each employee logs on and off. These logs often record whether the users are local or remote, so communications from remote systems is tracked.

Some communications software allows passwords to be entered in a command file, and they are sent when the workstation dials a remote computer.

This should never be allowed in business systems, since unauthorized local or remote users may read or copy the communications software's command files to learn the password(s).

17.3.3 Access Control in Microcomputers and Word Processors

With many multiuser microcomputer operating systems, separate directories can store accounting, business performance reports, financial analysis, data bases, and customer lists. Each area can be protected so that users work only in the areas they are allowed to access. The software that does this is either the micro's operating system, or a menu program that limits the user's movement throughout the system.

Some menu programs have automatic start-up upon logon. They prevent end users from exiting to the operating system, unless this choice is in the menu. Within the menus, users cannot delete a file or list a directory of files if these are not menu options.

Within permitted user areas, controlled access can be added, using password protection built into some software packages. A local office bookkeeper, for example, may enter only accounts payable invoices, and not be able to print checks or journal listings, or do any other accounting (such as accounts receivable). Remote users might not be given any access to the accounting software.

These carefully planned local systems are reasonably secure for remote access. Users dialing into them face four security measures, as shown in Figure 17.2: (1) password logon, (2) restriction to specific functional areas, (3) no access to sensitive software and data files, and (4) user access records with time and date stamping, on the computer's log.

17.3.4 Access Control in Mainframes

After remote employees gain authorized access to the mainframe computer, standard computer security keeps them in their approved areas of computer use, as illustrated in Figure 17.3.

While a variety of approaches are used, the most common one is as follows. The remote user enters the mainframe computer with an authorized password. A security table registers the level of authority assigned to the user. An access control table restricts the user to limited areas of the computer system. The user is restricted first to assigned functional areas, and second to specific files, records, and fields within permitted areas.

Security Method	Types of Security Possible
Operating System	Password Logon Computer log: records user access; time and date of access are logged Security is built into some operating systems, such as UNIX systems
Applications Software (selected packages)	Password Logon Password Logon with access control to specific portions of the application Password protection of sensitive data in some applications
Menu Software	Initial menu runs automatically when user logs on Password access to sensitive applications menus Controls access to limited range of applications and data files for each user Prevents exit to operating system and system utilities
Communications	Remote user access to local system(s): any combination of the above methods For secure transmission to remote systems: Only data encryption is secure; transmission lines are not secure

Figure 17.2   Security methods possible on many multiuser hard-disk micros or on a local area network of micros.

17.3.5 Data Encryption

Picture an office of remote users sending their authorized passwords over a thousand miles of transmission lines to access the computer in their company's main data center. Next picture a wiretap on that line. Finally, imagine what outsiders can do, at their leisure, with valid passwords on the mainframe computer.

Encryption is the accepted method for protecting against wiretaps. This turns passwords, text, and data into random bits that appear meaningless. At the receiving end, the bits are turned back into the original message.

From the end user's point of views, encryption hardware is an automatic and invisible way to do this, while encrypting messages with software usually requires users to run the software. This means that encryption software may not be used as often, because users may put getting their jobs done ahead of security. Since users probably won't encrypt routine messages, their passwords will be sent over the line, which is a serious security issue in many companies. If both user convenience and security are needed, then hardware encryption is the best choice.

17.4 OBSTACLES TO EFFECTIVE SECURITY

The two main causes of poor security are a shortage of people who are concerned about security and loose security procedures. This opens wide the door for end-user initiative—specialists are not needed for the majority of the above techniques.

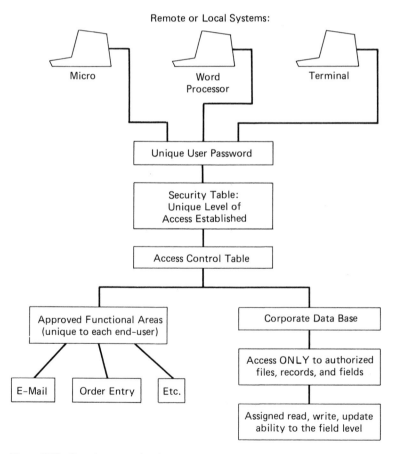

Figure 17.3 Security protection in a mainframe computer.

If security is added, it's like putting visible and invisible burglar alarms on a home. The alarms stop the honest people who might wander in by mistake. Most criminals will also avoid the house—they prefer easier, unprotected victims. All that's left are a few clever, malicious crooks who are willing to try to bypass the alarms.

Protecting micros, word processors, and workstations works in the same way. Security procedures help control the honest people, and visible security leads most crooks to prefer easier target computers—so many of them are becoming available. That leaves only the clever criminals, who definitely intend to penetrate smaller and larger computer systems.

Fortunately, these people are rare. The real question is whether you'll plan for their arrival, or be caught by surprise.

18

ON-LINE DATA BASES

Pity yesterday's best trained researcher. First she traveled from an office to the Library of Congress or some equally prestigious facility. Then she walked to its reference room and stood while thumbing through its card catalog one book at a time, searching the titles in each category being investigated.

To find related magazine articles, she went to shelf after shelf of magazine indexes, searching each index for several categories, with each year separated in its own bound book.

After she copied the best citations by hand, she requested them a few at a time at a central reference desk. Librarians went to the stacks and brought back the books and articles. She then reviewed each of them to see if it really fit her needs.

Hours later the researcher emerged blinking into the sunlight, weary, but knowing that she had acquired the best information available.

In today's age of communicating micros, word processors, and workstations, you can do an even better job in less than 15 minutes. The same modem and software that provide instant communications within a company offer access to information utilities that, in their speed and scope, surpass professional research in the greatest libraries in the world. These tools are so exceptional that professional researchers often prefer them to every other approach.

18.1 INFORMATION UTILITIES

The telephone can link a workstation with computers that contain tens of millions of items of information (see Figure 18.1). These can be searched in minutes to find answers quickly. A few examples include:

Database (Supplier)	On-line Charge: $/Hour	Off-line Printing Charge: $/Record	Number of Records in Data base*
CIS (Congressional Information Service)	$ 90	$ 0.25	140,000
FOUNDATION GRANTS INDEX (Foundation Ctr.)	60	0.30	90,000
PAIS INTERNAT'L (Public Affairs Info. Serv.)	60	0.15	113,000
SSIE CURRENT RESEARCH (Smithsonian)	78	0.20	144,000
AGRICOLA	35	0.10	1,140,000
BIOSIS (Biosciences Information Service)	58	0.15	1,260,000
CA SEARCH (Chemical Abstracts Service)	64	0.20	5,102,000
EXCERPTA MEDICA (Excerpta Medica)	70	0.20	1,200,000
HEALTH PLANNING (US Natl. Library of Medicine)	35	0.15	185,000
MEDLINE (US National Library of Medicine)	35	0.15	3,300,000
CLAIMS/US PATENTS ABSTRACTS (IFI/Plenum)	95	0.15	1,782,000
ERIC (Educational Resources Info. Center)	25	0.10	383,000
PSYCINFO (Amer. Psychological Association)	65	0.10	325,000
SOCIAL SCISEARCH (ISI)	110	0.20	910,000
ADTRACK (Corporate Intelligence, Inc.)	95	0.25	150,000
PTS U.S. FORECASTS (Predicasts, Inc.)	90	0.20	196,000
PTS INTERNAT'L FORECASTS (Predicasts, Inc.)	90	0.20	230,000

*Some data bases are made of multiple data bases that cover various categories.
 For example, CA SEARCH includes File 2 (1967-71: 1,314,000 records),
 File 3 (1972-76: 1,772,000 records), File 104 (1977-79: 1,267,000 records),
 and File 4 (1980-present: 749,000 records).

Figure 18.1   A listing of some of the 180 data bases available from the DIALOG search service.

- Computer communications. What electronic mail software is available for a specific microcomputer?
- Chemical regulations. What occupational health regulations govern each of the specific chemicals in a cosmetic product?
- Legal resources. What kinds of government records can be accessed under the Missouri Sunshine Law?
- Grants. What foundations have given grants for cleaning up highway trash in Ohio?
- Current research. Which researchers are studying the decommissioning of nuclear power plants scheduled to be shut down?
- Medicine. Are there any new treatments for mountain frostbite that might help skiers?

Today's users of these data bases include corporations of all sizes, libraries, professionals, government agencies, individuals, and home computer users. An inexperienced researcher takes about 15 to 20 minutes to do a search. After gaining experience, a search often takes about ten minutes.

Each information utility offers its own range of data bases and services. Some of the largest include DIALOG, ORBIT, BRS, and LEXIS. An increasing number of information vendors are available around the world, especially in Europe and Latin America. Britain's Prestel, for example, has 200,000 pages on-line, and it is offered on both sides of the Atlantic.

The 250+ information utilities offer a wide variety of on-line services. Entire reference books are devoted to listing the data bases available on-line, and new editions of these directories are published each year. The number of data bases expands annually at a rate of about 40 percent.

As an industry, information utilities have passed one billion dollars a year in sales. Large investments are being made in developing new data bases, updating existing data bases, and marketing these to millions of users in easy-to-search formats over easy-to-access computers.

The information utility is a vendor that does not develop the data bases. It is like a print publisher that publishes books or magazines written by others. The information utility is an on-line publisher that sells on-line access to data bases prepared by other organizations.

The three main providers of data bases are the government, professional societies, and commerical companies. Typical government data bases are ERIC, which covers education; NTIS, which covers most nonmilitary government information sources; AGRICOLA, which offers agricultural information; and MEDLINE, a well-known data base developed by the National Library of Medicine.

Professional society data bases include almost every discipline. Literally millions of searchable records are available in fields like psychology, engineering, chemistry, physics, electronics, and geology.

During the 1980s the fastest-growing data bases are provided by commercial companies. Some of these include Congressional Information Service, which tracks government bills; Predicasts, which provides economic business data; and ADTRACK, which tracks the print advertising of companies in major publications.

The most popular information utilities available for home computer users are Dow Jones, The Source, and Compuserve. For a low hourly cost these allow people to access major data sources like the Dow Jones financial data base, UPI news wire, airline flight schedules, and articles in sources like the *World Book Encyclopedia* or newspapers like *The New York Times* and the *Washington Post*. They also offer electronic mail, computer games, and other kinds of home, personal, and health information.

Some of the largest information utilities have started low-cost services for home computer users, with access during evening and weekend hours. These include DIALOG's Knowledge Index and BRS's After Dark. Only a limited number of data bases are included in these services, compared to what is offered at full fees during daytime hours, but these still include millions of instantly searchable records. They may also provide a low-cost way for business users to try these services and gain experience, before bringing them into the office during daytime hours at full fees.

18.2 EXAMPLE SEARCH

The information utility most commonly found in libraries and corporations is Lockheed's DIALOG search service. There are many other excellent services, but the basic principles by which they operate are similar and can be illustrated best by selecting DIALOG as an example.

A password and an account on the DIALOG system do not cost anything, and new users receive $100.00 of free search time during their first month.

DIALOG offers over 180 data bases with over 80 million records, covering the majority of human knowledge. This is on-line and available for searching within minutes, 22 hours a day. A customer support staff is available on a toll-free number to answer users' questions.

With DIALOG's search service, your call goes through a carrier like Tymnet or Telenet. After logging on to the DIALOG computers, you select a specific data base. Once inside the data base, you request the information you need.

The computer tells you how many records are available in the category you requested. You then broaden or narrow your search until you find about five to 25 records on your precise subject.

The steps in doing a search are as follows:

18.2.1 Linking to an Information Utility

A workstation is linked to a nationwide computer network with a local phone call in most cities. The network links your workstation with the DIALOG computers in Southern California.

18.2.2 Logging On the Remote Computer

At the logon prompt, sign on to the search service by entering a user ID number and a password. Entering a password is like signing a credit card charge receipt. It tells the computer that this is a valid user who can be billed for the charges incurred. Within one company, different users or groups of users may have different passwords so that their searches are charged to their accounts.

18.2.3 Selecting the Data Base

Once you are in the search service (in the DIALOG computers), you select the data base you want to use. DIALOG user manuals are available for low fees, to guide searchers. These describe each data base, its supplier, a sample of the format of the records in each data base, and search tips that may be helpful. They can usually be supplemented with detailed manuals from each data base supplier. There is also direct telephone assistance from DIALOG or many of the data base suppliers, if it is needed.

Since only one data base can be searched at a time, and there are five or six large data bases in fields like medicine, it helps to choose the best one for each topic. DIALOG offers an optional data base called DIAL INDEX. By searching in DIAL INDEX first, one can learn how much information on a particular topic is found in each DIALOG data base.

18.2.4 Search Procedures

The search is based on the key words that describe what you need to learn. The key words of each information record are indexed. Such an index includes the title, the author, key words and concepts in the article or book, and all significant words in the abstract (description) that is part of the record in the computer. You enter the key words that you want to find; the computer searches the data base's index for them, and then tells you how many records are available.

To start, you can ask for the number of records that contain one term. Depending on how many records the computer reports, you can either expand your search or narrow it. For example, you might search a medical data base to investigate the relationship between coffee and sleeplessness. You could start by searching the number of records in the key concepts of caffeine, sleep, insomnia, and sleeplessness. See Figure 18.2.

The next step is to combine the concepts to make the search more specific. This is done by using the words *and* and *or* where *and* makes a search smaller and *or* makes it larger. If you add "caffeine *or* coffee," you receive the number of records that refer to both areas. If you request "caffeine *and* sleep" you receive the smaller number of records that apply to both of these at the same time.

After each request, the computer tells you how many records are available that meet your needs. You can start from either large broad categories and narrow them down, or begin with a narrow concept and expand until you reach a manageable number of records. See Figure 18.3.

The next step is to list some of the actual records in the data base to make sure that the information found is what is needed. For instance, if the first five

Set	Search Terms	Number of References Found
S1	caffeine	1,427
S2	sleep	5,866
S3	insomnia	583
S4	sleeplessness	14
S5	caffeine or coffee	1,684
S6	caffeine and sleep	28
S7	S3 and S5	8
S8	S4 and S5	0

Figure 18.2 An example of data base search logic using key words to focus on a topic.

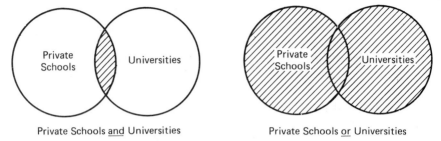

Private Schools <u>and</u> Universities   Private Schools <u>or</u> Universities

Figure 18.3   The first step in effective searching is understanding how the term *and* narrows a search, and the term *or* expands the search.

titles listed seem appropriate, the search can be ended there. If the titles aren't right, the search must be redirected.

It can be costly to spend time listing actual records, but it is important to confirm that the set of records created are the ones wanted. The payoff from a small amount of checking is a more accurate search, at a slightly increased cost.

At every point the user controls the search and the search service's computer. Searches can be temporarily suspended to refer to an on-line thesaurus that gives more terms to be searched, if this is needed. Then the search can be resumed until the right information is located.

When the final set of records is found, the user can have them printed off-line and mailed, which is the least costly way to get the information. If these records will be used later in word processing, it may be cheaper to have the records sent on-line into a disk file on the workstation. This saves the cost of typing them into the system again, though this is more expensive than off-line printing. For this option, 1200 bps communications speed is far more economical than 300 bps.

After the records have been reviewed, DIALOG offers an on-line service called DIALORDER. This allows specific articles, books, research reports, and other materials to be ordered on-line. They are photocopied and shipped, usually within seven days.

18.3 CONTROLLING ON-LINE COSTS

While it is possible to develop a search while on-line, this is the most expensive way to work. The faster a search is finished, the less it costs. If a search pattern is known, planned in advance, and done quickly on-line, a search can be done in about ten minutes. If alternative key words to search are chosen before beginning, the search can be revised quickly, if needed, while on-line.

Since a typical cost is a dollar per minute, plus printing the records off-line or having them sent on-line to your system, the value of searching experience and preparation can be measured in dollars and cents.

Is $15 to $40 expensive for a search? The user can answer that by asking three questions. First, what is the information worth? Second, how much would it cost to have a researcher find the information in the library? Third, how much is saved by finding the best answers in minutes, without moving from one's desk?

Who should do the data base searches? Should all workers be able to dial an information utility and run all the searches they want?

In most organizations, someone is responsible for conducting data base searches. Many companies have an information resource center or a corporate library. This has one or more information specialists who do searches. In other companies, nonspecialists in various departments run searches. In either case, a few people are responsible for planning and running searches for less experienced people.

There is a learning curve to data base searching. An experienced searcher knows that there may be a large difference between the first key words suggested by an end user and the best key words that will yield the data base's information. With experience, the quality of the search increases along with speed and savings.

The user and the specialist should plan the search together. If possible, the user should be present while the searcher is on-line, to answer questions as the search proceeds. This is valuable for end users, because it helps them to learn what can be achieved with data base searches and what cannot. As a result, their future requests will be more precise.

18.4 THE INFORMATION WORKSTATION

Many micros, word processors, or workstations can be used to create a local information system. A few command files, custom menus, and inexpensive software make access to information utilities easier and less expensive. Extensive information management can be done faster, and repetitive searches can be done at computer speeds, which saves money.

On-line searching has a definite procedure that is followed over and over: The local information system must be linked with a search service's computer, and this can be done by pressing one key at a "research" menu. All sessions should be saved to disk automatically to review the search strategy and improve it if it will be run again, and these instructions can be run automatically in the communications command files.

The kind of information that is needed by a business today will resemble the kind of information it will need in similar situations in the future. After a number of searches, a pattern begins to emerge.

Command files can be created from the saved searches. These command files can be checked with the search service, over the phone, to confirm the procedures. After the command files have been tested, they can be used as needed, to duplicate the same or slightly modified searches.

For example, many data bases are updated on a monthly basis. The same search can be run repeatedly against the latest records. A company may use this to run identical ADTRACK searches every month, to track the new print advertising of its competitors.

A pharmaceutical company may want to search multiple data bases at one time to monitor the published research and news stories on a new product it is releasing. Once the search pattern is set, this can be done quickly by using command files instead of manual searches.

Many information utilities offer the service of storing standard searches in their computer. The storage cost is billed to the user, however. By using a local information system to store standard searches in command files, the search computers work at their fastest possible speed, and the command files are stored for free in the local system.

At the local system, information from data bases can be analyzed and processed quickly by using word processing or data base software. Statistical data can be entered into spreadsheets for analysis or projections. Finished reports are produced for immediate dissemination by electronic mail. The information from various searches can be merged by using inexpensive data base software to build a privately managed information resource that is an up-to-the-minute reference in business, science, art, or government.

In addition, data base searching software is available that can accelerate and simplify searches on information utilities. This software guides users through searches with extensive help commands. It also offers on-line tutorials and a thorough reference manual.

By using this software's search editor, a search can be set up quickly before connecting to the information utility. Then the search can be run rapidly while on-line. A one-key index command brings a list of additional choices to the screen, and these can be reviewed off-line while a revised search is created. The search strategies can be saved for repeated use. The references produced by the search can be saved in memory to be read on the screen, stored in disk files, or printed. The software automatically titles and pages the references for printing.

Compared to every other kind of research that has been available, a local information system is a giant step into the future.

19

TIME-SHARING

What's the worst nightmare an DP director and an executive can share?

The executive's department is in a business crisis; a major new computer application is urgently requested, and the DP director says, "Sorry. Our programmers are backed up to the hilt. We won't be able to start your project for at least nine months."

This nightmare gets worse if the executive threatens to go to top management and the DP director takes on the new project. Instantly, part of the DP department is turned into a house of cards, risking existing projects as well as the new one. Key staff are yanked off current projects to tackle this unexpected priority. Since all the affected projects will be done on a crash basis, they have an excellent chance of being delivered late, failing to work properly, and winding up over budget. A breaking point looms if DP project managers and staff leave the company because of the pressures.

While the causes of this nightmare are common, it can be solved by taking advantage of instant communications on the user's micros, word processors, workstations, and minicomputers. This opens the world of time-sharing to executives who need a new mainframe application but can't arrange it with the DP department.

Once users know how to logon to a remote mainframe, it doesn't matter whether the mainframe is within the company or outside it. Through time-sharing, the range of immediately available computing resources is staggering, including the largest and best computers available, software that is already compatible with micros, and fast custom programming.

Whether the executive needs a large amount of raw processing power or a new software application, numerous time-sharing benefits are available:

- Use as a communications network.
- A wide range of state-of-the-art mainframe and micro software.
- Integrated micro/mainframe growth.
- Training and technical support.
- Custom programming.
- Low start-up costs.
- Testing useful software for the company's mainframe.

Above all, the option of time-sharing allows immediate progress when an DP director says, "I know it's important, but we can't touch it for months."

19.1 TIME-SHARING ALTERNATIVES

Instant communications allows every workstation to tie into any of the 2000-plus time-sharing companies in the industry. At the lower end of the scale are small local companies that offer some services, but mainly provide "plain vanilla" time-sharing. This is the raw computing power of a large system maintained by a professional staff, available to handle extra processing work during peak periods.

At the other end of the scale are the time-sharing industry giants, with revenues over $100 million per year. The prices here often include a monthly minimum use charge that starts at $300 to $500. Since it usually takes about 10 days notice to cancel an account, and only $10 to $25 to reinstate it, it is possible to use the resources of these large companies on an "as needed" basis.

Consider a fraction of what is available from two companies, CDC (Control Data Corporation) and GEISCO (General Electric Information Services Corporation), two of the largest time-sharing vendors in the world:

- Accounting/auditing.   International cash management with wire transfers, investment analysis, capital budgeting, corporate tax analysis, financial projection, custom accounting systems, and operating reports.
- Business graphics.   Interactive systems with many capabilities.
- Communications.   (1) Analysis of networks to determine line selection and minimize costs; (2) use of CDC or GEISCO networks for electronic mail.
- Distribution management.   Inventory control, including current stock levels, prices, and management reports.

- Electric utilities processing.   Power plant design, system planning, fuel management, control systems, schedule generation, cost analysis, and transmission network operations.
- Engineering analysis.   Complete structural analysis, mechanical and temperature loading, fracture mechanics, piping analyses, and system simulations.
- Financial analysis.   Decision-oriented modeling for profit planning, risk analysis, new product introductions, acquisitions, mergers, and evaluating alternative marketing strategies.
- Law.   Docket management, document control, time and practice management.
- Lease management.   Complete system for leasing companies.
- Project management.   Estimating, scheduling (machinery, work centers, manpower), cost allocation, billing, payroll, reporting.
- Purchasing.   Electronic purchase orders sent in purchaser's format and delivered electronically in vendor format, for immediate computer processing.
- Real estate.   Detailed investment analysis and projections.

This range of software is an example of why time-sharing companies can be so valuable. If the volume of work doesn't justify an expensive software purchase or development project, micros, word processors, and workstations offer access to mainframe quality computing at a fraction of the cost.

For customers who want to use their company's mainframe, many of the software packages can be leased from time-sharing vendors. This choice allows users to start with a small, flexible arrangement, and to expand if justified by the benefits.

19.2 SELECTING A TIME-SHARING VENDOR

The answers to three questions determine the need for time-sharing:

1. Can the job be done on installed local office systems, even if new software must be bought? (If the answer is yes, the user's own systems are the cost-effective choice.)
2. Is there capacity and appropriate software on the company's mainframe? (If yes, the mainframe is a better choice.)
3. Does the company have staff, time, and resources to write or buy the software? (If no, time-sharing may be the best choice.)

Where any kind of computer capacity and appropriate software are available within a company, that should come first. Sometimes there is available computer hardware only, so time-sharing may still be a good choice, because this may offer the software needed at a lower cost than writing it or buying it.

If the decision is to select a time-sharing company, then the following "tests" should be passed by the time-sharing vendor chosen:

- The time-sharing company's computer system should be compatible with the company's mainframe computer. Arrangements should be possible to buy or license the software used, if it really solves the business's needs. This is why hardware compatibility is valuable.
- The hardware and software that the time-sharing company uses should be the latest available, and should include all available interfaces needed to work with workstations in the company. For example, can data be downloaded to workstations and used locally?
- Is custom programming needed? Is this offered by the time-sharing company? Many time-sharing companies can get new applications up and running in seven to 60 days, so this can be a fast way to get ahead. If custom programming is done, answer a key question in advance and in writing: who owns the finished product?
- Enough training classes and support staff should be available to bring the projected number of end users up to speed quickly.

For some applications, unusual sources of time-sharing may be the best choice. For example, some companies sell excess capacity on their mainframe computer, including well-known software written for their own use. In the airline and banking industries, for example, it is common for some companies to sell the use of their software, along with time on their computers.

19.3 CONNECTING MICROS AND LARGER COMPUTERS THROUGH A TIME-SHARING SERVICE

Time-sharing companies must be totally dedicated to solving user problems quickly with the latest hardware and software. If they fail to meet this standard, customers easily switch to better alternatives. A rapidly increasing number of time-sharing vendors are on the cutting edge of micro-mainframe compatibility. They have installed micros throughout their organizations and offer to lease them to customers.

Since time-sharing companies are actively developing many ways to integrate micros and mainframes, they can be an excellent source of expertise for companies that need this assistance. Learning from their experience can accelerate a company's progress for reasonably low costs.

For example, a company may want to buy a mainframe financial planning package that is supposed to work effectively with micros. It is easy to set up an account on a time-sharing computer that offers this package, buy copies of the compatible microcomputer software, and have the appropriate end users test the software using live data, as if the financial planning system were running on the company's mainframe. This approach offers the start-up advantage of training and technical support from the time-sharing company, so any number of end users can be brought up to speed quickly.

Since many popular mainframe computer packages are available through time-sharing arrangements (though the micro software may have to be purchased separately), they can be evaluated at much lower cost than buying them. If suitable, they can often be bought or leased through the time-sharing vendor, who can also help install and support the new software, including its micro-mainframe links.

For example, two large time-sharing vendors that have made a major commitment to micros are GEISCO and Boeing Computer Services (BCS). Both of these companies sell or lease IBM PCs and the software they need to use a variety of GEISCO and BCS computing services.

Smaller time-sharing vendors have taken a different approach. Infoservices, an Atlanta service bureau, has used communications with micros to double the number of tax returns it processes for 400 accountants in five states. Now, micros that run four microcomputer operating systems can access and use Infoservices' Prime minicomputers for processing and laser printing taxes and forms. The 400 accountant-clients use more than 30 different brands of micros to create tax data files. These files are then sent via modem to Atlanta and processed by users while on-line. This gives them access to the latest software, greater processing power, and laser printers, as well as extensive support from Infoservices's staff.

19.4 REDUCING TIME-SHARING COSTS

While the initial cost of starting time-sharing is minimal, the more these services are used, the higher the total expense. If pricing is not understood up front and efforts are not made to control costs, time-sharing can be shockingly expensive. This is why it is important to know how to get the most for the money spent (see Figure 19.1):

- Volume discounts.   Prices should provide lower unit costs when more time-sharing services are used.
- Custom software costs.   If custom software is developed, it should be on a fixed-price basis. The customer should have the option of paying in monthly installments, over the life of the contract.

START-UP ITEMS	PROJECTED COST

Hardware (if bought)
  (desktop systems, modems)
  Hardware Maintenance
	_____
	_____

Management
  Research and Evaluation
  Installation
	_____
	_____

Conversion
  Data Entry
  Time Sharing Charges
	_____
	_____

TOTAL START-UP COST:	_____

ANNUAL EXPENSES	PROJECTED COST

Hardware (if leased)
  (desktop systems, modems)
  Hardware Maintenance
	_____
	_____

Time Sharing Charges	_____

Salaries
  Data Entry
  Management
	_____
	_____

Supplies	_____
TOTAL ANNUAL COST:	_____

Figure 19.1   How to project the cost of new time-sharing services.

- On-line storage costs.   End users should be cautioned to erase all data not needed on hard disk (on-line) storage at the time-sharing vendor, or write it to tape if it is not needed frequently. On-line storage is expensive, and its use should be limited.
- Processing speed.   Turnaround time should be overnight when possible, if money can be saved. Real-time (immediate) processing often costs twice as much as batch (overnight) processing.
- Off-line preparation.   Plan each session in advance, and do as much work as possible on company-owned systems, before going on-line with the time-sharing system.

If a cost comparison is needed between several alternatives, the same project request may be sent to an in-house computer department (if there is a chargeback system) and to a few time-sharing vendors. This brings to light the estimate that offers the best solution at the lowest cost, within the requested project deadline. Since the same applications software is often available from several time-sharing companies, money can often be saved by picking a less expensive one.

20

EXTERNAL COMMUNICATIONS

The dream of computer communications is to do the same thing that is done daily with telephones: Anyone can pick up a phone, press a few buttons, and be connected to any phone almost anywhere around the world. It doesn't matter whether the phones are made by two different companies, or if the phone lines are copper wire, microwave, fiber optics, or satellite links provided by still more companies. Compatible standards makes an immediate, world-spanning phone conversation possible.

In the comparatively young history of computer communications, national and international organizations are working to produce these same kinds of standards. One of these, for example, is the International Standards Organization's (ISO) open systems reference model. This approach separates communications from computer applications, so that different computer systems and communications protocols are compatible with a single set of internationally accepted standards.

The idea of "open systems" is not new. Because computers are still infants compared to the telephone, however, this is still being developed today. It is only starting to become available for interested users.

20.1 ADVANTAGES AND PROBLEMS

Even if every computer could instantly communicate with every other, total compatibility would not exist. The most that is accomplished by "open systems communications" is information exchange. Total compatibility means having applications software on the sending end work at computer speed with software in the receiving computer: If a chain of 100 department stores sends 30,000 separate purchase orders from its computer into the computers of 100 distributors, the purchase orders must be read, understood, and processed by the receiving computers without anyone's being involved.

While it is possible for many computers to exchange information, most software has been custom-written for one company's use by its DP department. Different companies in the same industry thus use unique data formats, and their computers cannot communicate with each other.

Until most companies write or buy programs to match their computer data with industry-standard formats designed for universal communications, information exchange using text (electronic mail) is still possible. This offers them valuable time savings by eliminating days wasted by sending purchase orders and other communications in the mail.

There is a real value today to the interim step of electronic mail between computers and word processors in different companies. It helps build the new standards, protocols, user experience, and interfaces between companies that leads to expanding data communications. This is a real step on the road to software compatibility, and it is also faster than using the mail.

When two companies do not have compatible communications, the value-added networks (such as Telenet, Tymnet, AT&T, and those operated by large time-sharing companies support enough communications protocols to make electronic mail reasonably easy. Tymshare, for example, offers Edi-Net. This service supports direct computer-to-computer transmission of business documents between companies that have different computers using dissimilar document formats. A highly formatted message is delivered that can be processed immediately by the recipient's computers.

For most organizations, however, there are three stages of growth in developing external communications.

20.2 EXTERNAL ELECTRONIC MAIL

For the majority of companies, communications with customers, clients, and suppliers will begin with text transfers and electronic mail. For many kinds of external communications, this is all that is needed. A closer look can be taken by tracking information from system to system.

In a patent infringement case, High Tech, Inc., is suing its rival, claiming that the rival's newest product infringes patents and copyrights owned by High Tech. The pretrial depositions are transcribed by a court reporting service using word processors. These transcripts are sent via modems over the phone lines into the word processors of the independent trial lawyer retained by High Tech. There, global searches are made to locate key personal and corporate names,

USERS	ACTIVITY	METHOD OF COMMUNICATIONS
Court Reporting Service	Transcribe depositions on Word Processors	Transcriptions sent over phone lines to law firm
Law Firm	Creates summary report on a Word Processor	Sent over phone lines to corporate client
Law Department at the corporate client	Archives report and opens access to three users	Uploads report to mainframe computer for storage
Director of Research and Development Director of Marketing Senior Vice-President	Use Micros and Word Processors to print, read, and review the report	Downloaded report from mainframe for local reviews
Director of Research and Development Director of Marketing Senior Vice-President	Prepare answer memos (or have them entered) on Micros or Word Processors	Memos are sent via electronic mail directly to the Law Department
Law Department at the corporate client	Summary reply prepared on Word Processor	Sent over phone lines to outside Law Firm

Figure 20.1 High-speed text communications between outside legal services meshes smoothly with a corporation's internal electronic mail.

dates, and facts. These searches speed up the first reading of the depositions, because they note relevant passages and pages for special attention.

Using cut-and-paste techniques, the word processor helps create a master report that shows the known facts about people and events relating to the patent infringement. This report lists these items in chronological order, and each one is footnoted so that it can be found in the depositions and other documents in the case.

This master report is sent over the phone lines into a word processor in the law department at High Tech, which has a compatible communications protocol. The word processor uploads it into High Tech's mainframe for mass storage and access by various departments. See Figure 20.1.

Within hours, the law firm's report is downloaded to workstations in the offices of the directors of Research & Development, Marketing, and Engineering, where it is printed for review. Each relevant executive writes an answering memo directly on a workstation or has it typed into a workstation by a secretary.

These memos are sent via electronic mail to the company's internal legal counsel who is supervising the lawsuit. She reviews all the memos and the report, and acquires copies of new High Tech documents mentioned in the memos. After preparing her summary reply for the trial lawyer, she phones him to let him know she's sending it from her word processor to his, so he will have a printed copy within hours. He promises to call back by the next morning, after he has read it.

By using instant communications and the powerful search abilities of word processors, trial preparation is completed more rapidly, more easily, and with less expense compared to slower manual methods. A week is saved by cutting out the first step alone, sending the trial lawyer's report through the mail, photocopying it, and distributing it to three executives. Since computer applications were not involved, all the information exchanged was text files. With protocol translation and electronic mail, these can be transferred from system to system, whether the systems are micros, word processors, or mainframe computers.

20.3 DATA COMMUNICATIONS WITH OPERATOR ENTRY

A slightly more complex level is reached when a company receives a message via electronic mail that needs to be entered into a computer and run by its applications software.

Suppose a computer supplies company in Atlanta uses electronic mail from a workstation to place an order for 200 boxes of computer paper from a paper mill in Alabama. Since the paper mill does not have applications software that interfaces with the purchase order sent by the Atlanta company, they use operator entry to get new orders into their computer that day so that they can process it that night. See Figure 20.2.

At the paper mill, one of the order entry clerks who used to work from purchase orders sent by mail now scans the incoming electronic mail file several times a day to see what arrived. After he prints the electronic mail orders on a fast dot matrix printer, the clerk calls up the mill's standard order entry screen. He enters each of the electronic mail orders, using normal keypunching, as if it came in through postal delivery. These orders are stored in the same batch file as the rest of the day's orders, for processing by the mill's usual software.

Even though they used electronic mail, the computer supplies vendor in Atlanta and the Alabama paper mill do not have applications software that is integrated with each other. The link is made by an order entry clerk who provides the bridge by entering electronic mail orders into the mill's computer. It does not matter whether the order entry clerk is working at a terminal on a mainframe computer, or on a workstation. Any one can serve equally well, and offer the electronic mail benefit of having orders sent and received right away.

USERS	ACTIVITY	METHOD OF COMMUNICATIONS
Computer supplies company in Atlanta	Purchase order for 200 boxes of computer paper	Sent over phone lines to paper mill in Alabama
Order Entry Clerk at paper mill	Prints P.O.'s received via electronic mail	Manual keyboarding of order into paper mill's computer
Order Entry Clerk at paper mill	Standard confirmation form is sent to computer supplies company in Atlanta	Sent via electronic mail so order is confirmed the same day it is sent, or the next morning
Paper mill's computer	Processes day's orders each night, in batch runs, for faster shipping of orders	Standard WATS lines are used to eliminate the delays from paper mail, at low cost

Figure 20.2   People can provide the bridge between different computers, such as at this paper mill, which has added electronic mail with its customers.

20.4 DATA COMMUNICATIONS BETWEEN EXTERNAL COMPUTER SYSTEMS

The most powerful stage of integrated applications is reached when outside customers or suppliers use communications that is compatible with the software of the computer with whom they are communicating. Now, an order entry clerk is not needed. The information is transferred directly from one computer system to the next.

There is a reasonably easy way to implement this. Outside customers can dial directly into a computer that presents the order entry form directly to them on their screen. Customers can "fill in the blanks" while they are on-line using the applications software in the host system. Editing and procedural commands can be listed in a short menu that is on the top or bottom lines of the screen, with on-line help available for those who might need it.

The on-line order-entry software can be in the computer of an intermediary, such as a large time-sharing organization like GEISCO, or a network like AT&T's Net 1000. In either of these cases, customers dial into the intermediary's computer, and after logging on see the "fill in the blanks" order form on their screen so that they can fill it out while on-line.

The advantage of using an intermediary is off-loading what could grow to be a sizable order entry operation, with many different computer interfaces, onto outside computers designed to handle this type of communications. This lowers the work load for the DP department at the receiving company. The disadvantage is that the receiving company's computers need to dial in and pick up their orders frequently, or the delay lowers the value of offering instant electronic purchasing.

If this kind of fast communications is designed properly, almost any customer can place an order in minutes. If a micro, word processor, or workstation is used to place these orders, communications software should be used that can save the communications to disk. This automatically stores an electronic copy of all orders placed while on-line. See Figure 20.3.

There is another way to integrate software, and that is to run compatible software at many computers in an industry. Today, this is the fastest growing approach, even though it requires an industry-standard data format that cannot be changed by any company, because all the compatible communications and applications software is built on this. Currently, entire industries are being standardized, and the experts forecast a 1000 percent increase in *electronic document interchange* (EDI) usage within the near future.

Two new factors make this possible. First, after 15 years of gradual development, industrywide standards for EDI have matured and have been widely accepted. Second, the proliferation of micros as everyday business tools brings EDI to every user who needs it.

The grocery industry, for example, has already begun a rapid expansion in EDI use. This started in 1981 by pilot testing the Uniform Communication Standard (UCS). Within two years, over 55 companies started using UCS, including retailers, manufacturers, distributors, and brokers. Super Valu is just one participant, but it soon started using EDI at all 17 company divisions. As micros are installed in more companies and offices, the advantages of faster

BUYING COMPANY'S COMPUTER	SELLING COMPANY'S COMPUTER
Request for a price quotation	Price quotation, perhaps with availability and delivery information
Purchase order	Order confirmation
Request status of order	Shipping update
	Shipping notice
	Invoice
Payment(s)	Statement(s)

Figure 20.3   Some of the types of automated communications that can be developed between computers in making a purchase.

turnaround on orders and reduced bookkeeping errors result in wider company and industry use of EDI.

The National Association of Realtors (NAR) has begun testing a national mortgage data network for realtors, called "Rennie Mae" (or Realtors National Mortgage Access Network). Using microcomputers that cost less than $6000 for hardware and software provided by the NAR, any realtor can log on to the network. In their offices, realtors can give property buyers an instant opportunity to review mortgage choices available at lending institutions all over the country. The software and network also provide immediate analysis of which types of mortgages are best suited for the buyer's budget. Finally, interested buyers can receive a rapid indication of whether they might qualify for the mortgages they select. This program is being developed in conjunction with the investment firm of Salomon Brothers, Inc., so that any corner realtor can offer the most sophisticated financial services available.

Even a field as loose as international free-lance photographers now has not one, but two worldwide telecommunications networks that are designed not just for micros, but for lap-size portables. Photo-1 is restricted to the top photojournalists and the editors at major publications such as *Time, Forbes,* and *National Geographic*. These photographers may be on the road up to 80 percent of the time, with flexible itineraries that make contact difficult. The Photo-1 electronic mail service allows editors to leave messages for individual photographers, or for those in the field to send information and photo captions to any of the member publications. The network also has a bulletin board where editors post free-lance assignments. If a photographer happens to be in Argentina on assignment, the bulletin board can be checked to see if another publication is looking for photos of Argentina. The publication saves the cost of a separate assignment, while the photographer earns extra income. The second network, Photonet, is more open and has subscribers in 130 cities and 30 countries.

The National Automated Clearing House Association (NACHA) unveiled a system that electronically replaces paper checks in all types of transactions between participating companies. Any of 30 automated clearinghouse networks can be used by banks, savings and loan associations, and credit unions to replace up to 400 million paper checks annually. Each clearinghouse forms its own membership policies, prices, and operating policies. In addition to banks, over 50 major corporations have joined NACHA's work in this area, including Sears, Xerox, Exxon, Westinghouse, and Equitable Life Insurance. The dollar volume on individual checks processed has ranged from $400 to over $1 million. NACHA's role is to provide the rules, standards, and technical support for exchanging automated clearinghouse payments on a nationwide basis.

This kind of communications takes hard work and persistence to develop, but it is being advanced by those willing to invest time and effort to build the growing movement into external computer communications.

GLOSSARY*

ACK A communication control character transmitted by a receiver as an affirmative response to a sender. It indicates that the preceding transmission block has been received, and that the receiving unit is ready to accept the next block of the transmission.

algorithm A defined set of operational steps to be taken to effect a desired calculation. An example of its use is the Data Encryption Standard algorithm (DES) of the National Bureau of Standards, which is used in the encryption of transmitted data to protect its security.

alphanumeric A generic term for alphabet letters, numerical digits, and special characters which are machine-processable. Describes a character set containing both letters and digits, and, usually, additional characters such as punctuation marks and other symbols.

analog In data communications, the description of the continuous wave or signal (such as the human voice) for which conventional telephone lines are designed. For transmission on these lines, the digital, or pulse, output of a computer or terminal must be converted to an analog signal.

ASCII An acronym for "American Standard Code for Information Interchange," an 8-level code (7 bits + parity bit).

asynchronous transmission A transmission method in which each character of information is individually synchronized, usually by the use of "start" and "stop" elements. (Compare with *synchronous transmission.*)

baud A unit of signaling speed. Speed as expressed in bauds is equal to the number of signaling elements per second.

*The terms and definitions in this glossary are provided courtesy of Racal-Milgo.

bps   Bits per second (also expressed as b/s), a measure of speed in serial transmission. Also used to describe hardware capabilities, as in a 9600-bps modem.

buffer   A storage device or routine used to compensate for a difference in the rate of data flow or the time of occurrence of events when data is transmitted from one device to another. A buffer permits a change of speed, voltage, or interface characteristic between two devices.

CCITT   A European advisory committee—*Comite Consultatif International Telegraphique et Telephonique*—established by the United Nations to recommend worldwide standards of transmission within the International Telecommunications Union (ITU).

circuit   In communications, a means of two-way communication between two or more points; usually a physical, metallic path such as a telephone line.

common carrier   A government-regulated company charged with furnishing public communications facilities, such as a telephone company or a telegraph company.

conditioning   The addition of equipment to a leased voice-grade channel in order to provide the appropriate line characteristics required for data transmission.

contention   A method of line control in which the individual terminals contend with each other for access to the transmission channel. A terminal requests to transmit, and if the channel is free, transmission takes place; if not, a queue of contention requests is built up, and the terminal must wait for its turn for access to a free channel.

data base   The aggregate body of all information stored in a computing system that is fundamental to the enterprises which own or operate the system. Access to the data base may be limited to certain specific users and/or application programs.

data communications   The movement of encoded information by an electrical transmission system. The transmission of data from one point to another.

data collection   The act of bringing data from one or more points to a central point.

data-phone   A trademark of the AT&T Company to identify the data sets manufactured and supplied by the Bell System.

data set   A device containing the electrical circuitry necessary to connect data processing equipment to a communications channel, usually through modulation and demodulation of the signal.

data source   The equipment which supplies the data signals to be transmitted.

data stream   Generally, the flow of information being transmitted in a communications system, or the path along which it flows.

dedicated line   A leased telephone line, reserved for the exclusive use of one customer.

demodulation   The process of retrieving an original signal from a modulated carrier wave. The technique used in data sets to make communication signals compatible with business machine signals.

diagnostics   The detection and isolation of a malfunction or mistake in a communications device, network, or system.

dial-up   The use of a dial or pushbutton telephone to initiate a station-to-station call.

digital   In data communications, the description of the binary (off/on) output of a computer or terminal. Modems convert the pulsating digital signals into analog waves for transmission over conventional telephone lines.

distributed processing   A general term usually referring to the use of intelligent or programmable terminals for processing at sites remote from a company's main computer facility.

EBCDIC   Abbreviation for "Extended Binary Coded Decimal Interchange Code," a 9-level code (8 bits + parity bit), which is one of the two basic codes used in IBM systems. (The other is an 8-bit version of the USASCII code, USASCII-8.)

error control   An arrangement for detecting the presence of errors, including refinements for correcting the detected errors, either by operations on the data received or by retransmission from the source.

error detecting code   A code in which each data signal conforms to specific rules of construction so that departures from the norm—errors—are automatically detected. (Synonymous with *self-checking code*.) Such codes require more signal elements than are necessary for conveying the fundamental information.

error detecting and feedback system   A system wherein any signal detected as an error automatically initiates a request for retransmission of the data in error. (Also called *decision feedback system, requests repeat system,* and *ARQ system.*)

error rate   The ratio of incorrectly received data (bits, elements, characters, or blocks) to the total amount of data transmitted.

facsimile   (Also called **FAX**) The transmission of photographs, maps, diagrams, and other graphic data by communications channels. The image is scanned at the transmitting site, transmitted as a series of impulses, and reconstructed at the receiving station to be duplicated on paper.

four-wire circuit   A circuit containing two pairs of conductors, one pair for the "go" channel and the other for the "return" channel. A communication path in which there are two wires for each direction of the transmission.

frequency division multiplex   A system of transmission in which the available frequency transmission range is divided into narrower bands, so that separate messages may be transmitted simultaneously on a single circuit.

full duplex   Used to describe a communications system or component capable of transmitting data simultaneously in two directions.

half duplex   Used to describe a communications system or component capable of transmitting data alternately, but not simultaneously, in two directions.

home loop   The physical part of a communication circuit involving only the lines and/or devices within or adjacent to the local terminal.

intelligent terminal   A "programmable" terminal which is capable of interacting with the central site computer and performing limited processing functions at the remote site.

interface   A shared connection or boundary between two devices or systems. The point at which two devices or systems are linked. Common interface standards include

EIA Standard RS-232B/C, adopted by the Electronic Industries Association to ensure uniformity among most manufacturers; MIL STD 188B, the mandatory standard established by the Department of Defense; and CCITT, the world recommendation for interface, mandatory in Europe and closely resembling the American EIA standard.

line speed   The maximum rate at which signals may be transmitted over a given channel, usually measured in bauds or bps. Line speed varies with the capabilities of the equipment used.

local loop   The physical part of a communication circuit that lies between the subscriber's equipment and the equipment located at the telephone company exchange.

loopback tests   A test procedure in which signals are looped from a test center through a modem or loopback switch and back to the test center for measurement.

message format   The rules for placement of portions of a message to be transmitted: heading, address, text, end-of-message, etc.

modem   A contraction of **mo**dulator/**dem**odulator; a generic term for data sets manufactured by independent (non-AT&T) electronics firms.

modulation   The process by which a characteristic of one wave is varied in accordance with another wave or signal, as in modems, which transform computer signals into waves that are compatible with communications facilities and equipment.

multiplex   To interleave, or simultaneously transmit, two or more messages on a single channel.

multiplexing   The process of dividing a transmission facility into two or more channels.

multipoint circuit   A circuit that interconnects three or more stations.

NAK   A communication control character transmitted by a receiver as a negative acknowledgement: "message not received" or "transmission not acceptable."

network   A series of points interconnected by communication channels. The switched telephone network consists of public telephone lines normally used for dialed telephone calls; a private network is a configuration of communication channels reserved for the use of a sole customer.

network management system   A comprehensive system of equipment used in monitoring, controlling, and managing a data communications network. Usually consists of testing devices, CRT displays and printers, patch panels, and circuitry for diagnostics and reconfiguration of channels, generally housed together in an operator console unit.

noise   Generally, any disturbance that tends to interfere with the normal operation of a communication device or system. Random electrical signals introduced by circuit components or natural disturbances which denigrate the performance of a communications channel.

on-line   A general description of equipment or devices which are under the direct control of the CPU, or terminal equipment which is connected to a transmission line.

on-line system   A system in which the data to be input enters the computer directly from the point of origin (which may be remote from the central site) and/or the output data is transmitted directly to the location where it is to be used.

operating time   In data communications, the total time required to dial a call, wait for the connection to be established, and coordinate the transaction with the personnel or equipment at the receiving end.

redundancy   A computer or communications facility in which there is a spare backup device for each important component of the system.

real time   Generally, an operating mode under which receiving the data, processing it, and returning the results takes place so quickly as to actually affect the functioning of the environment, guide the physical processes in question, or interact instantaneously with the human user(s). Examples include a process control system in manufacturing, or a computer-assisted instruction system in an educational institution.

remote station   Data terminal equipment located at a distance from the data processing site and requiring electronic communication for access.

response time   The time a system takes to react to a given act; the interval between completion of an input message and receipt of an output response. In data communications, response time includes transmission time to the computer, processing time at the computer (including access of file records), and transmission time back to the terminal.

SDLC   Abbreviation for Synchronous DataLink Control, a communications line discipline associated with the IBM system network architecture (SNA), which offers several advantages to data network users. SDLC initiates, controls, checks, and terminates information exchanges or communications lines (in a full duplex operation).

short-haul modem   A data set designed for use in communicating data up to distances of 25 miles. The private line metallic circuits linking such devices permit extremely high-speed operation, up to 19,200 bps and faster.

store and forward   The act of receiving and holding complete messages and forwarding them as required.

synchronous transmission   A transmission method in which the synchronizing of characters is controlled by timing signals generated at the sending and receiving stations (as opposed to start/stop communication). Both stations operate continuously at the same frequency and are maintained in a desired phase relationship. Any of several data codes may be used for the transmission, so long as the code utilizes the required line control characters. (Also called *bi-sync*, or *binary synchronous*.)

switched telephone network   A network of telephone lines normally used for dialed telephone calls. Generally synonymous with the Direct Distance Dialing network, or any switching arrangement that does not require operator intervention.

tariff   The published rates and specifications for a specific unit of equipment, facility, or type of service provided by a communications common carrier, as regulated by state or federal agencies.

telex   An international network of teleprinter subscriber service; also, a domestic network of Western Union.

terminal   Any device capable of sending and/or receiving information over a communication channel, including input to and output from the system of which it is a part. Also, any point at which information enters or leaves a communication network.

text   That part of a message which contains the substantive information to be conveyed. Sometimes called the *body* of the message.

throughput   The total measure of useful information processed or communicated during a specified time period.

time division multiplexer   A device which permits the simultaneous transmission of many independent channels into a single high-speed data stream by dividing the signal into successive alternate bits.

time-sharing   A method of operation in which a computer or communications facility is shared by several users for different purposes at (effectively) the same time. Although the system actually services each user in sequence, the rapid electronic speeds make it appear that all users are accommodated simultaneously.

trunk   A single circuit between two points, both of which are switching centers and/or individual distribution points.

turnaround time   The actual time required to reverse the direction of transmission from send to receive (or vice versa) on a half-duplex circuit.

TWX   Western Union's teleprinter exchange service, providing a real-time direct connection between subscribers.

unattended operation   The automatic features of a station which permit the transmission and reception of messages without human intervention.

voice grade channel   A channel suitable for the transmission of speech, digital or analog data, or facsimile, generally having a frequency range of about 300 to 3000 hertz.

WATS   An acronym for Wide Area Telephone Service, a telephone company service which permits a customer to dial station-to-station calls via an access line to specific zones for a flat monthly charge, or to receive "collect" calls in specified numbers at a flat monthly charge, rather than on a per-call basis.

INDEX